AMERICAN HISTORY IN FOCUS SERIES

Under the Editorship of
William H. Goetzmann

THE COLONIAL HORIZON:
AMERICA IN THE SIXTEENTH AND SEVENTEENTH CENTURIES
William H. Goetzmann, University of Texas

THE AMERICAN REVOLUTION:
THE ANGLO-AMERICAN RELATION, 1763–1794
Charles R. Ritcheson, Southern Methodist University

YEARS OF TURMOIL:
CIVIL WAR AND RECONSTRUCTION
John Niven, Claremont Graduate School

THE GILDED AGE: AMERICA, 1865–1900
Richard A. Bartlett, The Florida State University

THE AGE OF INSECURITY: AMERICA, 1920–1945
Robert A. Divine, University of Texas

YEARS OF TURMOIL: CIVIL WAR AND RECONSTRUCTION

Interpretive Articles and Documentary Sources

Edited by
JOHN NIVEN
Claremont Graduate School

ADDISON-WESLEY PUBLISHING COMPANY
Reading, Massachusetts / Menlo Park, California / London / Don Mills, Ontario

 Printed in the United States of America. Published simultaneously in Canada. Library of Congress Catalog Card No. 72–86584.

PREFACE: THE AMERICAN HISTORY IN FOCUS SERIES

History is the recorded deeds, ideas, and emotions of men. Living history is the re-recording of these deeds, ideas, and emotions by interpreters in each new generation. *The American History in Focus Series* seeks to provide the student with what might be called "the varieties of living historical experience," from a mid-twentieth century point of view. Each of the major historical epochs in American history is brought into focus by means of modern interpretive articles written by major scholars in the field, scholars who may be said to be on "the growing tip" of historical knowledge. Their interests span a vast range of historical methods and commitments. Collectively, they represent the multiple points of view of political, social, economic, diplomatic, military, and intellectual historians —historians who are nonetheless very much products of our own times and affected by current interests. These selections are concerned in almost every instance with answering that simple but all-important question—"so what?"—as it relates to our historical heritage. Of what relevance has past American historical experience been to the total course of human development, to the emergence of American values, achievements, problems, and predicaments? How did I, a citizen of the United States, get to be where and what I am today with all the privileges, burdens, and responsibilities that are entailed? What experiences of quality and nobility of conduct can be noted in the past against which we can measure our own aspirations and behavior—for we can the better recognize quality in our own lives for having seen it somewhere before in the recent or distant past?! By portraying realistically the complexities, relativisms, and ambiguities in the interpretations of time past, the editors and authors represented in these volumes provide new perspectives for determining our cultural identity.

Each of the volumes concentrates on a major period in American history, from colonial times to the present. Each is structured around focal, interpretive articles of modern historians with several varieties of history represented. These focal articles are supplemented by important and revealing historical documents of the particular era with which the historian is concerned. These are samples of the kinds of materials out of which he has constructed his interpretation. They are intended to serve two purposes: first, to give today's student a "feel" for the language and perspectives of the people of earlier generations; second, to provide materials with which to *test* the generalizations of the modern interpreters—to provide a laboratory situation whereby the student may critically examine some of the interpreter's answers and hopefully even some of his questions. For serious historical study requires constant criticism of historical generalizations, and it is too little recognized that such criticism might properly begin with the question, "did the historian ask the right questions of the period?"

Given the above, it should be obvious that these are experimental books especially designed as tools for learning. They are neither exercises in belletristic virtuosity, nor are they "canned" problems where the rules are clear and for the clever, the answers pat. Rather they are intended to be sophisticated, broad-based springboards to future discussion. As an added dimension we have experimented with the addition of pictorial materials which are not intended as idle embellishment but should rather serve as integral parts of the text—as further documents of the time. These, too, when examined with care, afford points of focus.

In attempting to draw a distinction between the nature of science and the nature of history, an historian of science, Derek de Solla Price, makes a striking analogy. He sees science as a "many-brained" machine into whose circuits all of the latest "growing tip" discoveries, however limited, can be wired so that advances in knowledge can result without the necessity for retracing in detail the historical steps involved in previous discoveries. History, on the other hand, is a "single-brained" enterprise in which each historian has to go back over all the sources and interpretations of the past before making his own generalization.* The *American History in Focus Series* attempts to draw upon the advantages of both. For the individual student it is clearly a "single-brained" experience. But in assembling between two covers modern interpretations, along with documents from the past, both written and pictorial, we have attempted to provide the advantages of a "many-brained" approach as well, so as to encourage the student to examine the nature of historical enquiry as a process of thought, and to address himself to the problem of cultural identity in a changing world.

William H. Goetzmann, General Editor

---

* Derek D. Price, "Two Cultures and One Historian of Science," *Teachers College Record*, **64**, 7, April 1963, pp. 528–531.

CONTENTS

GENERAL INTRODUCTION

GENERAL INTRODUCTION

The American Civil War was a startling occurrence even to a century in which turmoil and violence were scarcely exceptional. The apparent swiftness of its approach, the dimensions and duration of the struggle, were as perplexing to Europeans as they were agonizing to the American people. After the first wave of popular enthusiasm—parades, emotional oratory, martial music—the war became a grim business, a frightening beast that seemed to feed upon itself. Never before had a people of common heritage so gaily yet so thoughtlessly thrown themselves at each other for ends that their leaders had not worked out with any sharp-edged clarity.

True, the Confederate government cast itself in the hallowed Revolutionary role, invoking the spirit of '76 to defend its lands and its institutions from "an alien and aggressive majority." The Lincoln administration similarly called upon the "mystic chords of memory," the image of "patriot graves," to sustain a "new nation" that had evolved from the War for Independence. Both sides appealed to the Constitution—the one to justify secession, the other to deny it. Later the North, and more especially the radical North, citing the Declaration of Independence, added emancipation to its war aims. Yet at no time during the war and the reconstruction that followed was there any consensus on the causes of the conflict or what should be the legitimate aims of victory. It would be safe to say that leading elements among the Republican factions in the North believed that secession and the Confederacy were the results of a long-term conspiracy. This thesis, first offered by Stephen A. Douglas (a Democrat, and a firm supporter of the Union before his premature death in the summer of 1861), was taken up by moderates and radicals alike among the Republicans and the War Democrats. Lincoln asserted it on more than one occasion, as did Gideon Welles, his Navy Secretary, Horace Greeley, editor of *The New York Tribune,* Senator Benjamin Wade of Ohio, and a host of others. Secretary of State William H. Seward believed it too, but added a penetrating suggestion of his own when he told the historian Motley that the underlying cause of the war was a complete failure of the sections to understand each other's characters.

Tension between the slave states and the free states had been building for years. Social and economic differences were mirrored in the stormy politics of the thirties and early forties. It was not until the Mexican War that these divisions began to escalate beyond the traditional process of debate and compromise. The vast land acquisitions resulting from the war dramatically modified and magnified previous issues. How were the new territories and, indeed, all the undeveloped lands of the trans-Mississippi West to be organized and opened to settlement? Were they to become a part of the expanding slave-plantation system? Were they to become the domain of small farms owned and operated by free, white settlers? Or were they to be divided, and if divided, where would the line be drawn? There were irreconcilables on both sides, but even after Lincoln's election as a minority President on a sectional platform, a majority of the American people, North, South, and West, were opposed to armed conflict. Unfortunately, by this time a decade of political excitement had weakened the forces of moderation. During the year 1860–61 skillful manipulators of public opinion on both sides of the Mason and Dixon line had all but paralyzed the orderly processes of government in the Presidency, in Congress, and especially in the slave states. Reason in many instances gave way to passion or obstruction. Had the aging President Buchanan been a more resolute man, he might have bought time and restored a measure of tranquility, so that the new President, moving carefully but firmly, could have rallied the moderates in the nation. Lincoln did what he could, with the options he had, to uphold national authority, to contain, and if possible, to isolate the "fire eaters" in the South. If the Confederacy were deprived of the rich and populous border states, there was a chance that the Union might be restored eventually without bloodshed. The provisional Confederate government was well aware of this, too, and while reluctant to open hostilities, was also concerned about maintaining its leadership. In dealing with a crisis situation, however, decision makers are always confronted with the problem of uncertainty. Trivial errors in judgment or timing can lead to unforeseen consequences. The actual attack on Fort Sumter was triggered by just such a failure on both sides to assess accurately each other's intentions.

Once the issue was drawn and conflict began in earnest, the historian searches in vain for any coherent, all-embracing war aim among soldiers North and South. Many, like the Connecticut volunteer officer Henry Ward Camp, fought to preserve the Union—not to abolish slavery. Others enlisted for the sheer adventure of it and then gave their loyalty to their particular company or regiment, or became so integrated into the military organization that they thought little about anything except personal survival—food, clothing (especially shoes), and small comforts. Some, of course, had idealistic motives from the beginning; to them the war for the Union was also a crusade for human freedom. Or they accepted Lincoln's position as he expressed it to John Hay: "if we fail, it will go far to prove the incapability of the people to govern themselves." Popular government itself was on trial. Idealists, however, were rare among the rank and file, though emancipation of the slaves gained rapid acceptance.

The Confederate soldier, when he thought about the war in abstract terms, saw it as a defense of his homeland and its institutions. Slavery was accepted as a matter of course, an essential factor in the southern way of life, a practical adjustment of the troublesome race problem. Total emancipation would have been inconceivable, at least until near the very end of the conflict. Yet once the war ended, the Confederate veteran accepted the thirteenth amendment to the Constitution with little complaint. He would not accept, nor would most of the southern whites (and for that matter, many northern whites), significant social or economic reform measures that would have improved the status of the freedman.

The politicians and the officeholders, not subject to the disciplines, the demands, and the actual perils of the battlefield, could afford the luxury of speculation, particularly when they sensed an issue that might be useful in an election or in speeding up the war effort. The Davis regime had less trouble with politics and more with the war effort than its counterpart in Washington. The image of a "defensive war" was a satisfactory explanation for the civilian population until the strain on manpower and material resources became acute in 1864. The desperate efforts of Richmond to squeeze the last conscript and the last bushel of corn from a people harried on all sides provoked serious constitutional challenges to Confederate authority. In contrast, the material superiority of the Union was such that the Lincoln administration never had to employ Draconian measures which might have provoked a dangerous reaction.

On the political side, however, Washington was assailed from all quarters. The war had scarcely begun when arguments about its conduct and its aims developed among factions of the Republican party. This situation stemmed from the hybrid composition of the party itself—old-line Whigs, Free Soil Democrats, North Americans, a sprinkling of Abolitionists. United at first only in their opposition to the extension of slavery, many Republican leaders clung to earlier partisan attachments and attitudes. By 1862 the War Democrats, who had joined with them in the Union party, added another restive element.

Opposition to the Administration's war aims was demonstrated in Congress. A minority group of powerful Congressmen looked ahead to an eventual Union victory when the nation would be reunified, slavery extinguished, and civil rights extended to the Negro. These men, who shared radical views on reconstruction, who were impatient with Lincoln's cautious border state policy, did not present a monolithic front either during or after the war. A few, such as Thaddeus Stevens and Charles Sumner, were unswerving in their convictions. In their view the southern black man had a right to education, to the equal protection of the law, to the tilling of his own soil. He was not just a political lever to establish party supremacy in the South after the war. Others of their more practical, though still radical, colleagues, like Zachariah Chandler of Michigan or Benjamin Wade of Ohio, had the same objectives on the postwar status of the Negro, but their idealism was secondary to their politics. What they feared above all else was the reestablishment of the prewar alliance between the conservative northern Democrats and old "cotton" Whigs and their former associates in the South. In this event it would be difficult for the radicals to satisfy their own consciences about the aims of the war, let alone explain those aims to their constituents. As they saw it, a reestablishment of the conservative alliance would make a mockery of the billions of dollars spent for the war effort, and the quarter of a million lives lost on the battlefield. They held that the Lincoln-Johnson moderate course on reconstruction would result in both political and moral bankruptcy.

Whatever partisanship was involved, if the various radical factions had anything to say about it, the freedman would not be cast back into peonage, his personal liberty a mere high-sounding sham. They would attempt to impeach the President and would treat the former Confederacy as conquered territory rather than abandon the black man to his former masters. Ultimately, of course, they failed in the face of southern intransigence and northern indifference. The radical program—moderate, even conservative in a modern context—was still too far in advance of public opinion.

The Peace Democrats were poles apart from the radicals, yet in a curious way shared their idealism, their factionalism, and their opposition to the Lincoln administration. The Peace Democrats too ranged in opinion from the loyal opposition of a man like Governor Horatio Seymour of New York to the possible subversion of Clement L. Vallandigham, a former Democratic congressman from Ohio. Just as Lincoln did not prosecute the war vigorously enough and was too moderate on the slavery question for the radicals, he was too arbitrary and dictatorial in the use of executive powers for the Peace Democrats. Frequent resort to peremptory arrest and confinement of alleged agitators was to them a flagrant violation of civil rights. It is significant that Henry Winter Davis, a radical of radicals, also disliked this sort of executive "usurpation." In some rare instances Democrats had even been imprisoned, without due process of law, for partisan opposition. Another source of conflict was the belief of almost all Peace Democrats in white supremacy. They thought the Emancipation Proclamation an unconstitutional measure that struck at property rights, raised the issue of race adjustment, opened the door to a black invasion of the white North, and at the same time closed the door on any negotiated peace with the South. Common to all Democrats and Republicans, if they happened to be members of Congress during the war, was their sensitivity to any executive encroachment on the legislative prerogative. Lincoln was a strong executive, the first in over a decade of congressional supremacy. The Wade-Davis Manifesto, included in this book, was a stern reminder of legislative power, a bold assertion that reconstruction was not to be attempted by presidential fiat.

While the Confederacy also had a potentially strong executive in Jefferson Davis, its military and material position was so desperate that by 1862 its Congress could not indulge in searching political debate. Davis had his political opponents, his problems with factions. He had to contend with secret organizations dedicated to peace at any price. Still his administration and the Confederate Congress were quite scrupulous about civil rights. When the Congress suspended the privilege of the writ of habeas corpus, as it did three times during the war, it stipulated time limits and enumerated the offenses to which suspension applied. Despite waning military and civilian morale after Gettysburg, the Confederate government was more tolerant of criticism, less prone to arbitrary arrests, than was Washington.

The historical literature dealing with the war and reconstruction is not only abundant but controversial. A recent survey of articles and books on the subject has underscored this point with the arresting title: "The Dark and Bloody Ground of Reconstruction Historiography." * One trend, however, seems to mark all of the work—a fascination, if not an absorption, with the political issues involved. Only in recent years, excepting two or three major works—Robert Sharkey's and Irwin Unger's studies of the greenbacks, for example—have the economic impact and consequences of the period attracted significant scholarly attention. The "robber baron" thesis and the flagrant public corruption of the Grant administration have left us with a distorted picture of the post-Civil War era. In reality the 60's and 70's were a time of social flux and outstanding philosophical, artistic, and scientific achievement, as well as economic change. The war and reconstruction acted as powerful stimuli on technology, which was indispensable to the development of the modern industrial state. Experience in mass organization during the war had a profound influence on the structure of postwar industrial enterprise. Promotional and merchandizing techniques pioneered by the Philadelphia banker Jay Cooke in his market-

---

* Bernard A. Weisberger, "The Dark and Bloody Ground of Reconstruction Historiography," *The Journal of Southern History*, XXV, No. 4 (November 1959).

ing of government bonds directly to the people laid the basis for financing later railroad projects on a colossal scale. The age produced two of the greatest American philosophers, Charles Peirce and William James, one of the world's great scientists in Josiah Willard Gibbs, the superb novelist and wit Mark Twain, and fine artists in Winslow Homer and Thomas Eakins. Culturally, the period from 1861 to 1877 was the beginning of a brilliant display, not an Indian summer with the dying time near at hand.

The persistent concern for political and constitutional questions has led many historians to relate the war and reconstruction to the political and emotional issues of their own times. Currently, some specialists are restudying the events of a century ago in terms of the present civil rights struggle—attributing modern motives to the principal characters involved, and emphasizing achievements that were belittled or brushed aside by earlier scholars. For the past seventy years the contest has not only raged in academic circles, but has carried over into public discussion. Each generation of historians, searching for a more perfect explanation, is apparently conditioned in varying degrees by its particular environment, its convictions, the audience it hopes to reach.

Historical evidence has the same complexities and variations as any other body of data, whether it be gathered for a market analysis or for a new hypothesis in elementary particle physics. All of this may be confusing to the student, but if he considers that innovation is essential to the vitality of any intellectual process, he will perceive that knowledge, historical or otherwise, depends on the creative force of scholarly debate. Give-and-take, as with other disciplines, is a basic part of the historical method.

Historians have to deal with all manner of information, much of which would be ruled out by the natural and the behavioral sciences. Gossip, hearsay, untrustworthy recollections, the element of chance are but a few of the variables that must be examined and evaluated, accepted or discarded. The past can never be recaptured exactly as it was. Even "hard," quantitative data, such as roll-call votes in Congress, cannot account for the unrecorded deals, the logrolling, perhaps even the state of health of those voting on a key issue on a given day. Perspective is the most powerful tool in the historian's workshop, yet it is far from a precision instrument.

It is impossible within the limited confines of a source book to do more than suggest the many-dimensioned impact of the war and the reconstruction. This volume presents a brief series of introductions and interpretive articles, followed by documents which in one way or another suggest or represent the kinds of materials an author might use to formulate his interpretation. As for any basic change in the American character, that elusive and all-encompassing thing, the chance remark of the great historian Jules Michelet to Matthew Arnold during the 60's may be appropriate. Speaking of his beloved France, he said it had been "a nation of barbarians civilized by the conscription." Arnold amplified and defined Michelet's comment by noting that he meant "through their military service the idea of public duty and of discipline was brought to the minds of these masses, in other respects so raw and uncultivated." DeForest came to a similar conclusion when describing some of the ex-Confederate soldiers he met while a Union officer in South Carolina during reconstruction. Perhaps, after all, this was the overriding impact of the war on the mind of the average American—this sense of being a part of the whole, of beginning to look at things in the aggregate rather than as so many independent units. Even the freedman, the prime cause, the major beneficiary, and ultimately the tragic victim of the war, for a brief moment identified himself with the nation, until forced back to his traditional alienation.

In many respects a nation had been made. The war developed the idea of coordination and organization of enterprise on a national scale, whether in business, the professions, or in labor. Those who resumed their farming occupations lent impetus to the Granger and the cooperative movements. Returning veterans who entered the working force carried with them the discipline to organize the first effective trade unions. Only the Negro had to wait—and is still waiting, though again war and conscription may provide a stimulus for the economic and social equality that was but a fitful shadow a century ago.

I/ESCALATION

INTRODUCTION

Planning and blundering on both sides provoked the Sumter incident as you will note in your reading of David Potter's admirable introduction to his new edition of *Lincoln and His Party in the Secession Crisis.* A partial list of the documents on which Potter drew for his thesis is included for analysis. Implicit in the Potter approach is the reluctance of either side to precipitate hostilities. Seward and Lincoln seemed resigned to let matters take their course in Charleston harbor until the tiny garrison ran out of supplies and evacuated the post. Certainly Seward and probably Lincoln had selected the far more defensible, less politically sensitive Fort Pickens off the Florida coast as the place to maintain national authority. This might well have occurred had not a bizarre chain of circumstances and command confusion cast doubt on whether Pickens could be held. Only then did Lincoln despatch the Fox expedition to support the garrison at Sumter. Seward, desperate to avoid a collision at Charleston harbor, had the President detach from the expedition the powerful warship *Powhatan,* which Fox considered essential to the success of his plans. And in a final effort, Lincoln emphasized the peaceful nature of the expedition—supplies only—when he gave official notice of his administration's intent to the governor of South Carolina. He was, however, prepared for resistance, as his telegram of warning to Governor Curtin of Pennsylvania demonstrates. One might argue that in permitting the relief expedition to sail, Lincoln was taking a calculated risk by committing a provocative act, and was fully aware of the probable result. This is a question that still deserves critical attention.

INTERPRETATION

David Potter of Stanford University, an eminent political and social historian, has written the best general analysis of the events in the critical five-month period between the election of Abraham Lincoln and the attack on Fort Sumter. Though he emphasizes the Republican-northern reaction to the secession crisis, he does not gloss over events in the southern states. In this preface to the new edition of his original 1942 monograph, Potter has carefully evaluated the more significant newer contributions concerning the immediate causes of the war, the last-ditch efforts to stave off hostilities, and finally the assignment of responsibility for the firing of the first shot.

DAVID POTTER, Preface to *Lincoln and His Party in the Secession Crisis*

. . . Certainly, the historical literature on Lincoln and on the precipitation of the Civil War have witnessed [some] transformation in [the] twenty years [that have passed since the first edition]. To recognize the extent of this change, it is necessary to remember something of the state of the literature in 1942. At that time the papers of Abraham Lincoln had never been opened to any writers other than the authorized biographers, John G. Nicolay and John Hay, and they were still impounded in the Library of Congress, awaiting the expiration of the twenty-one-year period which Robert Todd Lincoln had provided should elapse after his death before the papers became public (he died in 1926). The only full-scale documented account of Lincoln's presidency was the work of his personal secretaries, the same Nicolay and Hay, who had used the papers and had published their ten volumes in 1890. (In saying this, I omit Sandburg's great epic which made Lincoln's War Years live again, but was hardly a history of his presidency.) The only extensive, detailed history of the crisis period was one published between 1893 and 1906 by James Ford Rhodes, a man who had been twelve years old when Lincoln became President. The only book devoted entirely to the policy of Northern leaders during the seces-

---

David Potter, Preface, *Lincoln and His Party in the Secession Crisis* (New Haven: Yale University Press, 1962).

sion crisis was a study by an attorney in Montgomery, Alabama, who argued that Fort Sumter did not even need relief, and implied that Lincoln's claim to be acting on a letter from Major Anderson, stating the need of relief, was a fabrication, since such a letter did not exist and had probably never existed. In short, Lincoln precipitated the crisis needlessly and on deliberately false grounds.

Since 1942 the flow of literature has been not only profuse but continuous. In 1947 the Lincoln Papers were at last opened to scholars. They have not yielded much data of large importance (Nicolay and Hay had combed them thoroughly), although David C. Mearns has published two volumes of selections from them. The Papers also helped pave the way for a long-awaited scholarly edition of Lincoln's writings. Before the Lincoln Papers were opened, J. G. Randall brought out, in 1945, the initial volumes of his history of Lincoln's presidency—the first full-scale scholarly study of this subject, and in 1955 this work was completed in a fourth volume, finished by Richard N. Current after Professor Randall's death. In 1952 the late Benjamin P. Thomas published his one-volume biography, *Abraham Lincoln,* a masterly summary of a vast amount of scholarship. In 1960 Reinhard Luthin added another, more extensive, one-volume treatment, *The Real Abraham Lincoln.* All of these far surpass in scholarship the earlier works, though it is questionable whether anyone has yet sized Lincoln up with more wisdom and perception than Lord Charnwood did in 1916. Meanwhile, an extraordinary profusion of good monographs has dealt with many aspects of Lincoln's career. The ones pertinent to the secession crisis include especially William E. Baringer, *A House Dividing: Lincoln as President Elect,* which, however, did not go beyond the inauguration, and which emphasized the problems of the cabinet rather more than the problems of secession; and William B. Hesseltine, *Lincoln and the War Governors,* which showed how the demands of the governors of the Northern States bore upon Lincoln's policy.

In the broader field of literature on the antecedents of the Civil War, again there has been a sweeping transformation. In 1942 the so-called revisionist view was just beginning to gather momentum. Avery O. Craven published his *Coming of the Civil War* in that year, and followed it with his *Growth of Southern Nationalism, 1848–1861* in 1953 and his *Civil War in the Making, 1815–1860* in 1959. I must return to the question of the relation of my own work to revisionism later in this introduction, but to continue here with this overview of the literature, the basic line of development is that Randall's work, mentioned above, as well as essays by him published in 1940, also became a cornerstone of revisionism, and that Roy F. Nichols' *The Disruption of American Democracy* partook of the revisionist view without fully adopting it. Since then, revisionism has come under fire from Arthur Schlesinger, Jr., Pieter Geyl, Harry V. Jaffa, and others, and a considerable body of critical discussion has accumulated concerning this controversy. While this dispute was raging, Allan Nevins was moving steadily ahead with a monumental history, which was neither strongly revisionist nor antirevisionist, and which gave us, in place of Rhodes' history, a massive survey of the entire crisis period, from the year 1850, using fully the vast body of information now available. Nevins' two-volume *Ordeal of the Union* came in 1947, followed by two more volumes, *The Emergence of Lincoln,* in 1950, and by a single volume, *The War for the Union: The Improvised War,* in 1959.(*) Since then, David Donald has added a contribution of importance in his *Charles Sumner and the Coming of the Civil War,* and Bruce Catton has given a detailed and illuminating account of the final crisis in his *The Coming Fury.*

While these writers dealt with the question of sectional antagonism in general, others have focused intensively on the Sumter crisis in particular. Kenneth Stampp did this, first in an article, "Lincoln and the Strategy of Defense in the Crisis of 1861," in 1945, and later in a book, *And the War Came: The North and the Secession Crisis, 1860–1861,* in 1950. Richard N. Current also did so, in an unpublished paper delivered at the annual meeting of the American Historical Association in 1955, and in a chapter, "The Bringer of War," in his *The Lincoln Nobody Knows,* in 1958. David R. Barbee renewed the extreme Southern attacks upon Lincoln as a warmonger in an article, "The Line of Blood—Lincoln and the Coming of the War," in 1957. Other writers have written criticisms, more or less extensive, concerning the views of these writers.

In the light of all this flood of new literature, it might be supposed that there is no longer place for a study of the secession crisis written in 1942. Yet, in another sense, it is surprising how little of the new evidence is really out of line with the evidence available in 1942. There are, to be sure, some changes. For instance, the late Frank Maloy Anderson has demonstrated conclusively, in my opinion, that the *Diary of a Public Man* was, if not a forgery, at least not what it purported to be; and if I were writing now I would not use it as a source . . . . Major Robert Anderson's letter, telling of the imminent exhaustion of his supplies at Sumter has been found in the Lincoln Papers, and I would now cite it directly instead of using elaborate indirect evidence to prove its existence. The papers of Charles Francis Adams have been opened, and I would now use them in my account of developments in the Committee of Thirty-Three, and would not rely so much upon what Henry Adams reported. Yet Martin Duber-

---

(*) In 1960, a second war volume appeared, *The War for the Union: War Becomes Revolution, 1862–1863.* Ed.

man's very able biography, based upon the papers, does not appreciably alter the story, and it shows that Henry Adams was remarkably accurate. Two letters have turned up in the Lincoln papers, giving Lincoln's statements in 1863 that he had offered to evacuate Fort Sumter in 1861 if the Virginia Convention would adjourn. But I had already concluded on the basis of testimony by C. S. Morehead and John Hay that Lincoln had made such an offer. We have some interesting new material on Republican opposition to compromise and some striking additional evidence that many Republicans did not believe that the secession threat was in earnest, and therefore that they did not really face the choice between disunion and war, and I would like to exhibit some of this material; but to do so would be merely to extend my original argument.

Where diverging views have developed on the interpretation of the events of 1861, they have resulted no less from the discovery of new evidence than from the development of conflicting interpretations of evidence which had been known for some time and which I used in my account. On the whole, I would still interpret this evidence today very largely as I did before, and I have therefore decided not to make revisions, which would be rather limited if I did make them, and which would only compel thorough scholars to use both editions in order to find how far I might have altered my original position. I admire the decision of David Riesman and Reuel Denney in their 1953 revision of *The Lonely Crowd* "not . . . to take into account the criticism made of the original work, because we believed it would be more helpful to our readers to be loyal to our original errors than to try to conceal them."

At the same time, however, it would be dated indeed to reissue this book without giving some attention to the bearing of the scholarship of the last two decades upon it. For inasmuch as my study dealt with the coming of the Civil War, it was almost by definition controversial, and it touched upon two questions which have been the focus of sharp and extensive dispute. One of these is the question whether the Civil War could have been and should have been avoided. This, of course, is a vast problem, and in its full extent reaches back to the earliest divergence between Northern and Southern societies. In its philosophical aspects, it involves all the great questions of causation, of historical inevitability, and of determinism. Obviously my book, with its sharp focus on the events of a five-month interval, did not attempt to deal either with the broad background of sectional antagonism or with the nature of historical forces. I was working on the immediate circumstances which led to the outbreak of war at a particular time—April 1861—and not on the underlying forces of antagonism which were back of these circumstances. If my narrative helps to explain anything, it helps to explain why war came when it did; it certainly does not explain at all why North and South were antagonistic to one another at this time; nor does it measure the depth of their antagonism. In a sense, therefore, there is hardly occasion for me to discuss whether a result was unavoidable from the operation of forces which I have not examined.

But I did suggest very strongly . . . that the Crittenden Resolutions represented a possible basis for compromise, and I presented evidence throughout that the Crittenden Plan commanded a great deal of support both in the North and in the South—so much, in fact, that if Lincoln had supported it, it might have been adopted. I still think the evidence is impressive, and I still believe that if Lincoln had supported the Compromise it might have been adopted.

This, of course, means that I believed there was a possible alternative to war in 1861. It does not mean that I regarded the crisis as an artificial one, or the sources of sectional antagonism as being in any sense superficial. It does not mean that I subscribed to the doctrine that conflict was "needless" or "repressible," for, as I asserted, "the slavery issue was certain to arouse emotions which no compromise could pacify—therefore it was beyond compromise." Yet to say that the fundamental source of friction was bound to cause deep antagonism is not, I think, the same as to say that this antagonism had inevitably to take the form of armed combat, and it is certainly not the same as to say that it had to take the form of armed combat at an exact time—April 1861—no sooner, no later.

The Crittenden Compromise had many of the same qualities and the same limitations as the Compromise of 1850. The chief limitation was that it did not and could not settle the slavery question. But within this limitation, it was perhaps less heavily freighted with bones of potential controversy than the Compromise of 1850. At least, it contained no Fugitive Slave Law, and it did not hold any such built-in ambiguities as later made the formula of popular sovereignty a source of chronic conflict. Perhaps it had almost as much popular backing at the beginning of 1860 as the Compromise of 1850 commanded at the beginning of the earlier year. Perhaps, also, it would have been a stopgap, or, as some would say, a "mere stopgap." The Compromise of 1850 is now widely regarded as such a stopgap; yet there is some question whether it failed in its own provisions or whether it was undone by the repeal of the Missouri Compromise in 1854.

I am very reluctant to dismiss Crittenden's plan as a stopgap so long as we maintain a double standard on the subject of stopgaps. For our evaluation of them depends very much upon whose gaps are being stopped. Thus no *modus vivendi* with the Soviet Union can be much more than a stopgap today, given our basic disagreements with that country. But we would be prone to regard it as most praiseworthy to defer a showdown, even for as much as five years. Our attitude is not unrelated to the fact that this would assure us of five years of immunity from being killed by the Russians. It is quite true, no doubt, that if war had been averted in 1861, it would not have meant a settlement of the issues. It would only have meant an indeterminate interval of immunity from being killed by the Rebs or the Yanks, as the case may be—immunity specifically for those who were killed between 1861 and 1865. Since all of these individuals would be dead by now even if the Rebs or the Yanks had not killed them, we can afford to be very bland about how right it was that the issue was met in 1861, and was not put off. All I suggest is that historians who believe so zealously in the virtue of facing up to issues in the past ought not to believe in the expedients of peace in the present. If an interval of peace, without any fundamental solution of issues, is worth something today, it was worth something in 1861. In 1861, as today, it would be worth a great deal less than a real peace—a real settlement of the basic issues.

Those who despise the advantages of a stopgap peace will point out, of course, that the Civil War did settle the basic issues. It saved the Union, and it freed 4,000,000 slaves. Certainly this is true, and it is important. But it can hardly be said that these immense values were gained at a bargain. For every six slaves who were freed, approximately one soldier was killed; for every ten white Southerners who were held in the Union, one Yank or one Reb died. A person is entitled to wonder whether the Southerners could not have been held and the slaves could not have been freed at a smaller per-capita cost. Certainly few would have purchased these gains at the time if they had known the price, and the mere fact that it has already been paid is not a reason for historians to let it go without questioning now.

The so-called revisionists, who have been most explicit in questioning the necessity for the war, have stressed certain themes: namely that the Republicans were quite prepared to guarantee the continued existence of slavery in all the slave states, and that the difference between what the Republicans proposed to do about slavery and what the Democrats proposed to do was not worth a war (this is, of course, very different from saying that slavery was not worth a war); that North and South had formed unreal, emotional stereotypes of one another, and that the opposing groups fought against these illusory stereotypes, rather than against one another; and that the war resulted from a breakdown of reason and would not have happened if reason had prevailed. In connection with these themes, they have been severely criticized for their moral indifference concerning slavery; for their failure to perceive that overwrought emotions and exaggerated stereotypes are the reflex rather than the cause of deep antagonisms; and for the fallacy that irrational forces are unreal forces. On all of these counts, it seems to me that revisionism is vulnerable, though it by no means follows that everyone associated with revisionism is open to these criticisms. For myself, to repeat, my study makes no attempt to analyze the long-range history of sectional antagonism, and I do not think that a compromise averting war in 1861 would have solved the basic issues or cleared up the basic problem any more than the Compromise of 1850 did. I certainly do not think the issues or the antagonisms were in any sense unreal, nor of anything less than major importance. If I believe there was an alternative course available in 1861, it is not because I am abstractly converted to the power of rationality but because the concrete evidence seems to me to show that a majority in the South did not want disunion and that a majority in the North did not want to press the question of slavery in the territories. I have discussed this evidence at length in my book, but here let me merely point out that in the election of 1860 the combined vote for Douglas and Bell in the slave states exceeded the vote for Breckinridge, and that the combined vote for Douglas, Bell, and Breckinridge in the states which stayed with the Union exceeded the vote for Lincoln. Over all, Lincoln received almost precisely the same proportion of the popular vote in 1860 that Herbert Hoover received in 1932 (39.9% and 39.6%). The evidence further seems to me to show that the Crittenden proposals commanded so much support in 1861 that if the President-elect had thrown his weight in the balance for them rather than against them, they would have been voted in Congress. If this had occurred, the fire-eating secessionists would still have resisted them bitterly, but again the evidence indicates that the fire-eaters almost failed to carry their program anyway, and if the Crittenden proposals had been thrown into the balance against them, they could hardly have gained the minimum support which they needed and which they only barely gained as it was. The Southern Unionists had beaten them in 1850 and might have done so again.

This, of course, would not have solved the ultimate problem. It would have resulted only in temporary peace. But what peace is more than temporary? Peace is essentially finite and temporal, and can be gained only by installments—not in perpetuity. Our peace with the Soviet Union for some seventeen years now has never appeared more than temporary, and indeed future historians may say that it was not worth our while to preserve such a tenuous peace. If it has any merit, it is only the merit of being better than war, and that is the merit which peace in 1861 might have had.

Along with the debate as to what policy ought to have been adopted in 1861, there is also a disagreement as to what policy actually was adopted, for there has been a spirited dispute concerning the real intent of the Lincoln administration. This brings me to the second controversial aspect of my study. My narrative emphasized the idea that Lincoln wanted peace and believed until the last moment that he might be able to preserve it. Many very able historians, like Bruce Catton, David Donald, and Allan Nevins, hold a similar view, but there are other scholars whose work must be taken very seriously who deny that Lincoln wanted peace or, if not that he wanted it, that he either expected it or thought it practicable to seek.

When I wrote in 1942, the chief exponent of this view was the late Professor Charles W. Ramsdell. Ramsdell, a Texan and a man of Southern sympathies, took a fairly clear-cut position. Lincoln, he said, was in a dilemma from which he perceived that he could escape if the Southerners "could . . . be *induced* [his italics] to attack Sumter." Therefore Lincoln deliberately "maneuvered the Confederates into firing the first shot." He adopted a "stratagem," and when Sumter was fired upon he knew that his "strategy had been completely successful." Ramsdell compared Lincoln's handling of the Sumter situation to Bismarck's handling of the Ems telegram.

Professor J. G. Randall challenged this argument, and my book here challenged it also. . . .

A few years after Ramsdell's paper, Kenneth M. Stampp published another interpretation of Lincoln's policy, which was formulated in his paper entitled "Lincoln and the Strategy of Defense in 1861" and in his book *And the War Came,* both mentioned above. Stampp's argument was a subtle and balanced one, less easy to summarize than Ramsdell's, but he seemed to say first that, without really wanting war, Lincoln *expected* war—he saw it was on the way, and he prepared not to be caught at a disadvantage by its coming; and second, that without actually *inducing* (Ramsdell's word) the Confederates to start a war, Lincoln took a position to which he foresaw the Confederates would react by starting a war. In Stampp's opinion, Lincoln was quite satisfied with the outcome. Both writers spoke of Lincoln's action as a "maneuver," and Stampp spoke distinctly of Lincoln's "coercionist views," and of his policy as one of "casting coercion in the mold of defense." According to Stampp, Lincoln saw the possibilities in the situation where "the Union government could easily pretend to forego aggressive action and simulate a defensive pose."

It would be a neat question to determine wherein Ramsdell and Stampp agreed, and wherein they disagreed. Certainly Ramsdell laid emphasis upon the thought that Lincoln actually desired war, while Stampp stressed the thought that he accepted it as something that could not be averted and must be handled in an advantageous way. Also, Ramsdell pictured him as scheming to provoke the Confederates to attack, while Stampp portrays him rather as taking a position which he shrewdly foresaw that they would attack. But these differences sometimes blur at the edges, and to some extent both writers are saying the same things: Lincoln concluded that he could only save the Union by means of war; he perceived that it would be greatly to his advantage if the adversary did the first shooting; he therefore worked out a policy at Fort Sumter which he clearly foresaw would result in an initiation of hostilities by the Confederates; his claims of a peaceful intent merely to provision the fort were disingenuous; and when war came, he was well satisfied with the result.

The most substantial difference between Ramsdell and Stampp clearly turns not upon what they think Lincoln was doing but upon how they feel about what they think he was doing. Ramsdell, with his Southern sympathies, was shocked and disapproving. Stampp, on the contrary, with solidly Northern sympathies, says in effect that the War was worth what it cost, that it had to be, and that Lincoln is to be admired for putting his adversaries in the wrong and for facing up to the situation without shirking it.

Professor Stampp is a most resourceful scholar, and so is Richard N. Current, who has to some extent associated himself with Stampp's position. They make an impressive presentation. For instance, Stampp adduces a very strong argument that Lincoln must have known that war was likely to result from sending provisions to Sumter. He knew that the Confederates had fired on the *Star of the West* when it brought provisions; members of the cabinet told him plainly that the sending of provisions would result in war; and, as Current emphasizes, his special emissary to Charleston, Stephen A. Hurlbut, reported to him on March 17 that any attempt to send provisions would result in war.

It is certainly true, as Stampp and Current contend, that Lincoln must have seen the likelihood of war, and that his thought must have reckoned with that contingency. I now believe that I should have recognized this fact more clearly and explicitly than I did, and if I were rewriting my account now, I would do so. But for reasons which I will indicate further on, it seems to me that, whatever other effects his recognition of the increasing likelihood of war may have had upon Lincoln, it did not cause him to deviate a single step from a course of action which can be precisely defined. This course was to avoid any menacing action or any action which might precipitate a clash, just as far as was possible consistently with maintaining the principle of Union. As I have argued at some length, Lincoln pointedly refrained from the exercise of all the customary forms of federal authority in the seceded states, any of which he would have been perfectly justified in asserting.

Not all of Stampp's and Current's arguments seem to me as convincing as their demonstration that Lincoln must have realized the increasing likelihood of war. For instance, they have made very detailed computations to discredit Lincoln's statement in his message to Congress in July 1861 that he had decided upon sending the final expedition to Fort Sumter only after his attempt to reinforce Fort Pickens had failed. He stated that he had wanted to demonstrate, by the reinforcement of Pickens, "a clear indication of policy," and that if he had been able to do this it would have "better enable[d] the country to accept the evacuation of Fort Sumter as a military necessity." Stampp's analysis emphasizes, quite correctly, that Lincoln had certainly ordered the Sumter expedition prepared before he learned that the reinforcement of Pickens had miscarried. It also emphasizes the even more important points that Lincoln had actually gone to the length of ordering the expedition to move, and of sending word to Major Anderson that it would move. But it is crucial that the evidence still indicates that Lincoln did not inform the Governor of South Carolina that the Sumter expedition would be sent until exactly the time when news reached Washington that the orders of March 11 for the reinforcing of Pickens had not been carried out. This news left Pensacola on April 1 and arrived at Washington on April 6, the same day on which Lincoln's message to the Governor of South Carolina was sent. The labored nature of Stampp's and Current's arguments on this point makes it all the more striking that they have found the essential point unassailable: the one irrevocable step, the message to the Governor, was taken on the very day when news arrived of the failure to reinforce Pickens. The first ships of the Sumter expedition did not leave port until two days later.

The assertions, therefore, that Lincoln's later statement about this matter is "scarcely consistent with the known facts" and that "the President had dealt with Sumter and Pickens as separate problems" seem to me arbitrary and insufficiently proved. Also it seems unsatisfactory to say that Lincoln did not need to wait for news of the reinforcement of Pickens, since he "had no reason to doubt that his order would be executed." In fact, his order instructed Union troops to occupy a position which he knew that Confederate forces might try to prevent them from occupying, and he had very real reason to await the result with anxiety. And, of course, his order was not executed, though the Fort was later reinforced.

Another case in point is the question of Lincoln's offer to the Virginians to evacuate Fort Sumter if they would adjourn the Virginia Convention. Historians have fallen into an endless dispute over the insoluble question whether Lincoln made such an offer to John B. Baldwin. But this focus upon Baldwin is unfortunate, for the testimony of Governor Morehead of Kentucky and of John Hay, reporting the statement of Lincoln himself, has long given evidence that Lincoln did propose to the Border State men terms on which he would abandon the Fort. Since the opening of the Lincoln Papers, new evidence in the form of a letter from George Plumer Smith to John Hay on January 9, 1863, asking Hay to secure Lincoln's confirmation of the fact that Lincoln had told him (Smith) of the offer to Baldwin, and a reply from Hay to Smith on January 10 giving this confirmation, tend to corroborate this further. Professor Stampp deals with this evidence by doubting that Lincoln "seriously expected the Virginians to accept the offer," and Professor Current by saying that "these letters, it seems to me, by no means settle the controversy as to whether Lincoln actually made an offer to give up the fort."

There is certainly a substantial amount of evidence, whether it is conclusive or not, both in general terms and in specific terms, that Lincoln thought, until very late in the crisis, if not until the end, that he could achieve both peace and Union and would not have to choose between them. In this connection it is important to remember how consistently the Republicans had ridiculed all threats of secession, and how much they were the captives of their own mental set when secession came. In the light of this mental set, it is not really necessary to attribute such adroit hidden purposes as Stampp attributes to Lincoln in explaining his statement that "there is no crisis but an artificial one."

It is also important to remember that in some respects the secession movement, as of March 1861, had failed and that Seward, at least, regarded it as a failure. Eight slave states were still in the Union; only seven had seceded. The secessionists had been beaten in Virginia, North Carolina, Tennessee, Arkansas, and Missouri, and the efforts to create a united South had divided the South as never before.

Another point which it is essential to keep in view if Lincoln's thinking is to be understood is that the President-elect made all his calculations, until March 5, on the assumption that Major Anderson's position at Fort Sumter was secure and that the existing status could continue for some time without any positive action on the part of the new administration. Not until March 5 did Secretary Holt and General Scott confront him with the news that a decision would have to be made at once either to abandon Fort Sumter or to take positive action for the support of the Fort.

Without being repetitious about evidence which is discussed more fully in the main body of this work, I would argue also that there are several items of evidence which indicate that Lincoln did quite seriously consider the evacuation of Fort Sumter. For instance: the fact that he made overtures to the Virginians about this possibility; the fact that Seward expected evacuation with enough confidence to make promises to the

Confederates, based upon the expectation; the fact that Trumbull feared evacuation enough to introduce monitory resolutions in the Senate reminding the new head of the Republican party of his duty "to hold and protect the public property." Could these things have happened if the idea of evacuation had not seemed very much a reality?

The dispute concerning evidence, however, could go on endlessly for two reasons. First, because there were large factors working toward war and large factors working for peace, and both left a substantial residue of evidence. Thus one can marshal extensive material to show the magnitude of the demands upon Lincoln to hold Sumter or the extent of the pressure upon him to evacuate the Fort. Applying this ambivalence to Lincoln's own situation, one can legitimately stress his seeming expectation in March that he would abandon Sumter, or one can with equal validity emphasize the deep reluctance with which he arrived at this expectation. The historian can show that many of Lincoln's contemporaries regarded the first inaugural address as a threat of coercion, or he can show that many others thought it was too mild and was a promise of peace. That this disagreement continues is evident from the fact that, in our own time, Stampp sees it primarily as a statement "in which he [Lincoln] took such enormous pains to absolve himself from the charge of aggression," while Allan Nevins sees it as "one long plea for patience, forbearance, and the avoidance of rash action," and Roy F. Nichols calls it "a stirring plea to avoid hostilities."

A second reason that the review of evidence can never be conclusive is that the dispute turns not only upon what Lincoln did but upon what he thought. In other words, it is a question of motive as well as of action. Motive lies to a considerable extent beyond historical proof, partly because historical judgments must depend upon acts, and the same act may be performed with diverse motives by different persons. Thus a man may perform an act which is honest in its effect because he is an honest man on principle, or because he wants whatever policy will prove most advantageous to him and he believes that honesty is the best policy. This example is not far from the point at issue here, for essentially I am arguing that Lincoln followed a peaceable-seeming course because he was a peaceable man who wanted peace and thought he could attain it. Stampp and Current are essentially arguing that he wanted an effective policy, knew that a peaceable-seeming policy would be most effective, and therefore took care to make his policy appear peaceable, though there was a covert element of coercion and of aggressiveness in it. They contend that he did not really mind fighting a war to protect the national interest.

If motive cannot be accurately determined, there will always be room both for the beliefs that Lincoln's purposes were peaceable or, alternatively, that the peaceable appearance of his position cloaked a purpose far from pacific. But if the question of motive must, by its very nature, be forever open to doubt, it becomes doubly important to turn back to the question of actions. At this level, the historian faces a different problem: given Lincoln's determination to save the Union, and given his belief that the loss of Fort Sumter, without being sure of Fort Pickens, would make it impossible to save the Union, could he have followed any more peaceable course than he did? Was there any possible means of holding Sumter that would have been less provocative than informing the Confederates that "an attempt will be made to supply Fort Sumter with provisions only and that if such attempt be not resisted, no effort to throw in men, arms, or ammunition will be made, without further notice or [except] in case of an attack upon the Fort." The existence of such an alternative and the demonstration that Lincoln rejected it is essential to any argument that Lincoln was not following the most peaceable course available to him.

Unless the historians who charge Lincoln with coercive or covertly aggressive policies can name a less provocative course that he might have followed, they are in the curious position of arguing that a man may pursue a course which offers the maximum possibility of peace and may at the same time be open to the accusation of scheming to bring about war.

If the very nature of human motivation is such that no one can ever say categorically whether Lincoln's purposes were peaceable, perhaps it is more nearly possible to say categorically whether his course of action was peaceable. Here the crucial fact is that no one who attributes to him a purpose to see that the war got started in a way that would be advantageous to him has yet said what else he could have done that would have been more peaceable than what he did, given his purpose not to abandon the principle of Union.

No doubt he must have recognized that war might ensue; no doubt he must have seen that if it did ensue, it would come in a way disadvantageous to the Confederacy; no doubt he was glad this was true. But when we say this, we are back in the realm of motive again. If we confine ourselves to scrutinizing his overt course, the question persists: what could he have done that would have been more peaceable? Two outstanding scholars have defined this point well. J. G. Randall stated it with superb precision when he wrote: "To say that Lincoln meant that the first shot would be fired by the other side, *if a first shot was fired* [Randall's italics], is by no means the equivalent of saying that he deliberately maneuvered to have the shot fired. This distinction is fundamental." Allan Nevins stated it with wonderful force when he said: " 'In your hands, not mine,' he [Lincoln] had told Southerners, 'lies the issue of peace or war.' The shells that burst over a Federal fort awaiting a victualizing expedition which had orders not to fire unless it was fired upon, gave the answer to that statement."

A PROPHECY

The following letter was written not one month after the election of James Buchanan to the Presidency. Remarkably perceptive, it forecasts the disruption of the Democratic party in 1860 and a Republican victory in that year. Public opinion in the free states, it noted, had crystallized against the extension of slavery. John Murray Forbes, who wrote this prophetic letter to a Florida friend, was a Boston capitalist and railroad entrepreneur. A staunch Republican, he was to render invaluable service to the Lincoln administration during the Civil War.

JOHN MURRAY FORBES, *Letter to J. Hamilton Cowper*

(Private) Boston, December 4, 1856

My dear Sir—Your favor of the 6th ulto. reached me in due course and I am much obliged for your valuable information and suggestions in regard to Chinese labor in Florida, which will probably nip that scheme in the bud or reduce it to a very safe experiment.

I thank you too for your frankness in regard to the great question of the day. You say truly that it is too delicate for profitable discussion among friends, but this makes it only the more important that the real state of public opinion, outside of partisan politics, should be better known than it is.

I had supposed that there existed a party of great latent strength at the South who value the Union much more than they do the extension of the institution of slavery, and who would put forth their strength whenever any real danger came. Knowing how far you are above being influenced by any desire for office, or for any popular extravagance, I take it as the very worst indication of the coming storm to find that you are not on that side of the question. Regretting deeply that it is so, I thank you for the warning, which coming on top of the election of Mr. Buchanan assures me that we are doomed to continued agitation until 1860, and then to the first real experiment of the strength of our confederacy. You have thrown a gloomy shadow over the hopes I had entertained of help for the Union from the conservatism of the South; but it is far better to know the truth, and I owe it to you in return to tell you what seems to me the state

---

John Murray Forbes, *Letters and Recollections*, ed. Sarah Forbes Hughes (Boston: Houghton Mifflin, 1900), Vol. I, pp. 152–158.

of public opinion here. Upon the only real point of difference suggested by you—which indeed is the only real issue between the North and South, viz.: the constitutionality of the principle of the Jefferson Proviso—there is hardly any division of opinion at the North excepting among the partisans of squatter sovereignty; and the experience in Kansas has, I think, reduced the advocates of this doctrine to a small minority. We are then all united here in the opinion that either Congress or the squatters (some looking to one and some to the other) have a clear right to prohibit slavery in the territories from the moment that settlement begins. We have been brought up in the faith that this was settled constitutional doctrine, held as it has been by all the men we are accustomed to look upon as great authorities at the North, and by many of your own best men, and confirmed too by the adoption of the Ordinance of 1787, at the very time when the Constitutional Convention was in session, as also by the adoption of the Missouri compromise when Mr. Calhoun was a member of the Cabinet.

But it is not my purpose to argue. I only mean to state the almost universal conviction at the North that the restriction of slavery is as clearly within the constitutional rights of the majority as any of our admitted and daily exercised rights; and the only real difference of opinion here is as to the expediency of exercising that right. Mr. Webster, with a respectable body of Whigs and a large body of Democrats, was, in 1850, against exercising that right unnecessarily; but it is a very solemn conviction that there is, as nearly as possible, unanimity here, since the repeal of the Missouri compromise, in favor of exercising that (real or supposed) right at all hazards whenever practically necessary to prevent the extension of slavery into territories now free.

Beyond and above all this, the conviction is being daily forced upon the North that the designs of the South do not stop with introducing slavery into our own territories, but that the question to be settled in Kansas is whether the whole power of the confederacy shall be exercised for buying or conquering all the territory and islands north of Panama for the mere extension of your institution. Some of your more bold and ultra men plainly avow this intention so far as Cuba, Mexico, and Central America are concerned; and the Cincinnati platform is certainly so framed as to warrant this apprehension on the part of the North.

Mr. Buchanan, if aided by the conservative men of the South, may allay the apprehension that the South seek anything more than the assertion of their (supposed or real) right to take their slaves into our own territories, but even if he does succeed thus far, it is my belief that the issue has been so sharply defined to be a struggle for political power between the North and South, that it is too late to change it until one or the other side yield, or until we separate and begin again on a new basis. I believe that the public mind in the non-slaveholding States has been in a state of revolution for some years, but of active change since the passage of the Nebraska Bill, and that the change will go on during the next four years in a progressive ratio, until in 1860 there will be not the ghost of a chance for any man's getting an electoral vote in the North and West who is not sharply opposed to the extension of slavery at home and abroad; and, moreover, that it will take all the strength of the moderate men of the North to draw the line there—to keep within the Republican platform of 1856.

It is hard for you to appreciate justly our position here without knowing more of the parties who rule the North than you can know through the expression given us by the press, the pulpit, and the rostrum.

I will try to sketch the elements that now move the Northern mind. The abolitionists have never had much direct influence, and they have been losing ground for several years; they may be thrown entirely out of account. The conservative men of both political parties have hitherto believed that they could occupy a common ground with those of the South in advocating the policy of letting slavery alone where it existed, and still retain their proper influence with the masses; but the issue at last made of slavery extension leaves them no choice between opposition to it and political annihilation. They have very extensively joined the Fremont party, and unless the issue can be changed they must continue to go there, until the remainder who take the Southern side becomes so small as just conveniently to fill the federal offices and the easy chairs of their drawing-rooms and clubs. But it is the masses, the democracy (call it by what name we may), which must rule; and they are hopelessly against the Southern policy, whether it be called the extension of slavery, or the establishment of a balance of power between the two sections.

Buchanan owes his Northern success to the Fillmore diversion, and to the name of Democrat which in certain slow-moving regions, like parts of Pennsylvania, still retained its power, under the representations of his partisans that he was for popular sovereignty (squatter) and for free Kansas. But, my dear sir, depend upon it the Northern democracy can never again be depended upon for a Southern alliance. Fifteen or twenty years ago the abolition men and women were mobbed everywhere, and their lives endangered and their halls burned; now the mob are all the other way, but it is not that they have become abolitionists. The wrong of slavery preached to them from the pulpit, the waste and inexpediency of slavery reiterated to them by the press, doubtless weigh with the masses, but all other influences sink into insignificance compared with that brought to bear for two years past, and especially during the past four months from the stump and by the tremendous machinery of the campaign press, to convince the laboring classes here of the aristocratic nature of the institution of slavery; of the small number of slaveholders compared with the white population North and South, and of the coming issue being whether this small class (supposed to rule the South) shall own half the Senate and shall use the national arm to extend their institution at home and abroad.

So long as there is a pretext, a color, for holding up to the people such an issue, there can be but one result.

The masses in all countries can be roused upon two points, their nation's interests and their own prejudices; and if there is anything in this country fixed, it is the prejudice against aught which has the appearance even of aristocracy. Are you entirely free from danger from this prejudice at home?

Unless then some strange and almost impossible change takes place in Mr. Buchanan's policy from that of his predecessor, you may count upon the popular vote of 1860 being against the increase of Southern power with as much certainty as you could upon its being thrown against the reëstablishment in our territories of the feudal institutions of the Middle Ages. I have said far more than I intended, but I have not that power of condensation which you so happily possess.

I cordially respond to your hope that difference of opinion as to public policy may never interfere with friendly private relations between individuals of the North and South, and am with great respect,

Yours very truly,

J. M. Forbes

P.S.—In reading over what I have hastily written I see that I have omitted to explain what I mean by the danger from Mr. Buchanan's election. Any attempt on his part to strengthen the South immediately or prospectively in the Senate, by foreign acquisitions of territory or otherwise, will only precipitate the crisis and increase the agitation. The only hope of safety for the Union seems to me to be for the South now, when they apparently have the power through their own President, and can do so without sacrifice of their pride, to recede from their position in regard to slavery extension, and from their struggle for that fatal chimera "the balance of power." Let it give up this, and by its compact union it will always have more than its fair share of the government; then by taking ground on which the conservatives of the North can stand with them (and still retain their due influence at home), the true interests of the whole country may be secured by putting down radical and dangerous experiments in government, and by avoiding those foreign wars which our turbulent spirits, North and South, will always be only too ready to engage in against the despotisms of the Old World.

Yours truly,

J.M.F.

CABINET CONSENSUS

Immediately after his inauguration President Lincoln was confronted with the problem of whether to maintain what was left of Federal property and authority in the seceded states. For political reasons, it seemed imperative that the flag be shown. By March 4, 1861 his options had dwindled to Fort Sumter in Charleston Harbor and Fort Pickens just off Pensacola, Florida. The Provisional Confederate government at Montgomery, Alabama was just as anxious to eliminate these symbols of national authority as the Lincoln administration was to maintain them. Yet each side was reluctant to take the first step. Lincoln's military and naval chiefs and his entire Cabinet except Montgomery Blair, the Postmaster General, felt that Sumter could not be relieved with the forces at hand.

ABRAHAM LINCOLN, *Memorandum on Fort Sumter*

March 18[?] 1861

Some considerations in favor of withdrawing the Troops from Fort Sumpter, by President Lincoln.

1. The Fort cannot be permanently held without reinforcement.
   This point is too apparent too [*sic*] need proof.
   The cutting off supplies and consequent starvation, not to mention disease, would compel surrender in a few months at farthest, without firing a gun.

2. The Fort cannot now be re-inforced without a large armament, involving of course a bloody conflict and great exasperation on both sides, and when re-inforced can only be held by sufficient number to garrison the post and to keep open communication with it by means of the harbor.

3. The Fort in the present condition of affairs is of inconsiderable military value, for: It is not necessary for the Federal Government to hold it in order to protect the City of Charleston from foreign invasion, nor: Is it available under existing circumstances for the purpose of collecting the revenue: and, It is difficult to see how the possession of the Fort by the Secessionists can be rendered a means of annoyance to the Federal Government. Every purpose for which the fort can now be made available would be better subserved by Ships of War, outside the harbor.

Gideon Welles Papers, Library of Congress.

4. The abandonment of the Post would remove a source of irritation to the Southern people and deprive the secession movement of one of its most powerful stimulants.

5. It would indicate both an independent and a conservative position on part of the new administration, and would gratify and encourage those, who while friendly to the Union are yet reluctant to see extreme measures pursued.

6. It would tend to confound and embarrass those enemies of the Union both at the North and South who have relied on the cry of "Coercion" as a means of keeping up the excitement against the Republican Party.

7. If the garrison should, while in an enfeebled condition be successfully attacked, or from want of proper supplies should be cut off by disuse the administration would be held responsible for it and this fact would be used by their opponents with great effect.

8. The moral advantage to the Secessionists of a successful attack would be very great.

Objections

1. The danger of demoralizing the Republican Party by a measure which might seem to many to indicate timidity or in common parlance, "want of pluck."

That this may be the first impression is probable but if the measure is justified upon the double ground of the small importance of the post in a military point of view and the desire to conciliate wherever this can be safely done a second thought will discover the wisdom of the course, and increase rather than diminish the confidence of the party in its leaders.

2. The danger of the movement being construed by the Secessionists as a yielding from necessity, and in so far a victory on their part.

WASHINGTON ON THE EVE

While President and Cabinet remained in a quandary regarding the Sumter-Pickens situation, the noted Crimean war correspondent William H. Russell visited Washington. An intimate of Thackeray and Dickens, a gifted storyteller, a bold, incisive writer, Russell gives us fine profiles of Lincoln, of Seward, and of other Cabinet members while the crisis was developing in South Carolina and Florida. He was impressed by Lincoln's unusual qualities, and thought the President, despite his rude appearance, an altogether striking individual. Commenting on Administration policy, he shrewdly remarked that the President and his Cabinet were not committed to any inflexible policy but were "waiting for events to develop themselves."

WILLIAM H. RUSSELL, *My Diary North and South*

March 27th, 1861. This morning, after breakfast, Mr. Sanford called, according to promise, and took me to the State department. It is a very humble—in fact, dingy—mansion, two stories high, and situated at the end of the magnificent line of colonnade in white marble, called the Treasury, which is hereafter to do duty as the head-quarters of nearly all the public departments. People familiar with Downing Street, however, cannot object to the dinginess of the bureaux in which the foreign and state affairs of the American Republic are transacted. A flight of steps leads to the hall-door, on which an announcement in writing is affixed, to indicate the days of reception for the various classes of persons who have business with the Secretary of State; in the hall, on the right and left, are small rooms, with the names of the different officers on the doors—most of them persons of importance; half-way in the hall a flight of stairs conducts us to a similar corridor, rather dark, with doors on each side opening into the bureaux of the chief clerks. All the appointments were very quiet, and one would see much more bustle in the passages of a Poor Law Board or a parish vestry.

In a moderately sized, but very comfortable, apartment, surrounded with book-shelves, and ornamented with a few engravings, we found the Secretary of State seated at his table, and enjoying a cigar; he received me with great courtesy and kindness, and after a time said he would take occasion to present me to the President, who was to give audience that day to the minister of the new kingdom of Italy, who had hitherto only represented the kingdom of Sardinia. . . .

. . . We accordingly set out through a private door leading to the grounds and within a few seconds entered the hall of the moderate mansion, White House, which has very much the air of a portion of a bank or public office, being provided with glass doors and plain heavy chairs and forms. The

William Howard Russell, *My Diary North and South* (Boston: T. H. O. P. Burnham, 1863), pp. 36–40.

domestic who was in attendance was dressed like any ordinary citizen, and seemed perfectly indifferent to the high position of the great personage with whom he conversed, when Mr. Seward asked him, "Where is the President?" Passing through one of the doors on the left, we entered a handsome spacious room, richly and rather gorgeously furnished, and rejoicing in a kind of *"demi-jour,"* which gave increased effect to the gilt chairs and ormolu ornaments. Mr. Seward and the Chevalier stood in the centre of the room, whilst his son and I remained a little on one side: "For," said Mr. Seward, "you are not to be supposed to be here."

Soon afterwards there entered, with a shambling, loose, irregular, almost unsteady gait, a tall, lank, lean man, considerably over six feet in height, with stooping shoulders, long pendulous arms, terminating in hands of extraordinary dimensions, which, however, were far exceeded in proportion by his feet. He was dressed in an ill-fitting, wrinkled suit of black, which put one in mind of an undertaker's uniform at a funeral; round his neck a rope of black silk was knotted in a large bulb, with flying ends projecting beyond the collar of his coat; his turned-down shirt-collar disclosed a sinewy muscular yellow neck, and above that, nestling in a great black mass of hair, bristling and compact like a ruff of mourning pins, rose the strange quaint face and head, covered with its thatch of wild republican hair, of President Lincoln. The impression produced by the size of his extremities, and by his flapping and wide projecting ears, may be removed by the appearance of kindliness, sagacity, and the awkward bonhommie of his face; the mouth is absolutely prodigious; the lips, straggling and extending almost from one line of black beard to the other, are only kept in order by two deep furrows from the nostril to the chin; the nose itself—a prominent organ—stands out from the face, with an inquiring, anxious air, as though it were sniffing for some good thing in the wind; the eyes dark, full, and deeply set, are penetrating, but full of an expression which almost amounts to tenderness; and above them projects the shaggy brow, running into the small hard frontal space, the development of which can scarcely be estimated accurately, owing to the irregular flocks of thick hair carelessly brushed across it. One would say that, although the mouth was made to enjoy a joke, it could also utter the severest sentence which the head could dictate, but that Mr. Lincoln would be ever more willing to temper justice with mercy, and to enjoy what he considers the amenities of life, than to take a harsh view of men's nature and of the world, and to estimate things in an ascetic or puritan spirit. A person who met Mr. Lincoln in the street would not take him to be what —according to the usages of European society—is called a "gentleman;" and, indeed, since I came to the United States, I have heard more disparaging allusions made by Americans to him on that account than I could have expected among simple republicans, where all should be equals; but, at the same time, it would not be possible for the most indifferent observer to pass him in the street without notice.

As he advanced through the room, he evidently controlled a desire to shake hands all round with everybody, and smiled good-humoredly till he was suddenly brought up by the staid deportment of Mr. Seward, and by the profound diplomatic bows of the Chevalier Bertinatti. Then, indeed, he suddenly jerked himself back, and stood in front of the two ministers, with his body slightly drooped forward, and his hands behind his back, his knees touching, and his feet apart. . . .

The minister forthwith handed his letter to the President, who gave it into the custody of Mr. Seward, and then, dipping his hand into his coat-pocket, Mr. Lincoln drew out a sheet of paper, from which he read his reply, the most remarkable part of which was his doctrine "that the United States were bound by duty not to interfere with the differences of foreign governments and countries." After some words of compliment, the President shook hands with the minister, who soon afterwards retired. Mr. Seward then took me by the hand and said—"Mr. President, allow me to present to you Mr. Russell, of the London 'Times.' " On which Mr. Lincoln put out his hand in a very friendly manner, and said, "Mr. Russell, I am very glad to make your acquaintance, and to see you in this country. The London 'Times' is one of the greatest powers in the world—in fact, I don't know anything which has much more power—except perhaps the Mississippi. I am glad to know you as its minister." Conversation ensued for some minutes, which the President enlivened by two or three peculiar little sallies, and I left agreeably impressed with his shrewdness, humor, and natural sagacity.

In the evening I dined with Mr. Seward, in company with his son, Mr. Seward, junior, Mr. Sanford, and a quaint, natural specimen of an American rustic lawyer, who was going to Brussels as Secretary of Legation. His chief, Mr. Sanford, did not appear altogether happy when introduced to his secretary, for he found that he had a very limited knowledge (if any) of French, and of other things which it is generally considered desirable that secretaries should know.

Very naturally, conversation turned on politics. Although no man can foresee the nature of the crisis which is coming, nor the mode in which it is to be encountered, the faith of men like Mr. Sanford and Mr. Seward in the ultimate success of their principles, and in the integrity of the Republic, is very remarkable; and the boldness of their language in reference to foreign powers almost amounts to arrogance and menace, if not to temerity. Mr. Seward asserted that the Ministers of England or of France had no right to make any allusion to the civil war which appeared imminent; and that the Southern Commissioners who had been sent abroad could not be received by the Government of any foreign power, officially or otherwise, even to hand in a document or to make a representation, without incurring the risk of breaking off relations with the Government of the United States. As regards the great object of public curiosity, the relief of Fort Sumter, Mr. Seward maintains a profound silence, beyond the mere declaration, made with a pleasant twinkle of the eye, that "the whole policy of the Government, on that and other questions, is put forth in the President's inaugural, from which there will be no deviation. Turning to the inaugural message, however, there is no such very certain indication, as Mr. Seward pretends to discover, of the course to be pursued by Mr. Lincoln and the cabinet. To an outside observer, like myself, it seems as if they were waiting for events to develop themselves, and rested their policy rather upon acts that had occurred, than upon any definite principle designed to control or direct the future. . . .

PICKENS VERSUS SUMTER

As Gideon Welles, Lincoln's Secretary of the Navy, remembered events of March and April 1861, Seward, in his anxiety to stave off conflict, encouraged the President to make the stand at Pickens rather than Sumter. Yet Lincoln, without informing either of his service secretaries about his decision on Pickens, authorized them to go ahead with the preparations for the relief of Sumter by the Fox squadron. Yielding to Seward, however, he detached the warship Powhatan *from the Sumter relief expedition, and under command of Lieutenant David Porter, she sailed for the Florida coast. When the President learned on April 6th that Pickens might also be in desperate straits, he tried unsuccessfully to recall the* Powhatan.

Excerpts from *The Diary of Gideon Welles*

. . . A strange state of things existed at that time in Washington. The atmosphere was thick with treason. Party spirit and old party differences prevailed, however, amidst these accumulating dangers. Secession was considered by most persons as a political party question, not as rebellion. Democrats to a large extent sympathized with the Rebels more than with the Administration, which they opposed, not that they wished secession to be successful and the Union divided, but they hoped that President Lincoln and the Republicans would, overwhelmed by obstacles and embarrassments, prove failures. The Republicans, on the other hand, were scarcely less partisan and unreasonable. Crowds of them at this period, when the storm of civil war was about bursting on the country, thronged the anterooms of the President and Secretaries, clamorous for the removal of all Democrats, indiscriminately, from office. Patriotism was with them no test, no shield from party malevolence. They demanded the proscription and exclusion of such Democrats as opposed the Rebel movements and clung to the Union, with the same vehemence that they demanded the removal of the worst Rebels who advocated a dissolution of the Union.

Neither party appeared to be apprehensive of or to realize the gathering storm. There was a general belief, indulged in by most persons, that an adjustment would in some way be brought about, without any extensive resort to extreme measures. It seemed probable there might be some outbreak in South Carolina, and perhaps in one or two other places, but such would, it was believed, be soon and easily suppressed. The threatened violence which the nullifiers had thundered for thirty years in the ears of the people had caused their threats to be considered as the harmless ebullitions of excited demagogues throughout the North, while at the South those utterances had so trained the Southern mind, and fired the Southern heart, as to cause them to be received as truthful. The South were, therefore, more united and earnest at this crisis, more determined on seceding, than either the Democrats or Republicans supposed. But, while the great body of the people and most of their leaders in the Northern States, listening to the ninety-day prophecies of Mr. Seward, were incredulous as to any extensive, serious disturbance, there were not a few whose forebodings were grave and sad. All the calamities which soon befell the country these men anticipated. Yet such as were in positions of responsibility would not permit themselves to despond, or despair of the Republic. Mr. Seward

---

John T. Morse, Jr., ed., *The Diary of Gideon Welles* (Boston: Houghton Mifflin, 1911), Vol. I, Ch. 1, *passim.*

possessed a hopeful and buoyant spirit which did not fail him in that dark period, and at no time were his party feelings more decided than during the spring of 1861. . . . In the confident belief that he could, if once in place and power, effect conciliation and peace, it had been an object with him to tide the difficulties past the 4th of March. He therefore had operated to that end, and so had Mr. Buchanan, though for different reasons.

Through Mr. Stanton, after that gentleman entered Mr. Buchanan's Cabinet, Mr. Seward and others were secretly advised in regard to the important measures of the Buchanan Administration, and in the course of the winter Mr. Seward came to an understanding, as was alleged and as events and circumstances indicated, with certain of the leading Secessionists. Among other things it was asserted that an agreement had been entered into that no assault should be made on Fort Sumter, provided the garrison should not be reinforced. Mr. Buchanan was to observe the status thus understood during the short remaining period of his administration, and Mr. Seward, as the coming premier, was, on the change of administration, to carry forward the policy of non-reinforcement of Sumter. If not supplied or reinforced, famine would certainly effect the downfall of the fortress without bloodshed on either side. Until blood was spilled, there was hope of conciliation. In fulfillment of this arrangement, Mr. Seward opposed any and every scheme to reinforce Sumter, and General Scott, who was old and much under his influence, if not a party to the understanding, seconded or took a leading part in that opposition.

On the 5th of March commissioners from the Rebel Government arrived in Washington and soon put themselves in communication with the Secretary of State, but the specific object which they had in view, and the negotiations or understanding between him and the parties were not immediately detailed to the Cabinet. They undoubtedly influenced the mind and course of Mr. Seward, who did not relinquish the hope of a peaceful adjustment of difficulties, and he in conversation continued to allure his friends with the belief that he should be able to effect a reconciliation.

In the many, almost daily, discussions which for a time were held in regard to Sumter, the opposition to forwarding supplies gathered strength. Commodore Stringham, as well as Commander Ward, on a final application which I made to him, by request of the President, and finally by the President himself, said he was compelled to advise against it. The time had gone by. It was too late. The military gentlemen had satisfied him it was impossible, that nothing could be gained by it, were the attempt made, that it would be attended with a useless sacrifice of blood and treasure, and he felt constrained to state his belief of the inability of the Navy to give relief.

Postmaster-General Blair, who had been a close and near observer of what had taken place through the winter and spring, took an opposite view from Mr. Seward and General Scott. To some extent he was aware of the understanding which Mr. Seward had with the members of Buchanan's Administration, or was suspicious of it, and his indignation that any idea of abandoning Sumter should be entertained or thought of was unbounded. With the exception of Mr. Seward, all his colleagues concurred with Mr. Blair at the commencement, but as the subject was discussed, and the impossibility and inutility of the scheme was urged, with assurance from the first military men in the country, whose advice was sought and given, that it was a military necessity to leave Sumter to its fate, the opinions of men changed, or they began at least to waver. Mr. Blair saw these misgivings, in which he did not at all participate, and finally, observing that the President, with the acquiescence of the Cabinet, was about adopting the Seward and Scott policy, he wrote his resignation, determined not to continue in the Cabinet if no attempt were made to relieve Fort Sumter. Before handing in his resignation, a delay was made at the request of his father. The elder Blair sought an interview with the President, to whom he entered his protest against non-action, which he denounced as the offspring of intrigue. His earnestness and indignation aroused and electrified the President; and when, in his zeal, Blair warned the President that the abandonment of Sumter would be justly considered by the people, by the world, by history, as treason to the country, he touched a chord that responded to his invocation. The President decided from that moment that an attempt should be made to convey supplies to Major Anderson, and that he would reinforce Sumter. This determination he communicated to the members of the Cabinet as he saw them, without a general announcement in Cabinet-meeting. The resolve inspired all the members with hope and courage, except Mr. Seward, who was evidently disappointed. He said it was of vastly more importance to turn our attention to Fort Pickens. I told him this had been done and how; that we had a considerable naval force there, almost the whole of the Home Squadron, and we had sent, a fortnight before, orders to land the troops under Captain Vogdes from the *Brooklyn*. He said that still more should, in his opinion, be done; that it was practicable to save Fort Pickens, but it was confessedly impossible to retain Sumter. One would be a waste of effort and energy and life, would extinguish all hope of peace, and compel the Government to take the initiative in hostile demonstrations, while the other would be an effective and peaceable movement. Although, as already mentioned, stated Cabinet-meetings were not then established, the members were in those early days of the Administration frequently together, and the President had every day more or less interviews with them, individually or collectively. The Secretary of State spent much of each day at the Executive Mansion and was vigilant to possess himself of every act, move, and intention of the President and of each of his associates. Perhaps there was an equal desire on their part to be informed of the proceedings of the Administration in full, but less was known of the transactions of the State Department than of any other.

The President, after his interview with the elder Blair, asked me if a naval expedition could be promptly fitted out to relieve Sumter. Mr. Fox, who had in February proposed to the Buchanan Administration a plan for the relief of Sumter, again volunteered for the service, and was accepted by Mr. Lincoln. . . .

Mr. Fox visited the Fort and saw Major Anderson, and was confident he could reinforce the garrison with men and supply it with provisions. Commodore Stringham was tendered the command of the naval part of the expedition, but doubted the practicability of succeeding. The President, notwithstanding Stringham's reluctance, determined to accept the volunteer services of Mr. Fox, who, though then in no way connected with the Government, had formerly been an officer of the Navy. The object being the relief of a military garrison and the supplies and troops for reinforcement being from the army, the expedition was made a military and not a naval one, but with naval aid and coöperation. The transports which the War Department was to charter were to rendezvous off Charleston with the naval vessels, which would act as convoy, and render such assistance as would be required of them. The steam frigate *Powhatan,* which had returned from service in the West Indies and needed considerable repairs, had just arrived and been ordered out of commission, and the crew discharged the day before the final decision of the President was communicated. Dispatches were forthwith sent revoking the orders which had been issued, directing that the *Powhatan* be again put in commission, and to fit her without delay for brief service. The *Pawnee* and one or two other vessels, including the *Harriet Lane,* a revenue cutter transferred to the Navy for the occasion, there not being sufficient naval vessels available for the expedition, were ordered to be in readiness for sea service on or before the 6th of April with one month's stores on board. These preparatory orders were given on the 30th of March. . . .

The preparations for the Sumter expedition were carried forward with all the energy which the Department could command, for we were notified the provisions of the garrison would be exhausted on the 15th of April. It was arranged by the War and Navy Departments that their forces—the naval vessels and transports—should meet and rendezvous ten miles due east of Charleston lighthouse on the morning of the 11th of April. Each of the vessels was to report to Capt. Samuel Mercer, commanding the

Powhatan, and the following final instructions were sent to that officer:

Navy Department, April 5, 1861

(Confidential)
To Captain Samuel Mercer,
Commanding U. S. Steamer Powhatan, *N. Y.:*

The United States Steamers *Powhatan, Pawnee, Pocahontas,* and *Harriet Lane* will compose a naval force under your command, to be sent to the vicinity of Charleston, S. C., for the purpose of aiding in carrying out the objects of an expedition of which the War Department has charge.

The primary object of the expedition is to provision Fort Sumter, for which purpose the War Department will furnish the necessary transports. Should the authorities of Charleston permit the fort to be supplied, no further particular service will be required of the force under your command; and after being satisfied that supplies have been received at the fort, the *Powhatan, Pocahontas,* and *Harriet Lane* will return to New York, and the *Pawnee* to Washington.

Should the authorities at Charleston, however, refuse to permit, or attempt to permit the vessel or vessels having supplies on board from entering the harbor, or from peaceably proceeding to Fort Sumter, you will protect the transports or boats of the expedition in the object of their mission, disposing of your force in such manner as to open the way for their ingress, and afford as far as practicable security to the men and boats, and repelling by force if necessary all obstructions toward provisioning the fort and reinforcing it; for in case of a resistance to the peaceable primary object of the expedition, a reinforcement of the garrison will also be attempted. These purposes will be under the supervision of the War Department, which has charge of the expedition. The expedition has been intrusted to Captain G. V. Fox, with whom you will put yourself in communication, and coöperate with him to accomplish and carry into effect its object.

You will leave New York with the *Powhatan* in time to be off Charleston bar, ten miles distant from and due east of the light-house, on the morning of the 11th instant, there to await the arrival of the transport or transports with troops and stores. The *Pawnee* and *Pocahontas* will be ordered to join you there at the time mentioned, and also the *Harriet Lane,* which latter vessel has been placed under the control of this Department for this service.

On the termination of the expedition, whether it be peaceable or otherwise, the several vessels under your command will return to the respective ports as above directed, unless some unforeseen circumstance should prevent.

I am, respectfully,
Your Obd't Serv't,
Gideon Welles,
Secretary of the Navy

Sealed orders were given to Commander Rowan of the *Pawnee*, Commander Gillis of the *Pocahontas*, and Captain Tanner of the *Harriet Lane*, to report to Captain Mercer on the 11th of April, and the entire military and naval expedition was to be under the command of Mr. Fox, who was specially commissioned by the President and received his instructions from the Secretary of War. My instructions to Captain Mercer were read to the President on the 5th of April, who approved them. Although but brief time had been permitted us to fit out the expedition, I congratulated myself, when I went to my room at Willard's on the evening of the 6th of April, that it had been accomplished within the time given us, and that the force had probably sailed.

Between eleven and twelve that night, Mr. Seward and his son Frederick came to my rooms at Willard's with a telegram from Captain Meigs at New York, stating in effect that the movements were retarded and embarrassed by conflicting orders from the Secretary of the Navy. I asked an explanation, for I could not understand the nature of the telegram or its object. Mr. Seward said he supposed it related to the *Powhatan* and Porter's command. I assured him he was mistaken, that Porter had no command, and that the *Powhatan* was the flagship, as he was aware, of the Sumter expedition. He thought there must be some mistake, and after a few moments' conversation, with some excitement on my part, it was suggested that we had better call on the President. Before doing this, I sent for Commodore Stringham, who was boarding at Willard's and had retired for the night. When he came, my statement was confirmed by him, and he went with us, as did Mr. Frederick Seward, to the President. On our way thither Mr. Seward remarked that, old as he was, he had learned a lesson from this affair, and that was, he had better attend to his own business and confine his labors to his own Department. To this I cordially assented.

The President had not retired when we reached the Executive Mansion, although it was nearly midnight. On seeing us he was surprised, and his surprise was not diminished on learning our errand. He looked first at one and then the other, and declared there was some mistake, but after again hearing the facts stated, and again looking at the telegram, he asked if I was not in error in regard to the *Powhatan*—if some other vessel was not the flagship of the Sumter expedition. I assured him there was no mistake on my part; reminded him that I had read to him my confidential instructions to Captain Mercer. He said he remembered that fact, and that he approved of them, but he could not remember that the *Powhatan* was the vessel. Commodore Stringham confirmed my statement, but to make the matter perfectly clear to the President, I went to the Navy Department and brought and read to him the instructions. He then remembered distinctly all the facts, and, turning promptly to Mr. Seward, said the *Powhatan* must be restored to Mercer, that on no account must the Sumter expedition fail or be interfered with. Mr. Seward hesitated, remonstrated, asked if the other expedition was not quite as important, and whether that would not be defeated if the *Powhatan* was detached. The President said the other had time and could wait, but no time was to be lost as regarded Sumter, and he directed Mr. Seward to telegraph and return the *Powhatan* to Mercer without delay. Mr. Seward suggested the difficulty of getting a dispatch through and to the Navy Yard at so late an hour, but the President was imperative that it should be done.

The President then, and subsequently, informed me that Mr. Seward had his heart set on reinforcing Fort Pickens, and that between them, on Mr. Seward's suggestion, they had arranged for supplies and reinforcements to be sent out at the same time we were fitting out vessels for Sumter, but with no intention whatever of interfering with the latter expedition. He took upon himself the whole blame, said it was carelessness, heedlessness on his part, he ought to have been more careful and attentive. President Lincoln never shunned any responsibility and often declared that he, and not his Cabinet, was in fault for errors imputed to them, when I sometimes thought otherwise.

Mr. Seward never attempted any explanation. He was not communicative on that night, nor afterwards, though there were occasional allusions, by myself, to that singular transaction. Mr. Cameron was greatly incensed; complained that Mr. Seward was trying to run the War Department, had caused Captain Meigs to desert; said he would have Meigs arrested and tried by court martial, that he was absent without leave, was expending the military appropriations without authority from the Secretary of War. My grievance was somewhat similar. Although Lieutenant Porter had gone with the *Powhatan* to Pensacola, there was no order or record in the Navy Department of the facts. He was absent without leave; the last sailing-orders to the *Powhatan* were [sent to] Mercer. The whole proceeding was irregular and could admit of no justification without impeaching the integrity or ability of the Secretaries of War and Navy. No one was more aware of this than the President, and, solicitous that there should be no disagreement or cause for disagreement in his Cabinet, he was not comforted by any reflection or examination of the subject. A large portion of the Home Squadron was off Pensacola, and no additional vessels were required nor could well be spared for that station whilst we were wanting them and many more this side of Key West. I had, moreover, on the earnest application of Lieutenant-General Scott, sent the *Crusader* and *Mohawk* already into the Gulf with orders to Captain Adams, the senior officer off Pensacola, to land the troops in order to reinforce Fort Pickens. No additional frigate like the *Powhatan* was needed there, while she was indispensable here. That vessel gave no greater security to Pickens. The troops, with the naval force already there, were abundantly able to defend it, as results proved. Besides, the defense was military, not naval, and could easily have been reinforced. Hence the reinforcements were stolen away from Sumter and sent to Pickens.

When at a later date I saw the communication of the Rebel commissioners of the 9th of April to Mr. Seward and also Judge Campbell's letter of the 13th of that month, I had one of the keys to the mystery and movements of Mr. Seward. The commissioners state that "on the 15th of March Messrs. Forsyth and Crawford were assured by a person occupying a high official position in the Government, and who, as they believed, was speaking by authority, that Fort Sumter would be evacuated within a very few days, and that no measure changing the existing status prejudicially to the Confederate States as respects Fort Pickens was then contemplated; and these assurances were subsequently repeated, with the addition that any contemplated change as respects Pickens . . . would be notified to us. On the 1st of April we were again informed that there might be an attempt to supply Fort Sumter with provisions, but that Gov. Pickens should have previous notice of this attempt. There was no suggestion of any reënforcements."

Judge Campbell and Judge Nelson of the Supreme Court were the high officials alluded to, and the former in his letter of the 13th of April to Mr. Seward says, "On the 1st of April I received from you the statement in writing: I am satisfied the govt. will not undertake to supply Fort Sumter without giving notice to Gov. P.". . . It was on the 1st of April that *carte blanche* was given to the two young officers, investing them with full governmental powers and authorizing them to act independently of their superiors and of the heads of their respective departments, by which a military expedition was sent out without the knowledge of the Secretary of War and a naval ship under orders was taken from her destination, her commander displaced, and her cruise broken up without the knowledge of the Secretary of the Navy, whereby the whole plan of sending supplies and reinforcements to Fort Sumter was defeated. The Secretary of State writes the Rebel commission he is satisfied the Government will not undertake to supply Fort Sumter without giving notice to Governor P., when at the very moment he knew the whole energies of the War and Navy Departments were engaged by order of the President in preparations to forward supplies and reinforcements to Sumter. All was rendered abortive, however, by secretly detaching the *Powhatan*, the flagship to which the squadron was to report and which had the supplies.

On the night of the 6th of April, Secretary Seward was ordered by the President to send a telegram to Porter to restore the *Powhatan* to Mercer and the expedition to Sumter. But the vessel was not so restored, and on the following day Mr. Seward writes Judge Campbell, "Faith as to Sumter fully kept; wait and see." I make no comments on these proceedings, by which I, and the President, and others, as well as the Rebel commissioners, were deceived. These letters of Judge Campbell and the commissioners were not disclosed to me by Mr. Seward, nor do I think the President saw them when received.

Porter's instructions, recommended by Seward and signed by Abraham Lincoln, placed that officer in independent command at Pensacola, where his senior, Captain Adams, was in command of the squadron, and the latter was to coöperate with and be subject to the request of his junior in the great object and purpose of the force on that station. The strange and irregular proceeding embarrassed Captain Adams and became uncomfortable to Lieutenant Porter as well as embarrassing to the Secretary of State. Captain Adams could not receive or recognize the *Powhatan* as a part of his squadron; he had received no orders from the Secretary of the Navy in relation to the vessel or to Lieutenant Porter; and while he could not disregard the strange instructions to which the Secretary of State had persuaded the President to affix his signature, there was nothing requiring his action as commander of the naval forces. Porter could not report or write to the Navy Department, for he was off Pensacola, when by naval record he should have been in the Pacific, and [as he was] in command of the *Powhatan* by no order from the Secretary of the Navy—was without orders or instructions from the proper Department—the officer in command would not receive and forward his letters. Officers are required to send their letters to the Navy Department through their senior officers. The Secretary of State had therefore to correspond with that branch of the Navy, and awkwardly passed over the letters of the officer who was in command of a vessel surreptitiously detached and withdrawn from her legitimate duties.

I may here state that, as early as the 11th of March, I had, on the application of General Scott, who feared to trust the mails, and was unwilling to send a messenger through the infected region lest he should be arrested, detailed the *Crusader* to carry an officer with instructions to Captain Vogdes to land his forces and strengthen the garrison at Fort Pickens. When the vessel was ready to sail, General Scott concluded not to send his messenger, but dispatched written orders to Captain Vogdes, which he entrusted to the naval officer to deliver. But Captain Adams, the senior naval officer, would not recognize the orders of General Scott, nor permit Captain Vogdes and his command to land. His justification was an armistice, which had been entered into by Secretaries Holt and Toucey with prominent Rebels, not to reinforce the garrison at Fort Pickens, provided the Rebels would not attack it.

Captain Adams was not entirely satisfied with his own decision. Though technically he might be justified in adhering to the armistice or order of the Secretary of the Navy, rather than obey the order of General Scott, the emergency was one when a faithful and patriotic officer would have been justified in taking a reasonable responsibility. To relieve himself from embarrassment, he immediately dispatched Lieutenant Gwathmey with a secret confidential communication to me, dated the 1st of April, stating the facts and asking instructions. Lieutenant G., although a Secessionist, was faithful to his trust. He travelled night and day, not even stopping in Richmond, where he belonged, and reached Washington on the 6th of April. He came to me on his arrival before he went to his hotel, and took from a belt that was strapped around his body under his shirt, the letter of Captain Adams, which he delivered into my hands. A day or two after this affair, he tendered his resignation, which, however, was not accepted, but he was dismissed from the service.

I went immediately to the President with Captain Adams's communication, and we both deemed it absolutely essential that a special messenger should be forthwith sent overland with orders to immediately land the troops. Prompt action was all-important, for the Rebellion was rapidly culminating, and the hesitancy of Captain Adams had caused a delay which endangered the possession of Santa Rosa Island and the safety of Fort Pickens. But, in the general demoralization and suspicion which pervaded Washington, who was to be trusted with this important mission? It was then three o'clock in the afternoon, and the messenger must depart by the mail train which left that evening. Paymaster Etting was in Washington, and I sent for him to convey the message. Although not well, he prepared to obey orders, but had my consent to make inquiry for another officer, whose fidelity and energy were unquestioned, to perform the service. About five o'clock he reported to me that Lieut. John Worden had just arrived in Washington, that he would vouch for him as untainted by treason, and as possessed of the necessary qualifications for the mission. I directed that Lieutenant W. should immediately report to me, and in a brief interview I informed him of my purpose to dispatch him on a secret, responsible, and somewhat dangerous duty through the South, and that he must leave in about two hours. He expressed his readiness to obey orders, and, though the time was short and he indifferently prepared, he would be ready at the time designated. I directed him to make no mention of his orders or his journey to any one, not even to his wife, but to call on me as soon as ready and I would in the mean time prepare the document that was to be confided to him. The fact that he was an officer of the Navy passing South to Pensacola, and yet not a Secessionist or in sympathy with them, would be likely to cause him to be challenged and perhaps searched. I therefore wrote a brief dispatch to Captain Adams, which I read to him when he called, and gave it into his hands open, advising that he should commit it to memory, and then, if he thought best, he could destroy the paper. When he saw Captain Adams he could from recollection make a certified copy to that officer, stating the reasons why he did not produce the original. Everything was successful, for, though he was questioned at one or two points and asked if he was carrying a message, he managed to escape detection, and I believe was not searched.

He reached Pensacola and was put on board the *Brooklyn* on the 12th of April. That night the troops under command of Captain Vogdes with [a battalion of] marines were landed and Fort Pickens was reinforced. Instead of remaining with the squadron and improving the first opportunity to reach the North by steamer, Lieutenant Worden preferred to land as soon as his message was delivered, and commenced his return, going to Washington by the same route he had taken in going to Pensacola. It was not surprising that the Rebels, when they learned next day that the troops had been landed and were in Fort Pickens, connected the mission of that officer with the movement. Although he had been gone some hours on his homeward journey, the facts were telegraphed to the Rebel leaders at Montgomery, who had him arrested and confined in the prison at that place, where he remained several months until late in the fall, when an exchange was effected, and he reached the North in season to take command of the ironclad and turreted *Monitor,* the first vessel of that class, and fight the *Merrimac* in Hampton Roads. He was among the first, if not the very first, prisoners-of-war captured by the Rebels.

The order to Captain Adams to land the troops was received by him, as stated, on the 12th, and the fort was reinforced that night. Lieutenant Porter and the *Powhatan* did not reach Pensacola until the 17th, five days after Captain Vogdes and his command with the marines were in the fort —a force sufficient for its defense. In detaching the *Powhatan* from the Sumter expedition, no important or necessary aid was furnished by her or by Lieutenant Porter to Pickens. . . .

WASHINGTON, SUMTER, CHARLESTON, AND MONTGOMERY

The following exchanges between Washington, Sumter, Charleston, and Montgomery portray the mounting crisis. When the President learned of the danger at Pickens, he decided on the calculated risk of sending forward the Fox expedition, but he emphasized its peaceful character by informing the Governor of South Carolina that "provisions, only," not troops or ammunition, would be landed at Sumter. Upon receipt of this communication, the government at Montgomery authorized General Beauregard in command at Charleston to demand surrender, but agreed not to have him open fire if Anderson evacuated the fort peaceably. The appearance of the relief expedition off Charleston, in the early morning hours of April 12th, prompted Beauregard for military reasons to make an immediate demand of surrender. When the demand was rejected, the first shell was fired on the fort at dawn on a stormy April 12th.

Dialogue during the Sumter Crisis

[War Department] Washington, April 4, 1861

To Robert Anderson:

Sir: Your letter of the 1st inst. occasions some anxiety to the President.

On the information of Capt. Fox, he had supposed you could hold out till the 15th inst. without any great inconvenience; and had prepared an expedition to relieve you before that period.

Hoping still that you will be able to sustain yourself till the 11th or 12th inst. the expedition will go forward; and, finding your flag flying, will

---

The first two letters are from John G. Nicolay and J. Hay, eds., *Complete Works of Abraham Lincoln* (New York: Lamb, 1905), Vol. VI, pp. 239–241. The third letter is from the Robert Todd Lincoln collection of the papers of Abraham Lincoln, Library of Congress. The note from Lincoln to Curtin is owned by the Abraham Lincoln Association, Springfield, Illinois. The last letter is from Robert M. Thompson and Richard Wainwright, eds., *Confidential Correspondence of Gustavus Vasa Fox* (Naval Historical Society, 1920), Vol. I, pp. 43–44, and is reprinted by permission of The New York Historical Society. All the other letters are from *The War of the Rebellion, a Compilation of the Official Records of the Union and Confederate Armies* (Washington: Government Printing Office, 1880), Series I, Vol. I.

attempt to provision you, and, in case the effort is resisted, will endeavor also to reinforce you.

You will therefore hold out if possible till the arrival of the expedition.

It is not, however, the intention of the President to subject your command to any danger or hardship beyond what, in your judgment, would be usual in military life; and he has entire confidence that you will act as becomes a patriot and a soldier, under all circumstances.

Whenever, if at all, in your judgment, to save yourself and command, a capitulation becomes a necessity, you are authorized to make it.

Respectfully,

Simon Cameron

[War Department] Washington, April 6, 1861

To Robert S. Chew:

Sir—You will proceed directly to Charleston, South Carolina; and if, on your arrival there, the flag of the United States shall be flying over Fort-Sumpter, and the Fort shall not have been attacked, you will procure an interview with Gov. Pickens, and read to him as follows:

"I am directed by the President of the United States to notify you to expect an attempt will be made to supply Fort-Sumpter with provisions only; and that, if such attempt be not resisted, no effort to throw in men, arms, or ammunition, will be made, without further notice, or in case of an attack upon the Fort."

After you shall have read this to Governor Pickens, deliver to him the copy of it herein inclosed, and retain this letter yourself.

But if, on your arrival at Charleston, you shall ascertain that Fort Sumpter shall have been already evacuated, or surrendered, by the United States force; or, shall have been attacked by an opposing force, you will seek no interview with Gov. Pickens, but return here forthwith.

Respectfully,

Simon Cameron
Secretary of War

Charleston, S.C., April 8th, 1861

To the President:

Under the foregoing orders I left Washington at 6 p.m. Saturday April 6th, 1861, in company with Capt. Theodore Talbot, U.S. Army, and arrived at Charleston, S.C. on Monday at the same hour. Finding that Fort Sumter had neither been surrendered, evacuated nor attacked, I immediately thro' Capt. Talbot, requested an interview with Governor Pickens, which was at once accorded to me, and I then read to him the portion of said orders in italics [quotation marks], and delivered to him the copy of the same which was furnished to me for that purpose, in the presence of Capt. Talbot. Govr. Pickens received the Copy and said he would submit it to General Beauregard, he having, since the ratification of the Constitution of the Confederate States by South Carolina, been placed in charge of the Military operations in this vicinity. Genl. Beauregard was accordingly sent for, and the Governor read the paper to him.

In reply to a remark made by Governor Pickens in reference to an answer I informed him that I was not authorised to receive any communication from him in reply.

Respectfully submitted,

R. S. Chew

Executive Mansion, April 8, 1861

To Governor Andrew G. Curtin:

My dear Sir: I think the necessity of being *ready* increases. Look to it.

Yours truly,

A. Lincoln

Fort Sumter, S.C., April 8, 1861

To Col. L. Thomas, Adjutant-General, Washington, D.C.:

Colonel: I have the honor to report that the South Carolinians have since about noon yesterday been very actively engaged in strengthening their works on Morris Island. I pray that God will avert the storm which seems impending over us, and restore amicable and permanently-pacific relations between the States who still stick to the old Union and those who have formed another Government in the South.

I am, colonel, very respectfully, your obedient servant,

Robert Anderson
Major, First Artillery, Commanding

P.S.—I omitted acknowledging the receipt of the letter from the honorable Secretary of the 4th instant.

Fort Sumter, S.C., April 8, 1861

To Col. L. Thomas, Adjutant-General, U.S. Army:

Colonel: I have the honor to report that the resumption of work yesterday (Sunday) at various points on Morris Island, and the vigorous prosecution of it this morning, apparently strengthening nearly all the batteries which are under the fire of our guns, shows that they either have received some news from Washington which has put them on the *qui vive* or that they have received orders from Montgomery to commence operations here. I am preparing by the side of my barbette guns protection for our men from the shells, which will be almost continuously bursting over or in our work.

I had the honor to receive by yesterday's mail the letter of the honorable Secretary of War, dated April 4, and confess that what he there states surprises me very greatly, following as it does and contradicting so positively the assurance Mr. Crawford telegraphed he was authorized to make. I trust that this matter will be at once put in a correct light, as a movement made now, when the South has been erroneously informed that none such will be attempted, would produce most disastrous results throughout our country.

It is, of course, now too late for me to give any advice in reference to the proposed scheme of Captain Fox. I fear that its result cannot fail to be disastrous to all concerned. Even with his boat at our walls the loss of life (as I think I mentioned to Mr. Fox) in unloading her will more than pay for the good to be accomplished by the expedition, which keeps us, if I can maintain possession of this work, out of position, surrounded by strong works, which must be carried to make this fort of the least value to the United States Government.

We have not oil enough to keep a light in the lantern for one night. The boats will have, therefore, to rely at night entirely upon other marks. I ought to have been informed that this expedition was to come. Colonel Lamon's remark convinced me that the idea, merely hinted at to me by Captain Fox, would not be carried out. We shall strive to do our duty, though I frankly say that my heart is not in the war which I see is to be thus commenced. That God will still avert it, and cause us to resort to pacific measures to maintain our rights, is my ardent prayer.

I am, colonel, very respectfully, your obedient servant,

Robert Anderson
Major, First Artillery, Commanding

Washington, D.C., April 9, 1861

To General Beauregard, Charleston:

The messenger speaks doubtless by authority. He gives the promised notice to Governor Pickens. Diplomacy has failed. The sword must now preserve our independence. Our gallant countrymen will do their duty.

Martin J. Crawford

Montgomery, April 10, 1861

To General Beauregard, Charleston:

If you have no doubt of the authorized character of the agent who communicated to you the intention of the Washington Government to supply Fort Sumter by force you will at once demand its evacuation, and if this is refused proceed, in such manner as you may determine, to reduce it. Answer.

L. P. Walker

Charleston, April 10, 1861

To L. P. Walker:

The demand will be made to-morrow at 12 o'clock.

G. T. Beauregard
Brigadier-General

Headquarters Provisional Army, C.S.A.,
Charleston, S.C., April 11, 1861

To Maj. Robert Anderson,
Commanding at Fort Sumter, Charleston Harbor, S.C.:

Sir: The Government of the Confederate States has hitherto forborne from any hostile demonstration against Fort Sumter, in the hope that the Government of the United States, with a view to the amicable adjustment of all questions between the two Governments, and to avert the calamities of war, would voluntarily evacuate it.

There was reason at one time to believe that such would be the course pursued by the Government of the United States, and under that impression my Government has refrained from making any demand for the surrender of the fort. But the Confederate States can no longer delay assuming actual possession of a fortification commanding the entrance of one of their harbors, and necessary to its defense and security.

I am ordered by the Government of the Confederate States to demand the evacuation of Fort Sumter. My aides, Colonel Chesnut and Captain Lee, are authorized to make such demand of you. All proper facilities will be afforded for the removal of yourself and command, together with company arms and property, and all private property, to any post in the United States which you may select. The flag which you have upheld so long and with so much fortitude, under the most trying circumstances, may be saluted by you on taking it down.

Colonel Chesnut and Captain Lee will, for a reasonable time, await your answer. I am, sir, very respectfully, your obedient servant,

G. T. Beauregard
Brigadier-General, Commanding

Fort Sumter, S.C., April 11, 1861

To Brig. Gen. Beauregard,
Commanding Provisional Army:

General: I have the honor to acknowledge the receipt of your communication demanding the evacuation of this fort, and to say, in reply thereto, that it is a demand with which I regret that my sense of honor, and of my obligations to my Government, prevent my compliance. Thanking you for the fair, manly, and courteous terms proposed, and for the high compliment paid me,

I am, general, very respectfully, your obedient servant,

Robert Anderson
Major, First Artillery, Commanding

Charleston, April 11, 1861

To Hon. L. P. Walker, Secretary of War:

Major Anderson replies: "I have the honor to acknowledge the receipt of your communication demanding the evacuation of this fort, and to say in reply thereto that it is a demand with which I regret that my sense of honor and of my obligations to my Government prevent my compliance." He says verbally: "I will await the first shot, and if you do not batter us to pieces we will be starved out in a few days."

Answer.

G. T. Beauregard

Montgomery, April 11, 1861

To General Beauregard, Charleston:

Do not desire needlessly to bombard Fort Sumter. If Major Anderson will state the time at which, as indicated by him, he will evacuate, and agree that in the mean time he will not use his guns against us unless ours should be employed against Fort Sumter, you are authorized thus to avoid the effusion of blood. If this or its equivalent be refused, reduce the fort as your judgment decides to be most practicable.

L. P. Walker

Washington, April 11, 1861

To General G. T. Beauregard:

The Tribune of to-day declares the main object of the expedition to be the relief of Sumter, and that a force will be landed which will overcome all opposition.

Roman.
Crawford.
Forsyth.

Headquarters Provisional Army, C.S.A.,
Charleston, S.C., April 11, 1861

To Maj. Robert Anderson,
Commanding Fort Sumter, Charleston Harbor, S.C.:

Major: In consequence of the verbal observation made by you to my aides, Messrs. Chesnut and Lee, in relation to the condition of your supplies, and that you would in a few days be starved out if our guns did not batter you to pieces, or words to that effect, and desiring no useless effusion of blood, I communicated both the verbal observations and your written answer to my communications to my Government.

If you will state the time at which you will evacuate Fort Sumter, and agree that in the mean time you will not use your guns against us unless ours shall be employed against Fort Sumter, we will abstain from opening fire upon you. Colonel Chesnut and Captain Lee are authorized by me to enter into such an agreement with you. You are, therefore, requested to communciate to them an open answer.

I remain, major, very respectfully, your obedient servant,

G. T. Beauregard
Brigadier-General, Commanding

Fort Sumter, S.C., April 12, 1861

To Brig. Gen. Beauregard, Commanding:

General: I have the honor to acknowledge the receipt by Colonel Chesnut of your second communication of the 11th instant, and to state in reply that, cordially uniting with you in the desire to avoid the useless effusion of blood, I will, if provided with the proper and necessary means of transportation, evacuate Fort Sumter by noon on the 15th instant, and that I will not in the mean time open my fires upon your forces unless compelled to do so by some hostile act against this fort or the flag of my Government by the forces under your command, or by some portion of them, or by the perpetration of some act showing a hostile intention on your part against this fort or the flag it bears, should I not receive prior to that time controlling instructions from my Government or additional supplies.

I am, general, very respectfully, your obedient servant,

Robert Anderson
Major, First Artillery, Commanding

Montgomery, April 12, 1861

To General Beauregard, Charleston, S.C.:

What was Major Anderson's reply to the proposition contained in my dispatch of last night?

L. P. Walker

Charleston, S.C., April 12, 1861

To L. P. Walker:

He would not consent. I write to-day.

G. T. Beauregard

Fort Sumter, S.C., April 12, 1861—3:20 a.m.

To Maj. Robert Anderson,
U.S. Army, Commanding Fort Sumter:

Sir: By authority of Brigadier-General Beauregard, commanding the Provisional Forces of the Confederate States, we have the honor to notify you that he will open the fire of his batteries on Fort Sumter in one hour from this time.

We have the honor to be, very respectfully, your obedient servants,

James Chesnut, Jr.
Aide-de-Camp
Stephen D. Lee
Captain, C. S. Army, Aide-de-Camp

Headquarters Provisional Army,
Charleston, S.C., April 27, 1861

To Hon. L. P. Walker,
Secretary of War, Montgomery, Ala.:

Sir: I have the honor to submit the following detailed report of the bombardment and surrender of Fort Sumter and the incidents connected therewith:

Having completed my channel defenses and batteries in the harbor necessary for the reduction of Fort Sumter, I dispatched two of my aides at 2.20 p.m., on Thursday, the 11th of April, with a communication to Major Anderson, in command of the fortification, demanding its evacuation. I offered to transport himself and command to any port in the United States he might elect, to allow him to move out of the fort with company arms and property and all private property, and to salute his flag in lowering it. He refused to accede to the demand. As my aides were about leaving Major Anderson remarked that if we did not batter him to pieces he would be starved out in a few days, or words to that effect. This being reported to me by my aides on their return with his refusal, at 5.10 p.m., I deemed it proper to telegraph the purport of his remark to the Secretary of War. In reply I received by telegraph the following instructions at 9.10 p.m.: "Do not desire needlessly to bombard Fort Sumter. If Major Anderson will state the time at which, as indicated by him, he will evacuate, and agree that in the mean time he will not use his guns against us unless ours should be employed against Fort Sumter, you are authorized thus to avoid effusion of blood. If this, or its equivalent, be refused, reduce the fort as your judgment decides to be most practicable."

At 11 p.m. I sent my aides with a communication to Major Anderson based on the foregoing instructions. It was placed in his hands at 12.45 a.m. 12th instant. He expressed his willingness to evacuate the fort on Monday at noon if provided with the necessary means of transportation, and if he should not receive contradictory instructions from his Government or additional supplies, but he declined to agree not to open his guns upon us in the event of any hostile demonstrations on our part against his flag. This reply, which was opened and shown to my aides, plainly indicated that if instructions should be received contrary to his purpose to evacuate, or if he should receive his supplies, or if the Confederate troops should fire on hostile troops of the United States, or upon transports bearing the United States flag, containing men, munitions, and supplies designed for hostile operations against us, he would still feel himself bound to fire upon us, and to hold possession of the fort.

As, in consequence of a communication from the President of the United States to the governor of South Carolina, we were in momentary expectation of an attempt to re-enforce Fort Sumter, or of a descent upon our coast to that end from the United States fleet then lying at the entrance of the harbor, it was manifestly an imperative necessity to reduce the fort as speedily as possible, and not to wait until the ships and the fort should unite in a combined attack upon us. Accordingly my aides, carrying out my instructions, promptly refused to accede to the terms proposed by Major Anderson, and notified him in writing that our batteries would open upon Fort Sumter in one hour. This notification was given at 3.20 a.m. of Friday, the 12th instant. The signal shell was fired from Fort Johnson at 4.30 a.m. At about 5 o'clock the fire from our batteries became general. Fort Sumter did not open fire until 7 o'clock, when it commenced with a vigorous fire upon the Cummings Point iron battery. The enemy next directed his fire upon the enfilade battery on Sullivan's Island, constructed to sweep the parapet of Fort Sumter, to prevent the working of the barbette guns and to dismount them. This was also the aim of the floating battery, the Dahlgren battery, and the gun batteries at Cummings Point.

The enemy next opened on Fort Moultrie, between which and Fort Sumter a steady and almost constant fire was kept up throughout the day. These three points—Fort Moultrie, Cummings Point, and the end of Sullivan's Island, where the floating battery, Dahlgren battery, and the enfilade battery were placed—were the points to which the enemy seemed almost to confine his attention, although he fired a number of shots at Captain Butler's mortar battery, situated to the east of Fort Moultrie, and a few at Captain James' mortar batteries at Fort Johnson. . . .

G. T. Beauregard
Brigadier-General, Commanding

Steamer *Baltic*,
New York, April 19, 1861

To Hon. Simon Cameron,
Secretary of War, Washington:

Sir: I sailed from New York in this vessel Tuesday morning, the 10th instant, having dispatched one steam-tug, the *Uncle Ben*, the evening previous to rendezvous off Charleston. The *Yankee*, another chartered tug, followed us to the Hook, and I left instructions to send on the *Freeborn*.

We arrived off Charleston the 12th instant, at 3 a.m, and found only the *Harriet Lane*. Weather during the whole time a gale. At 7 a.m. the *Pawnee* arrived, and, according to his orders, Captain Rowan anchored twelve miles east of the light, to await the arrival of the *Powhatan*. I stood in with the *Baltic* to execute my orders by offering, in the first place, to carry provisions to Fort Sumter. Nearing the bar it was observed that war had commenced, and, therefore, the peaceful offer of provisions was void.

The *Pawnee* and *Lane* immediately anchored close to the bar, notwithstanding the heavy sea, and though neither tugs or *Powhatan* or *Pocahontas* had arrived, it was believed a couple of boats of provisions might be got in. The attempt was to be made in the morning, because the heavy sea and absence of the *Powhatan's* gunboats crippled the night movement. All night and the morning of the 13th instant it blew strong, with a heavy sea. The *Baltic* stood off and on, looking for the *Powhatan*, and in running in during the thick weather struck on Rattlesnake Shoal, but soon got off. The heavy sea, and not having the sailors (three hundred) asked for, rendered any attempt from the *Baltic* absurd. I only felt anxious to get in a few days' provisions to last the fort until the *Powhatan's* arrival. The *Pawnee* and *Lane* were both short of men, and were only intended to afford a base of operations whilst the tugs and three hundred sailors fought their way in.

However, the *Powhatan* and tugs not coming, Captain Rowan seized an ice schooner and offered her to me, which I accepted, and Lieutenant Hudson, of the Army, several Navy officers, and plenty of volunteers agreed to man the vessel, and go in with me the night of the 13th. The events of that day, so glorious to Major Anderson and his command, are known to you. As I anticipated, the guns from Sumter dispersed their naval preparations excepting small guard-boats, so that with the *Powhatan* a re-enforcement would have been easy. The Government did not anticipate that the fort was so badly constructed as the event has shown.

I learned on the 13th instant that the *Powhatan* was withdrawn from duty off Charleston on the 7th instant, yet I was permitted to sail on the 9th, the *Pawnee* on the 9th, and the *Pocahontas* on the 10th, without intimation that the main portion—the fighting portion—of our expedition was taken away. In justice to itself as well as an acknowledgment of my earnest efforts, I trust the Government has sufficient reasons for putting me in the position they have placed me.

I have the honor to be, your obedient servant, *G. V. Fox*

Washington, D.C., May 1, 1861

To Capt. G. V. Fox:

My dear Sir: I sincerely regret that the failure of the late attempt to provision Fort Sumter should be the source of any annoyance to you. The practicability of your plan was not, in fact, brought to a test. By reason of a gale, well known in advance to be possible, and not improbable, the tugs, an essential part of the plan, never reached the ground; while, by an accident, for which you were in no wise responsible, and possibly I to some extent was, you were deprived of a war vessel, with her men, which you deemed of great importance to the enterprize.

I most cheerfully and truly declare that the failure of the undertaking has not lowered you a particle, while the qualities you developed in the effort have greatly heightened you in my estimation. For a daring and dangerous enterprize, of a similar character you would to-day be the man, of all my acquaintances, whom I would select.

You and I both anticipated that the cause of the country would be advanced by making the attempt to provision Fort Sumter, even if it should fail; and it is no small consolation now to feel that our anticipation is justified by the rest.

Very truly your friend,

A. Lincoln

WAR FEVER SOUTH

On April 15th, William H. Russell was traveling south on a rickety railroad. He describes the initial war spirit in North Carolina, just seceded from the Union. By April 17th he was in Charleston, which recalled memories of Paris during the '48 uprising.

WILLIAM H. RUSSELL, *My Diary North and South*

April 15, 1861. . . . By degrees we got beyond the swamps, and came upon patches of cleared land—that is, the forest had been cut down, and the only traces left of it were the stumps, some four or five feet high, "snag-

William Howard Russell, *My Diary North and South* (Boston: T. H. O. P. Burnham, 1863), pp. 90–93, 98–99.

ging" up above the ground; or the trees had been girdled round, so as to kill them, and the black trunks and stiff arms gave an air of meagre melancholy and desertion to the place, which was quite opposite to its real condition. Here it was that the normal forest and swamp had been subjugated by man. Presently we came in sight of a flag fluttering from a lofty pine, which had been stripped of its branches, throwing broad bars of red and white to the air, with a blue square in the upper quarter containing seven stars. "That's our flag"—said the engineer, who was a quiet man, much given to turning steam-cocks, examining gauges, wiping his hands in fluffy impromptu handkerchiefs, and smoking tobacco—"That's our flag! And long may it wave—o'er the land of the free and the home of the ber-rave!" As we passed, a small crowd of men, women, and children, of all colors, in front of a group of poor broken-down shanties or log-huts, cheered—to speak more correctly—whooped and yelled vehemently. The cry was returned by the passengers in the train. "We're all the right sort hereabouts," said the engineer. "Hurrah for Jeff Davis!" The right sort were not particularly flourishing in outward aspect, at all events. The women, pale-faced, were tawdry and ragged; the men, yellow, seedy looking. For the first time in the States, I noticed barefooted people. . . .

At Goldsborough, which is the first place of importance on the line, the wave of the Secession tide struck us in full career. The station, the hotels, the street through which the rail ran was filled with an excited mob, all carrying arms, with signs here and there of a desire to get up some kind of uniform—flushed faces, wild eyes, screaming mouths, hurrahing for "Jeff Davis" and "the Southern Confederacy," so that the yells overpowered the discordant bands which were busy with "Dixie's Land." Here was the true revolutionary furor in full sway. The men hectored, swore, cheered, and slapped each other on the backs; the women, in their best, waved handkerchiefs and flung down garlands from the windows. All was noise, dust, and patriotism.

It was a strange sight and a wonderful event at which we were assisting. These men were a levy of the people of North Carolina called out by the Governor of the State for the purpose of seizing upon forts Caswell and Macon, belonging to the Federal Government, and left unprotected and undefended. The enthusiasm of the "citizens" was unbounded, nor was it quite free from a taint of alcohol. Many of the volunteers had flint firelocks, only a few had rifles. All kinds of head-dress were visible, and caps, belts, and pouches of infinite variety. . . .

April 17th. The streets of Charleston present some such aspect as those of Paris in the last revolution. Crowds of armed men singing and promenading the streets. The battle-blood running through their veins—that hot oxygen which is called "the flush of victory" on the cheek; restaurants full, revelling in bar-rooms, club-rooms crowded, orgies and carousings in tavern or private house, in tap-room, from cabaret—down narrow alleys, in the broad highway. Sumter has set them distraught; never was such a victory; never such brave lads; never such a fight. There are pamphlets already full of the incident. It is a bloodless Waterloo or Solferino.

After breakfast, I went down to the quay, with a party of the General's staff, to visit Fort Sumter. The senators and governors turned soldiers wore blue military caps, with "palmetto" trees embroidered thereon; blue frock-coats, with upright collars, and shoulder-straps edged with lace, and marked with two silver bars, to designate their rank of captain; gilt buttons, with the palmetto in relief; blue trousers, with a gold-lace cord, and brass spurs—no straps. The day was sweltering, but a strong breeze blew in the harbor, and puffed the dust of Charleston, coating our clothes, and filling our eyes with powder. The streets were crowded with lanky lads, clanking spurs, and sabres, with awkward squads marching to and fro, with drummers beating calls, and ruffles, and points of war; around them groups of grinning negroes delighted with the glare and glitter, a holiday, and a new idea for them—Secession flags waving out of all the windows—little Irish boys shouting out, "Battle of Fort Sumter! New edishun!"—As we walked down towards the quay, where the steamer was lying, numerous traces of the unsettled state of men's minds broke out in the hurried conversations of the various friends who stopped to speak for a few moments. "Well, governor, the old Union is gone at last!" "Have you heard what Abe is going to do?" "I don't think Beauregard will have much more fighting for it. What do you think?"...

LAST ATTEMPT

In a last-ditch effort to keep Virginia in the Union, President Lincoln went as far as he could to reassure the convention assembled at Richmond that he planned no invasion of the South. Virginia seceded on April 17th.

ABRAHAM LINCOLN,
Reply to a Committee of the Virginia Convention, April 13, 1861

Gentlemen: As a committee of the Virginia Convention now in session, you present me a preamble and resolution in these words:

> *Whereas*, in the opinion of this Convention, the uncertainty which prevails in the public mind as to the policy which the Federal Executive intends to pursue toward the seceded States is extremely injurious to the industrial and commercial interests of the country, tends to keep up an excitement which is unfavorable to the adjustment of pending difficulties, and threatens a disturbance of the public peace: therefore
>
> *Resolved*, that a committee of three delegates be appointed by this Convention to wait upon the President of the United States, present to him this preamble and resolution, and respectfully ask him to communicate to this Convention the policy which the Federal Executive intends to pursue in regard to the Confederate States.
>
> Adopted by the Convention of the State of Virginia, Richmond, April 8, 1861.

In answer I have to say that, having at the beginning of my official term expressed my intended policy as plainly as I was able, it is with deep regret and some mortification I now learn that there is great and injurious uncertainty in the public mind as to what that policy is, and what course I intend to pursue. Not having as yet seen occasion to change, it is now my purpose to pursue the course marked out in the inaugural address. I commend a careful consideration of the whole document as the best expression I can give of my purposes.

As I then and therein said, I now repeat: "The power confided to me will be used to hold, occupy, and possess the property and places belonging to the government, and to collect the duties and imposts; but beyond what is necessary for these objects, there will be no invasion, no using of force against or among the people anywhere." By the words "property and places belonging to the government," I chiefly allude to the military posts and property which were in the possession of the government when it came to my hands.

But if, as now appears to be true, in pursuit of a purpose to drive the United States authority from these places, an unprovoked assault has been made upon Fort Sumter, I shall hold myself at liberty to repossess, if I can, like places which had been seized before the government was devolved upon me. And in every event I shall, to the extent of my ability,

---

John G. Nicolay and J. Hay, eds., *Complete Works of Abraham Lincoln* (New York: Lamb, 1905), Vol. VI, pp. 243–245.

repel force by force. In case it proves true that Fort Sumter has been assaulted, as is reported, I shall perhaps cause the United States mails to be withdrawn from all the States which claim to have seceded, believing that the commencement of actual war against the government justifies and possibly demands this.

I scarcely need to say that I consider the military posts and property situated within the States which claim to have seceded as yet belonging to the government of the United States as much as they did before the supposed secession.

Whatever else I may do for the purpose, I shall not attempt to collect the duties and imposts by any armed invasion of any part of the country; not meaning by this, however, that I may not land a force deemed necessary to relieve a fort upon a border of the country.

From the fact that I have quoted a part of the inaugural address, it must not be inferred that I repudiate any other part, the whole of which I reaffirm, except so far as what I now say of the mails may be regarded as a modification.

THE PROVISIONAL CONFEDERACY

Early May finds Russell at the provisional capital of the Confederacy—Montgomery, Alabama. After some pungent comments on the coarse fare and poor hotel accommodations, he visits Jefferson Davis, the new President.

WILLIAM H. RUSSELL, *My Diary North and South*

May 4, 1861. . . . I went to sleep, and woke up at eleven p.m., to hear we were in Montgomery. A very rickety omnibus took the party to the hotel, which was crowded to excess. The General and his friends had one room

---

William Howard Russell, *My Diary North and South* (Boston: T. H. O. P. Burnham, 1863), pp. 164–165, 172–173.

to themselves. Three gentlemen and myself were crammed into a filthy room which already contained two strangers, and as there were only three beds in the apartment it was apparent that we were intended to "double up considerably"; but after strenuous efforts, a little bribery and cajoling, we succeeded in procuring mattresses to put on the floor, which was regarded by our neighbors as a proof of miserable aristocratic fastidiousness. Had it not been for the flies, the fleas would have been intolerable, but one nuisance neutralized the other. Then, as to food—nothing could be had in the hotel—but one of the waiters led us to a restaurant, where we selected from a choice bill of fare, which contained, I think, as many odd dishes as I ever saw, some unknown fishes, oyster-plants, 'possums, raccoons, frogs, and other delicacies, and, eschewing toads and the like, really made a good meal off dirty plates on a vile table-cloth, our appetites being sharpened by the best of condiments.

Colonel Pickett has turned up here, having made his escape from Washington just in time to escape arrest—travelling in disguise on foot through out-of-the-way places till he got among friends.

I was glad when bedtime approached, that I was not among the mattress men. One of the gentlemen in the bed next the door was a tremendous projector in the tobacco juice line: his final rumination ere he sank to repose was a masterpiece of art—a perfect liquid pyrotechny, Roman candles and falling stars. A horrid thought occurred as I gazed and wondered. In case he should in a supreme moment turn his attention my way!—I was only seven or eight yards off, and that might be nothing to him!—I hauled down my mosquito curtain at once, and watched him till, completely satiated, he slept.

May 5th. Very warm, and no cold water, unless one went to the river. The hotel baths were not promising. This hotel is worse than the Mills House or Willard's. The feeding and the flies are intolerable. One of our party comes in to say that he could scarce get down to the hall on account of the crowd, and that all the people who passed him had very hard, sharp bones. He remarks thereupon to the clerk at the bar, who tells him that the particular projections he alludes to are implements of defence or offence, as the case may be, and adds, "I suppose you and your friends are the only people in the house who haven't a bowie-knife, or a six-shooter, or Derringer about them." The house is full of Confederate congressmen, politicians, colonels, and place-men with or without places, and a vast number of speculators, contractors, and the like, attracted by the embryo government. . . .

Montgomery has little claim to be called a capital. The streets are very hot, unpleasant, and uninteresting. I have rarely seen a more dull, lifeless place; it looks like a small Russian town in the interior. The names of the shopkeepers indicate German and French origin. I looked in at one or two of the slave magazines, which are not unlike similar establishments in Cairo and Smyrna. A certain degree of freedom is enjoyed by some of the men, who lounge about the doors, and are careless of escape or liberty, knowing too well the difficulties of either. . . .

May 9. . . . There before me was "Jeff Davis's State Department"—a large brick building, at the corner of a street, with a Confederate flag floating above it. The door stood open, and "gave" on a large hall white-washed, with doors plainly painted belonging to small rooms, in which was transacted most important business, judging by the names written on sheets of paper and applied outside, denoting bureaux of the highest functions. A few clerks were passing in and out, and one or two gentlemen were on the stairs, but there was no appearance of any bustle in the building.

We walked straight up-stairs to the first floor, which was surrounded by doors opening from a quadrangular platform. On one of these was written simply, "The President." Mr. Wigfall went in, and after a moment returned and said, "The President will be glad to see you; walk in, sir." When I entered, the President was engaged with four gentlemen, who were making some offer of aid to him. He was thanking them "in the name of the Government." Shaking hands with each, he saw them to the door, bowed them and Mr. Wigfall out, and turning to me, said, "Mr. Russell, I am glad to welcome you here, though I fear your appearance is a symptom that our affairs are not quite prosperous," or words to that effect. He then requested me to sit down close to his own chair at his office-table, and proceeded to speak on general matters, adverting to the Crimean War and the Indian Mutiny, and asking questions about Sebastopol, the Redan, and the Siege of Lucknow.

I had an opportunity of observing the President very closely: he did not impress me as favorably as I had expected, though he is certainly a very different looking man from Mr. Lincoln. He is like a gentleman—has a slight, light figure, little exceeding middle height, and holds himself erect and straight. He was dressed in a rustic suit of slate-colored stuff, with a black silk handkerchief round his neck; his manner is plain, and rather reserved and drastic; his head is well formed, with a fine full forehead, square and high, covered with innumerable fine lines and wrinkles, features regular, though the cheek-bones are too high, and the jaws too hollow to be handsome; the lips are thin, flexible, and curved, the chin square, well defined; the nose very regular, with wide nostrils; and the eyes deep-set, large and full—one seems nearly blind, and is partly covered with a film, owing to excruciating attacks of neuralgia and tic. Wonderful to relate, he does not chew, and is neat and clean-looking, with hair trimmed, and boots brushed. The expression of his face is anxious, he has a very haggard, care-worn, and pain-drawn look, though no trace of anything but the utmost confidence and the greatest decision could be detected in his conversation. . . .

WAR FEVER NORTH

After a leisurely tour through the southern states and up the Mississippi River, Russell learned when he reached Cairo, Illinois, in late June that a battle was expected between the Federal and Confederate forces in northern Virginia. He hurried east from Chicago, reaching New York on July 2nd. The city was in a blaze of patriotic sentiment and military preparation, quite different from its complacent attitude of some months before.

WILLIAM H. RUSSELL, *My Diary North and South*

July 2, 1861. . . . At about nine a.m., the train reached New York, and in driving to the house of Mr. Duncan, who accompanied me from Niagara, the first thing which struck me was the changed aspect of the streets. Instead of peaceful citizens, men in military uniforms thronged the pathways, and such multitudes of United States flags floated from the windows and roofs of the houses as to convey the impression that it was a great holiday festival. The appearance of New York when I first saw it was very different. For one day, indeed, after my arrival, there were men in uniform to be seen in the streets, but they disappeared after St. Patrick had been duly honored, and it was very rarely I ever saw a man in soldier's clothes during the rest of my stay. Now, fully a third of the people carried arms, and were dressed in some kind of martial garb.

The walls are covered with placards from military companies offering inducements to recruits. An outburst of military tailors had taken place

---

William Howard Russell, *My Diary North and South* (Boston: T. H. O. P. Burnham, 1863), pp. 368–371.

in the streets; shops are devoted to militia equipments; rifles, pistols, swords, plumes, long boots, saddle, bridle, camp belts, canteens, tents, knapsacks, have usurped the place of the ordinary articles of traffic. Pictures and engravings—bad, and very bad—of the "battles" of Big Bethel and Vienna, full of furious charges, smoke and dismembered bodies, have driven the French prints out of the windows. Innumerable "General Scotts" glower at you from every turn, making the General look wiser than he or any man ever was. Ellsworths in almost equal proportion, Grebles and Winthrops—the Union martyrs—and Tompkins, the temporary hero of Fairfax court-house.

The "flag of our country" is represented in a colored engraving, the original of which was not destitute of poetical feeling, as an angry blue sky through which meteors fly streaked by the winds, whilst between the red stripes the stars just shine out from the heavens, the flag-staff being typified by a forest tree bending to the force of the blast. The Americans like this idea—to my mind it is significant of bloodshed and disaster. And why not! What would become of all these pseudo-Zouaves who have come out like an eruption over the States, and are in no respect, not even in their baggy breeches, like their great originals, if this war were not to go on? I thought I had had enough of Zouaves in New Orleans. . . .

They are overrunning society, and the streets here, and the dress which becomes the broad-chested, stumpy, short-legged Celt, who seems specially intended for it, is singularly unbecoming to the tall and slightly-built Americans. Songs "On to glory," "Our country," new versions of "Hail Columbia," which certainly cannot be considered by even American complacency a "happy land" when its inhabitants are preparing to cut each other's throats; of the "star-spangled banner," are displayed in booksellers' and music-shop windows, and patriotic sentences emblazoned on flags float from many houses. The ridiculous habit of dressing up children and young people up to ten and twelve years of age as Zouaves and vivandières has been caught up by the old people, and Mars would die with laughter if he saw some of the abdominous, be-spectacled light infantry men who are hobbling along the pavement.

There has been indeed a change in New York; externally it is most remarkable, but I cannot at all admit that the abuse with which I was assailed for describing the indifference which prevailed on my arrival was in the least degree justified. I was desirous of learning how far the tone of conversation "in the city" had altered, and soon after breakfast I went down Broadway to Pine Street and Wall Street. The street in all its length was almost draped with flags—the warlike character of the shops was intensified. In front of one shop window there was a large crowd gazing with interest at some object which I at last succeeded in feasting my eyes upon. A gray cap with a tinsel badge in front, and the cloth stained with blood was displayed, with the words, "Cap of Secession officer killed in action." On my way I observed another crowd of women, some with children in their arms standing in front of a large house and gazing up earnestly and angrily at the windows. I found they were wives, mothers, and sisters, and daughters of volunteers who had gone off and left them destitute.

The misery thus caused has been so great that the citizens of New York have raised a fund to provide food, clothes, and a little money—a poor relief, in fact, for them, and it was plain they were much needed though some of the applicants did not seem to belong to a class accustomed to seek aid from the public. This already! But Wall Street and Pine Street are bent on battle. And so this day, hot from the South and impressed with the firm resolve of the people, and finding that the North has been lashing itself into fury, I sit down and write to England, on my return from the city. "At present dismiss entirely the idea, no matter how it may originate, that there will be, or can be, peace, compromise, union, or secession, till war has determined the issue."

As long as there was a chance that the struggle might not take place, the merchants of New York were silent, fearful of offending their Southern friends and connections, but inflicting infinite damage on their own government and misleading both sides. Their sentiments, sympathies, and business bound them with the South; and, indeed, till "the glorious uprising" the South believed New York was with them, as might be credited from the tone of some organs in the press, and I remember hearing it said by Southerners in Washington, that it was very likely New York would go out of the Union! When the merchants, however, saw the South was determined to quit the Union, they resolved to avert the permanent loss of the great profits derived from their connection with the South by some present sacrifices. They rushed to the platforms—the battle-cry was sounded from almost every pulpit—flag-raising took place in every square, like the planting of the tree of liberty in France in 1848, and the oath was taken to trample Secession under foot, and to quench the fire of the Southern heart forever.

The change in manner, in tone, in argument, is most remarkable. I met men to-day who last March argued coolly and philosophically about the right of Secession. They are now furious at the idea of such wickedness —furious with England, because she does not deny their own famous doctrine of the sacred right of insurrection. "We must maintain our glorious Union, sir." "We must have a country." "We cannot allow two nations to grow up on this Continent, sir." "We must possess the entire control of the Mississippi." These "musts," and "can'ts," and "won'ts,"

Courtesy of Prints and Photographs Division, Library of Congress. Photo by Mathew B. Brady.

Federal dead at Gettysburg—the first day.

are the angry utterances of a spirited people who have had their will so long that they at last believe it is omnipotent. Assuredly, they will not have it over the South without a tremendous and long-sustained contest, in which they must put forth every exertion, and use all the resources and superior means they so abundantly possess.

It is absurd to assert, as do the New York people, to give some semblance of reason to their sudden outburst, that is was caused by the insult to the flag at Sumter. Why, the flag had been fired on long before Sumter was attacked by the Charleston batteries! It had been torn down from United States arsenals and forts all over the South; and but for the accident which placed Major Anderson in a position from which he could not retire, there would have been no bombardment of the fort, and it would, when evacuated, have shared the fate of all the other Federal works on the Southern coast. Some of the gentlemen who are now so patriotic and Unionistic, were last March prepared to maintain that if the President attempted to reënforce Sumter or Pickens, he would be responsible for the destruction of the Union. Many journals in New York and out of it held the same doctrine.

One word to these gentlemen. I am pretty well satisfied that if they had always spoken, written, and acted as they do now, the people of Charleston would not have attacked Sumter so readily. The abrupt outburst of the North and the demonstration at New York filled the South, first with astonishment, and then with something like fear, which was rapidly fanned into anger by the press and the politicians, as well as by the pride inherent in slaveholders. . . .

II / ORGANIZATION

INTRODUCTION

By 1861 the factory system had taken firm root in various northern and midwestern states. These regions as a whole, however, had by no means reached industrial maturity. Factories were plentiful but small, individually owned and operated, fiercely competitive. The railroad system was far from complete, single track for the most part, dependent on connecting shipping lines for through traffic. Rail gauge was not standard, nor were rolling stock and other equipment. Railroads were owned and operated by scores of independent companies. Debt-ridden, poorly constructed, inefficient, they were competing among themselves as well as with coastal shipping and inland waterways for freight revenues. Had it not been for increasing passenger traffic, it would have been difficult for many to continue minimum service, much less expand and improve their facilities. Agriculture was still the mainstay of the northern economy. Commerce vied with manufacturing in importance.

Upon this semideveloped industrial plant, the great war burst with titanic force. Where before textile men and iron masters and shipbuilders had pared overhead and profits to the bone in order to win markets, now suddenly they were flooded with contracts from the Federal and the state governments. The hard-pressed War and Navy Departments, utterly unprepared for a major conflict, did not haggle over prices, though the Treasury was notoriously delinquent in payment.

Businessmen as a group had not courted war. Most of them had strong economic ties with the South and were distinctly dovish in their hopes for a compromise settlement. Although moderate in their understanding of war aims after Sumter, they were not cautious about piling up profits. Wartime Washington soon became a hive of influence peddlers, contract agents, and hungry manufacturers. Graft and corruption flourished until Edwin Stanton, who succeeded the inept Simon Cameron as War Secretary, wielded a broad broom. But even he and the tough-minded Navy Secretary, Gideon Welles, could not review every purchase order. With the Union in grave danger, the mounting needs of the military brooked no delay. Strict accountability in procurement could mean disaster.

What effect did all this spending—over three billion dollars in four years—have on an immature industrial economy which in 1861 had not fully recovered from severe depression? Some historians have suggested that the war produced extraordinary changes in the structure of industry. Unprecedented physical expansion and nearly full employment were obvious results. Less obvious was the distribution of government contracts. Who in effect were profiting the most? There is evidence that only those well-established firms with surplus capital could afford to make significant expenditures in new property, plants, and equipment. Conversion from consumer goods, except in the textile industry, was an expensive and risky proposition, involving as it did new mechanization and unfamiliar production skills.

The state of the public finances was always perilous. Secretary of the Treasury Chase's policy of inflation and internal taxation to meet staggering war costs caught the small businessman in a vise. Lacking the resources for expansion that would have given him a larger and more profitable share of war contracts, he was less able to cope with soaring labor and material costs. Thus a lion's share of war profits went to the larger operators, who used their new assets to improve their competitive position. Smaller, weaker rivals were squeezed out or bought up, or were forced to share profits on a subcontract basis. Wartime conditions are seen as giving a major boost to concentration of industry.

The trend toward bigness during the war is well-documented. Several important railroad mergers took place. The nation's telegraph companies were consolidated, largely as a result of war-earned capital and war-gained experience. Meat packers, paper plants, and iron mills joined the procession. But wartime demands could not be met solely by expansion, conversion, and concentration. Coordination of hundreds of diverse enterprises into a well-functioning war machine put a heavy premium on innovative management, as seen, for example, in the career of young Andrew Carnegie. The lessons Carnegie learned when for a time he supervised the military traffic of the Union's railroad and telegraph systems were applied with brilliant success in his organizing of the iron and steel industry.

Horizontal and vertical combinations marked the trend toward industrial consolidation. Cornelius Vanderbilt, who was adding to his millions with lucrative war contracts, began to expand his New York Central Railroad. He purchased other railroads, built rolling mills and machine shops, acquired connecting steamboat lines. Shortly after the war, even such freebooters as James Fisk and Jay Gould used a part of their speculative gains in Erie stock to recondition and reequip that road. Other entrepreneurs (men such as the meat packer, Philip Armour, or Thomas Scott, a transportation expert and Assistant Secretary of War under Simon Cameron), all of whom played important roles in organizing the Union war machine, saw the value of cooperation and coordination in broader terms. The South, with virtually no industry, created an extensive ordnance and munitions plant and adapted existing facilities to wartime production. Josiah Gorgas, the Confederate Ordnance Chief, ranks with great northern industrialists in his brilliant management of many highly complex activities under the worst possible conditions. Businessmen of lesser note found it both useful and profitable to pool their resources while still maintaining independent control of their enterprises. Prewar trade associations expanded their activities; many new associations were founded. Competition was as savage as ever within each industrial grouping, but coordination had proved its worth in securing contracts, in controlling prices and labor costs, in planning new ventures, and especially in shaping public policy.

What of the workingmen and the farmer? Wages and crop prices had risen rapidly in response to wartime demands, but real income for the worker declined in the inflation economy. During the immediate postwar period, both groups, following in the path blazed by management, organized themselves collectively on a national basis. Did prior service in the armies or in the Federal government provide group incentive? Leadership skills? Militancy? Robert W. Keen, founder of the Knights of Labor, the nation's first industrial (as opposed to craft) union, was a veteran of a Pennsylvania regiment. Another veteran, Major Samuel Leffingwell, was one of the Knights' chief organizers. Isaac Cline, of the 100th Pennsylvania Volunteers, became the first president of the Window Glass Workers Union. According to George McNeill, a contemporary observer, thousands of returning soldiers, accustomed to the discipline of army life, gave new vigor and scope to the labor movement. O. H. Kelley, founder of the Grange, described a similar drive for association among farmers who had served in the war. Kelley himself was a Washington clerk, as were all the founders of the Grange. They had witnessed at firsthand the focal point of the war effort. A government-sponsored trip through the South in January 1866 convinced Kelley that farmers also should be organized to promote their own special interests.

Neither the Grange nor the trade union movement had the economic power of the great postwar entrepreneurs. In almost every instance, they were merely able to fight rear guard actions against the new, highly efficient industrial combinations that emerged after 1865. Yet the student may speculate as to what would have happened had there been no organized countervailing power from farmers and workingmen. For big business did *not* win the battle to industrialize the nation on its own terms without being bloodied in the process. Indeed, the best it could achieve was an armed truce with labor and agriculture while the plant was being built. And eventually the great organizers would be forced to strike a balance with the public, as seen in the controlled economy of today. The Civil War had shown American capitalism how it could, with the help of the Federal government, industrialize the nation on a grand scale. It had shown the workers and the farmers how they could protect themselves and advance their own interests. War profits and inflation had stimulated economic growth.

Did the war so drastically alter patterns of American industry that it produced extraordinary, or perhaps revolutionary, changes? The interpretation excerpted from Thomas Cochran and William Miller's *Age of Enterprise* and the documents that follow may assist the student in answering this question.

INTERPRETATION: TRIAL BY BATTLE

This brief survey of the war's impact on the northern economy emphasizes structural change. There is no attempt to analyze whether the war advanced or retarded industrial growth, a question being hotly debated by economic historians. The authors, Thomas Cochran and William Miller, are concerned rather with the growth of big business. The war, they maintain, provided the profits, the experience, and the political climate for an entrepreneurial revolution.

THOMAS C. COCHRAN *and* WILLIAM MILLER, *The Age of Enterprise*

THE ROAD TO WAR

Northern business took advantage of the Civil War once it began and after it was over, but that does not prove that business wanted the war; it does not prove, certainly, that business started the war. Northern and western businessmen were bound to the South by ties which they deemed strongest—ties of profit. Secession strained these almost to the breaking point; war would shatter them altogether. New England cotton factories depended upon the South for raw materials; boot and shoe factories found their markets there, northern shippers their cargoes. All but the shippers could hope to preserve these ties with the South in or out of the Union, and the shippers certainly wanted no war. Commerce feeds on peace: no one knew it better than they.

From every section of the industrial North, from many types of industry, had come business spokesmen for peace. On December 19, 1860, August Belmont reported a meeting of "our leading men . . . composed of such names as Astor, Aspinwall, Moses H. Grinnell, Hamilton Fish, R. M. Blatchford, &c. They were unanimous for reconciliation, and that the first steps have to be taken by the North." From New Jersey came the voice of Abram Hewitt, who had suffered as much as any one from southern tariff and railroad policies but who in November, 1860, was "using every effort to induce the public mind to give up the idea of coercion, and to

---

Thomas C. Cochran and William Miller, *The Age of Enterprise,* rev. ed. (New York: Harper and Row, 1961), pp. 98–118. Footnotes deleted.

take that of peaceable separation." As late as March 1, 1861, George Lyman, Boston Associate, wrote hopefully of news "that an arrangement will be made in Washington satisfactory to the business men of the country if not to other persons, and that peace will prevail among the people." As late as April, 1861, the *New York Journal of Commerce* and the *New York Observer* were still clamoring for peace; and on the 9th of the month, but three days before Fort Sumter, the *New York Herald* had declared:

> Far better that the Union should be dismembered forever than that fraternal hands should be turned against one another to disfigure the land by slaughter and carnage.

With the South out of the Union, no one could deny northern business its tariffs, Pacific railroads, national banks, and free land. The opposition was removed: why fight to bring it back?

The South in turn wanted independence, not conflict. Robert Hunter of Virginia wrote in December, 1860:

> We already hear threats of coercing the seceding states by force. But if, unfortunately, such an experiment should ever be tried, even the stronger section would find the remedy worse than the disease. . . . I hold coercion by force to be almost impossible. It would fail if attempted, and would never be attempted, unless madness ruled the hour and passion raged where reason ought to govern.

The South knew it could win only freedom, not supremacy; that it could but escape the North, not conquer it. The South wanted to depart from the Union in peace; in the North, sentiment acquiesced in secession. The country's most influential editor, Horace Greeley, in November, 1860, declared in his *Tribune:*

> If the cotton states shall decide that they can do better out of the Union than in it, we insist on letting them go in peace. The right to secede may be a revolutionary one but it exists nevertheless.

Equally powerful in the pulpit, his *Independent* was almost as important as the *Tribune,* Henry Ward Beecher a little later announced his attitude:

> The time has come when the public mind must take some position and make some expression. I for one, do not believe in Union for the sake of it. . . . There is but one question: . . . "Do you think the South will secede?" My answer is: "I don't think they will; and I don't care if they do."

To be sure, there was war sentiment on both sides; there were short-sighted manufacturers looking for war profits, debt-ridden planters seeking excuses for repudiation of debts owed in the North, young fire-eaters clamoring for combat, professional military men eager to practice their trade. In the West, there was a strong faction that cried insistently for war. Governor Yates of Illinois asked in his inaugural address on January 14, 1861:

> Can it for a moment be supposed that the people of the valley of the Mississippi will ever consent that the great river shall flow hundreds of miles through a foreign jurisdiction, and they be compelled, if not to fight their way in the face of forts frowning upon its banks, to submit to the imposition and annoyance of arbitrary taxes and exorbitant duties to be levied upon their commerce?...I know I speak for Illinois and I believe for the Northwest, when I declare them a unit in the unalterable determination of her millions, occupying the great basin drained by the Mississippi, to permit no portion of that stream to be controlled by a foreign jurisdiction.

The *Illinois State Journal* seconded this declaration:

> The great Northwest will wage war with the Slave States bordering on that river [the Mississippi] as long as she has a man or a dollar, but what she will enjoy the right of free and unobstructed navigation of the natural southern outlet.

In January, 1861, however, these were but the war cries of extremists. After the secession convention of February, 1861, the federal post office collected and delivered mail in the South; federal customs men collected duties in southern ports; railroads ran unmolested across the borders of slave states and free; telegraph messages flew North and South; New Orleans handled southern and northern goods on equal terms. The instruments of peace, at least, seemed able to transcend new boundaries.

As days and weeks went by, however, and people watched developments, the crisis did not abate; neither side could satisfactorily adjust itself to the new arrangement. South Carolina's demand of federal forts in Charleston harbor went unheeded. The "Crittenden Compromise" failed, the Virginia Peace Convention failed, the attempt to reenforce Fort Sumter in January failed. Meanwhile, the Confederacy was taking form. Her constitution was published, her president elected, her government set up in Montgomery. While the North looked on with indecision, the South had become a sovereign nation, a foreign government on the borders of the United States, claiming federal territory within her limits, finally taking military measures to assert her independence.

Incident followed incident as the crisis worked on frayed nerves and the newspapers administered stimulants. So contagious, indeed, was the excitement the newspapers stirred up, that sometimes they fell prey to their own enthusiasm. By December 11, 1860, the pacific Greeley had discovered a dangerous paradox in the situation. A state could not "make herself really independent" without seizing all forts within her borders; and such seizure would render it incumbent upon the President "to repel force with force." Three weeks later, Greeley declared:

> Though we acknowledge prayer to be indispensable for the saving of individuals and nations, we nevertheless consider powder a good thing.

By April 3, 1861, he demanded that the "intolerable suspense and uncertainty give way to the alternative of war."

The publisher's business is to sell papers. Regardless of his own attitudes or the philosophy of his editorial page, he must compete with the field for patronage. Thus he seeks always to build up suspense, to enhance excitement even if he is opposed to the trend his headlines encourage. Secession made good copy. Every one was concerned with it, with all its aspects, with every incident created by the friction of the new arrangement. The newspapers, those for peace and those for war alike, could not afford to play down secession.

Three months of such agitation had led to a swelling cry in the North for decision. And while limp Buchanan, pledged to defend the Union but pledged as well to his southern Democratic colleagues, wavered between the two, there came from the West another cry that was to give direction to any decision that might be made.

Illinois, Indiana, Ohio, Michigan, Iowa, Wisconsin, Minnesota—none of these knew the time when they had been *sovereign* states. They had been brought into existence by the federal Congress; great numbers of their people had been naturalized by the federal government, had purchased their rich land from federal agents. "You cannot sever this Union," cried Stephen Douglas of Illinois in 1860, "without severing every hope and prospect that a Western man has on this earth." And he exclaimed to the farmers of the Ohio Valley in April, 1861:

> [Your] very existence depends upon maintaining inviolate and forever that great right secured by the Constitution, of freedom of trade, of transit, and of commerce, from the center of the continent to the ocean that surrounds it. [The question was not only one of Union or disunion but] of order, of the stability of the government; of the peace of communities. The whole social system is threatened with destruction.

Meanwhile, Lincoln had been inaugurated. Born in Kentucky, bred in Indiana and Illinois, he needed no instruction in western feeling, no mentor to guide him along the path chosen by his section. He would discuss anything with the South, but Union must be the basis for discussion. Seward, to remove the spotlight from domestic strife, devised fantastic schemes to conquer the world. Seward demanded time for southern tempers to cool, for the South to learn that independence was a hazardous if not foolhardy venture. Seward urged the President to surrender federal forts to the South. But Lincoln was adamant. The Union must be preserved. No concessions could be made, no wedge allowed for severance. In reply to Bennett's insistent demand for peace, throughout the month of April, he declared:

> I will suffer death before I will consent or advise my friends to consent to any concession or compromise which looks like buying the privilege of taking possession of the Government to which we have a constitutional right.

War, of course, is the business of armies; defense of the nation, their sworn duty. Sumter must be provisioned; Sumter was a northern fort. In southern territory? And the South was now sovereign in her own domain? Let her prove it. The instruments of peace may transcend new boundaries, the instruments of war must contest them. The North must provision her forts; the South must defend her sovereignty. For nations on edge, these were challenges. To refuse them was to admit weakness, to invite contempt; to accept them meant war.

In a last effort Lincoln appealed to the "leaderless people" of the South to cast off the yoke of the "slave profiteers" and return to the national fold. But in the South, too, publicists had been at work. The South had become a nation, proudly conscious of her new status. On the abolitionists' anvil her leaders had forged a unified people dedicated to white supremacy and impressed with the power such supremacy seemed to afford. As early as 1856, Robert J. Walker wrote:

> In all the slave states, there is a large majority of voters who are non-slaveholders; but they are devoted to the institutions of the South—they would defend them with their lives and on this question the South are a united people. The class, composed of many small farmers, of merchants, professional men, mechanics, overseers, and other industrial classes, constitute mainly the patrol of the South, and cheerfully unite in carrying out those laws essential to preserve the institution of slavery.

"In fact," said Rives of Virginia in 1861, to the Peace Convention called by his state, "it is not a question of slavery at all. It is a question of race."

In November, 1860, war could not have started. By April, 1861, it could scarcely have been avoided. The sides had been drawn, and as peace efforts one by one came to naught each side had gradually clarified its position and convinced its people of the righteousness of its cause. When Lincoln insisted at last on provisioning Fort Sumter, as an unmistakable token of northern determination, the South, if it was to succeed in what it had started, could not allow the act to pass unchallenged. After the firing of cannon, there was no turning back. On April 21, 1861, George Ticknor wrote:

> The heather is on fire. I never knew before what popular excitement can be. Holiday enthusiasm I have seen often enough, and anxious crowds I remember during the War of 1812, but never anything like this. Indeed, here at the North, at least, there was never anything like it; for if the feeling were as deep and stern in 1775, it was by no means so intelligent and unanimous; and then the masses to be moved were as a handful compared to our dense population now. The whole people, in fact, have come to a perception that the question is whether we shall have anarchy or no.

And on April 28 he explained how such unanimity had come about:

> Through the whole of the last six months, you see the working of our own political institutions most strikingly. The people were the practical sovereigns, and until the people had been appealed to, and had *moved*, the Administration, whether of Buchanan or of Lincoln, could act with little efficiency. We drifted. Now the rudder is felt.

FIRST THINGS FIRST

For the first time in almost fifty years, the crash of cannon was heard in the United States on April 12, 1861. War! Very few among the people knew what war meant. Very few of their leaders knew what was expected of them. Lincoln hoped the "insurrection" would be quelled in three months; it was five before hostilities seriously got under way. In either section there was practically no army, no machinery for organizing one or financing it when it would be ready. The North had railroads, factories, money, men. But it took two years to rig them into a war machine. The South, by comparison, had nothing—except generals. The South had to create, not adapt.

While military men were muddling their unaccustomed tasks, however, veteran northern politicians swung immediately into action. The Republican platform of 1860 had been a blunt appeal to businessmen—to manufacturers, railroad promoters, land speculators, bankers. It had promised protective tariffs, homesteads, Pacific railroads, easy admission for foreign laborers, federal appropriations for river and harbor improvements. Even before southern congressmen had fled the Capital, this program was being enacted.

Satisfied with the tariff of 1857, some New England manufacturers feared higher rates. Rice of Massachusetts said in 1860:

> The manufacturer asks no additional protection. He has learned among other things, that the greatest evil, next to ruinous competition from foreign sources, is an excessive protection, which stimulates a like ruinous and irresponsible competition at home.

To entice to the Republican banner iron manufacturers in Pennsylvania and woolgrowers in the West, however, the Morrill Tariff Act was passed by the House in 1860. At the next session, in February, 1861, the Union Senate approved it. Simply a political measure, this act was supplemented in August and December, 1861, by the first war tariffs.

Like all subsequent levies, these proved insufficient to meet rising costs of government; and as the conflict continued beyond its allotted ninety days, beyond six months, beyond a year with no sign of abatement, no sign of northern victory, new and drastic steps had to be taken. To avoid bankruptcy early in 1862, the government began to print huge quantities of "greenbacks," declaring them legal tender for all debts. By the middle of the year even these proved inadequate, and the government's position was further complicated by the refusal of many bankers who were opposed to the Treasury's regulations to market government bonds. To augment federal income, therefore, and to show good faith to the bankers, new taxes had to be levied. Among them were sales taxes on manufactured goods, income taxes on railroad, steamboat, and express companies. Novel measures, these duties encouraged tariff politicians to make novel demands. Tariffs for revenue had become traditional in America; tariffs for protection from foreign competition constantly had been sought. After the enactment of these internal excises in July, 1862, however, tariff men developed a new rationale. If manufacturers' costs were raised by excise and income taxes, they said, should not the old margin of protection be maintained? Under the whip of Morrill and Stevens, Congress agreed that it should. Camouflaged as "compensation," the tariff act of July 14, 1862, raised the rates to their highest level in thirty years—much higher, in many cases, than the new excise taxes warranted.

As war expenditures increased, internal taxes and "compensatory" duties increased with them until by 1864 tariff rates were higher than they had ever been. The tariff act of that year, says Taussig, "was in many ways crude and ill-considered; it contained flagrant abuses, in the shape of duties whose chief effect was to bring money into the pockets of private individuals."

When the war ended internal taxes were speedily repealed, but not import duties. Manufacturers, like railroad men before them, had grown rich through government aid. Now they were determined to retain control of the sources of such aid, come what might. In 1870, Morrill himself exclaimed: "It is a mistake of the friends of a sound tariff to insist on the extreme rates imposed during the war." In the ensuing years, he was heeded only to the extent that rates were reduced on articles America could not produce. The protective features stuck.

While Congress was erecting these almost insurmountable tariff walls, the army was decimating the ranks of labor, strikes were spreading, and employers complained. Friendly legislators tried to satisfy them with the Contract Labor Law, signed July 4, 1864. Besides validating contracts made abroad, Congress "took pains formally to declare" that no laborer imported under the terms of this law would be drafted for military service. Quickly, a group of industrialists formed the American Emigrant Company capitalized at $1,000,000. To every country in Europe they sent agents, and in all our large cities they opened branch offices where employers could make known their needs with the knowledge that cheap and docile hands promptly would be found for them. The contract with the laborer did not involve his person—it avoided any taint of "slavery" or "involuntary servitude." Under its terms the emigrant had but to pledge his wages for twelve months as compensation to the employer for the costs of emigration. Before its repeal in 1868 this act supplied business and agriculture with thousands of men, many of them serving effectively as strikebreakers.

While the Republican party was financed mainly by urban industrialists and promoters, its victory was won with the votes of western farmers hungry for free land. An Iowan wrote to the New York *World* in 1860:

> The people of the West have been deeply mortified by the failure of Congress to pass a proper homestead law. The question will enter largely into the political canvass, and will determine many votes against the Democratic party.

When westerners went to the polls this prediction was fulfilled, and when victorious Republicans organized Congress they seemed eager to satisfy their constituents. In 1860 New England and the Middle States had joined the West in voting almost unanimously for free homesteads only to have the successful act vetoed by Buchanan. In 1862 Buchanan and his followers were no longer in power and a homestead bill easily became law.

The West was jubilant; but not for long. The act granted 160 acres of unoccupied land in the public domain to any one who would cultivate it for five consecutive years. The act provided also, however, that within six months the "cultivator" could purchase his land at $1.25 an acre. The first part of the law was an invitation to any one who had money for the western trek; the second part was an Open sesame to land speculators. Their dummy "settlers" appeared in new areas almost always ahead of genuine farmers. They staked out quarter-sections there, recorded claims, and exercised options to purchase, until most of the best homesteads were gone. When authentic homesteaders came, their only choice was between buying at high prices and moving beyond civilization.

By the very act that offered "land to the landless poor," Congress thus had nullified its apparent gift. Subsequently it adopted other measures that confirmed its seeming sympathy with speculators rather than settlers, businessmen rather than farmers. To aid the Union, Central, and Northern Pacific railroads, chartered between 1862 and 1864, Congress gave them a potential 70,000,000 acres of the public domain. In 1862 Congress enacted the Morrill Act, granting to the states 30,000 acres for each of their senators and representatives, the income from the sale of this land to be used to endow and maintain in each state at least one college for instruction "in agriculture and mechanic arts." To the landless eastern states this act granted scrip to 7,500,000 western acres to be sold for the same purpose. Besides, as western territories became states they were given additional land totaling 140,000,000 acres, which thus became unavailable for free homesteads. For one reason or another, the federal government held out for sale, instead of distributing freely, another 100,000,000 acres, while the removal of the Indians to reservations added 175,000,000 acres more which were to be disposed of to the highest bidders and were closed to homesteaders.

Thus while 50,000,000 homestead acres were distributed in twenty years after 1862, many of them to speculators, almost half a billion acres of the public domain were reserved for businessmen or opened to farmers only at considerable cost. Most of this was the best land in the West. To encourage the colleges, the beneficiaries of the Morrill Act received land which would sell for the highest prices. The same was true of railroad companies which also profited handsomely by promising transportation facilities near their lands. Indian lands in many areas already were improved, making them much more desirable than the unbroken prairie. While the land held for sale by the national government was mainly timber and mineral land, it also included surveyed arable land in favorable locations.

Thus the land policies of the war government, like its tariff and labor legislation, had prepared a feast for eastern businessmen. The railroad grants were making "the whole Northwest and the whole West but little more than a province of New York," complained Senator Howe of Wisconsin, as early as 1864. "Perhaps the largest purchasers of land in Nebraska," writes Paul Wallace Gates, "were a group of Providence, Rhode Island, speculators consisting of Robert H. Ives, John Carter Brown, Charlotte R. and Moses B. J. Goddard." "With Agricultural College scrip of New York," Ezra Cornell located nearly 500,000 acres in Wisconsin, Minnesota, and Kansas. "A group of New York magnates, Thomas F. Mason, George B. Satterlee and William E. Dodge, entered 232,799 acres in the Marquette, Michigan, district, 10,850 acres elsewhere in that state, and 10,359 acres in Wausau, Wisconsin." "John C. Work and Rufus Hatch of New York, and John J. Blair of New Jersey, entered in western Iowa, in 1869 and 1870, 12,200, 28,671, 20,970, acres respectively." Amos Lawrence, Boston Associate, promoter, with others, of the Emigrant Aid Company, "located 58,360 acres in Kansas in 1866 with Agricultural College scrip," while the Emigrant Aid Company itself, "through transactions not always legitimate," purchased 800,000 acres of Cherokee lands at a dollar an acre, the settlers already on the land having no opportunity to claim their cultivated tracts. Soon, selling land became more important to this company than serving emigrants, and in its advertisements it gave publicity to the ills that befell independent farmers who were unaware that free homesteads were overgrown with thorns. Under the homestead law, according to one of its pamphlets,

> the settler must, in order to get a good location, go far out into the wild and unsettled districts, and for many years be deprived of school privileges, churches, mills, bridges, and in fact all the advantages of society.

The government created these conditions in the West; speculators capitalized them. In Kansas, between 1868 and 1872, for instance they successfully advertised for sale, up to $15 an acre, land that had once been free public domain. The State Agricultural College offered 90,000 acres of "the choicest land in the state." The Central Branch of the Union Pacific offered 1,200,000 acres, the Kansas Pacific Railroad, 5,000,000 acres. Competing with them were the Kansas & Neosho Valley Railroad, the Capital Land Agency of Topeka, Van Doren and Havens, Hendry and Noyes, T. H. Walker, and not least, the United States Government, offering 6,000 acres of Sac and Fox Indian lands. Such were the benefits of the homestead law.

The Republican party was a Union party, expressly opposed to states' rights. Perhaps as important as any of its specific measures was its rapid transfer of power from the states to the national government. The Union Pacific's was the first federal charter issued since 1816; its land grant was probably the first made by the federal government to a private corporation.

The national banking acts virtually eliminated state bank notes from circulation and relegated state banks to a secondary position in the country. The tariff, of course, always was a national matter, but its new protective features greatly extended federal control over the fate of business.

These changes combined to make the federal government stronger than it had ever been. Perhaps as important, they brought upon Washington rather than the state capitals a new army of lobbyists richly laden with gifts. By 1864 the railroads, already experienced in such devices, played for much higher stakes than ever before, and their handouts were commensurate. When the Union Pacific, in that year, had its charter revised, doubling its land grant, increasing its capital and relegating the government's lien to a second mortgage, it obtained these new benefits by spending almost half a million dollars in the nation's capital. J. B. Stewart, a company lawyer, alone dispensed $200,000 to smooth the way for the new bill. By 1865 representatives in Congress had become associated with the notorious Credit Mobilier, the Union Pacific's construction company which built a very poor railroad with money gotten from private investors, while its directors distributed among themselves and other insiders the proceeds of the government's lavish contributions.

Neither secession nor Civil War had called industrial businessmen to national leadership; both events only marked their ascension. When the southern states seceded from the Union they left with the conviction that the reign of agrarianism was over. That conviction prove correct. Businessmen had developed their plants, refined their techniques in the fifties. In 1860, aided by northwestern farmers, they had captured political power. By 1865 they had strengthened their control beyond agrarian recall.

PREPARING FOR "PROGRESS"

Northern politicians knew little about conducting a war, but they had few fears over the war's result. During the conflict, therefore, they concentrated not only on war emergencies but also on the future when the war would be over and the country their own. Their acts initiated new policies which, except for contract labor, continued in force long after 1865. While Congress was distributing the spoils of conquest, however, industrial businessmen were also making great strides in self-help, concentrating capital, organizing trade associations, extending factories, applying machinery to industry and agriculture. This program did not get under way immediately after 1861, but when the war was over and businessmen could devote themselves single-mindedly once again to peacetime enterprises, they found that their war activities had prepared the way for rapid forward strides.

Like many wars in modern society, the Civil War started during a business depression, and throughout the conflict many industries remained in the doldrums. The volume of American ocean shipping fell more than 60 percent between 1860 and 1864. Railroad building, in the fifties more extensive in the United States than in all the countries of Europe combined, virtually ceased during the war. The cotton textile industry, its supply of raw materials cut off, was severely depressed. While factory construction boomed in some industries and some areas, general construction steadily declined. Even those industries supplying indispensable war goods were slow in getting out of the rut. At the start of the war $300,000,000 of uncollectible southern debts dislocated northern credit activity, and optimistic government predictions of quick victory made businessmen wary of overexpansion to meet emergency needs. As the war continued, the government's haphazard fiscal policies disturbed businessmen still more, while the early series of northern defeats and Britain's undecided attitude toward the belligerents also sapped business confidence. As late as August, 1862, therefore, the *New York Tribune* could still complain of "our paralyzed industry, obstructed commerce, our over-laden finances, and our mangled railroads."

The summer of 1862, however, marked the nadir of depression. Jay Cooke's hectic door-to-door sale of the "five-twenties" had rescued the government from bankruptcy. The greenbacks had helped raise commodity prices. The chartering of the Pacific railroads and the great opportunities they promised for speculation in western lands had revived business confidence, and the imposing victories at Vicksburg, Gettysburg, and Chattanooga, following Farragut's success at New Orleans and McClellan's at Antietam, seemed to assure in the end a northern victory and kept business confidence high. In addition the national banking laws were soon to rationalize the crazy state bank-note currency system. They were to create also a great market for government securities and, through these securities, a huge reservoir of credit for private business. When the government, therefore, its treasury now replenished and its armies triumphant, began to place orders for huge quantities of shoes, hats, blankets, uniforms, munitions, flour, corned beef, pork, businessmen showed a new eagerness to fill these orders. Protected against foreign competition by high tariffs, and presented with a steadily growing demand for uniform goods, manufacturers no longer hesitated to extend and mechanize their plants. The money market became active, employment began to increase, and wartime prosperity thus began to brighten many sections of the land.

During the war two thousand new sets of woolen cards were erected. In the boot and shoe industry, sewing machines became so widely used that the inventor McKay received annual royalties of $750,000. "Operatives are pouring in as fast as room can be made for them," declared the *Lynn Reporter*, "buildings for shoe factories are going up in every direction; the hum of machinery is heard on every hand." Until 1863, soldiers' uniforms had still to be imported from abroad. After that date, the domestic industry, concentrated in Boston, New York, Philadelphia, and Cincinnati, began to supply all the requirements of an enlarged army. At the start of hostilities, North and South alike had to import munitions. By 1863 the North was able to supply itself, and by the end of the war its light-gun industry was filling orders from Europe as well as Washington. American farms also used more machines to replace the labor lost to the army. In 1862, 35,000 mowers were produced; in 1864, 70,000. In July, 1863, the editor of the *Scientific American* declared:

> In conversation a few days since with a most intelligent Western farmer he told us that manual labor was so scarce last autumn that but for horse rakes, mowers, and reaping machines one-half of the crops would have been left standing in the fields. This year the demand for reapers has been so great the manufacturers will not be able to fill their orders.

From much of this prosperity, however, small industrialists were shut out. Mechanization was expensive, and small manufacturers had neither the surplus cash nor the credit to expand their plants. Neither did they have access to friendly ears at Washington where orders were dispensed. Besides, sales taxes on manufactured goods in all stages of production put a premium on integration, and the independent spinning factory, for instance, could not compete in bids for government contracts with corporations handling all stages of the manufacture of blankets or soldiers' uniforms. The result was the concentration of manufacturing capital in fewer hands than before, the construction of larger plants, and the appearance of a new class of war millionaires. The New York *Independent*, during the war, declared that in New York alone there were already "several hundred men worth $1,000,000 and some worth $20,000,000 while twenty years back there had not been five men in the whole United States worth as much as $5,000,000 and not twenty worth over $1,000,000."

While business reorganized for war production, it did not neglect its pressure groups. Trade associations had been formed in the fifties chiefly to control prices and combat labor unions. To these functions during the war were added tax and tariff lobbying. Many new associations were formed, organized on a national basis in sympathy with the shift of power from the states to the federal government. Among those starting or extending their activities between 1861 and 1865, were the California Wine Growers' Association, the Cap and Hat Manufacturers Association of New

York, the National Association of Wool Manufacturers, the National Woolgrowers Association, and the American Iron and Steel Association.

The goods that farms and factories produced had, of course, to be shipped to armies, ports, towns, and villages. Though little railroad track was laid between 1861 and 1865, railroad traffic was enormous and some eastern roads paid dividends for the first time. Cutting into profits, however, was cutthroat competition among different roads and between railroad and water transportation companies. Manufacturers and farmers benefited from this competition and joined with a public afraid of great monopolies to resist efforts at transportation rate agreements or consolidations. In many cases this resistance was successful. The New York Central tried to combine with the Harlem, the Hudson River, and the Lake Shore railroads, but failed. Five lines along Lake Erie, between Buffalo and Chicago, tried futilely to come to an agreement. The Boston & Worcester and the Western in Massachusetts tried to form a through line between Boston and Albany but could not come to terms. As businessmen who shipped long distance and army officials who waited anxiously for goods coming from far away became increasingly annoyed during the war by lack of uniformity in railroad operation, however, they demanded more and more consolidation of transportation companies, more and more pooling of facilities and centralizing of management. And their demands did not go entirely unheeded. As in manufacturing, therefore, the war accelerated the growth of large transportation enterprises. Perhaps the most important combination made between 1861 and 1865 was the acquisition by the Pennsylvania of the Pittsburgh, Fort Wayne & Chicago Railroad, completing the first trunk line between Lake Michigan and the Atlantic coast. The Erie purchased several small roads to extend its western terminal from Dunkirk to Buffalo. Seven local lines combined to run from Boston to Ogdensburg, New York, while four western roads between Quincy, Illinois, and Toledo, Ohio, were brought under one management. The Chicago & North Western, among other acquisitions, absorbed the Peninsular line, uniting the lake city with the new iron and copper mines in northern Michigan.

Almost unanimously desired and therefore much more popular was the concentration of telegraph capital into the Western Union monopoly. Combination started in this infant industry when Western Union, organized in 1851, began to gobble up smaller lines in the Middle West. By 1863 it shared the entire country with the American Telegraph Company, though innumerable local independent companies were scattered outside their net. Some of these companies in New England and New York were linked to terminals in Buffalo, Pittsburgh, Cleveland, Chicago, St. Louis, and

Milwaukee by the United States Telegraph Company, which invaded the industry during the war. This company, or those from which it had been formed, constructed between 1861 and 1865 about 13,000 miles of line, creating a veritable "telegraph fever" and projecting a new giant into the business.

Telegraph profits were huge during the war though competition was acute in many areas and cooperation among the companies was subject to all the hazards of business rivalry. As use of the systems increased, these hazards became more obstructive and businessmen and government officials urged the companies to unite. By 1865, Western Union had built or acquired 50,000 miles of line, twice as much as its two rivals combined. It was best able, therefore, to press for consolidation. Its efforts were successful in 1866. Business had become accustomed, in a short time, to instantaneous communication between distant offices and factories. The telegraph monopoly made this service available uniformly throughout the nation. Under one management it united 75,000 miles of line, serving 2,250 offices in every region. Business celebrated the achievement.

Consolidations also were made in the sale and paper industries while Rockefeller's petroleum empire was beginning to take form. During the war, the first combination of five refineries was completed. The cause leading to its formation, Rockefeller declared,

> was the desire to unite our skill and capital in order to carry on a business of some magnitude and importance in place of the small business that each separately had theretofore carried on.

The demands of war and economics were combining during the military struggle to enlarge the typical American industrial plant and concentrate American capital. By 1866 the editor of the *Commercial and Financial Chronicle* could observe:

> There is an increasing tendency in our capital to move in larger masses than formerly. Small business firms compete at more disadvantage with richer houses, and are gradually being absorbed into them. Thus we have more men worth one hundred thousand dollars in some of our large commercial cities than were reputed five years ago to be worth fifty thousand dollars. No doubt much of this reputed capital is fictitious. But the power accumulating in the moneyed classes from the concentration of capital in large masses is attracting the attention of the close observers of the money market. It is one of the signs of the time and will probably exert no small influence over the future growth of our industrial and commercial enterprise.

PROFITS FOR WHOM?

In his first annual message, President Lincoln declared:

> Labor is prior to and independent of capital. Capital is only the fruit of labor and could never have existed if labor had not first existed. Labor is the superior of capital and deserves much the higher consideration.

Northern industrialists probably were pleased that Lincoln was so occupied with other things he could not try to enact these principles. Even so, Lincoln probably stayed the hand of some of his less liberal colleagues when strikes during the early years of the war hindered preparations for conflict.

In February, 1861, the national convention of workmen, meeting regularly after 1858 under the leadership of William Sylvis of the Moulders, had resolved:

> That our Government never can be sustained by bloodshed, but must live in the affections of the people; we are, therefore, utterly opposed to any measures that will evoke civil war.

When fighting began, however, Sylvis and other labor leaders actively supported the government. Labor shortages between 1861 and 1865 stimulated unionization and encouraged strikes, most of them successful. Lincoln's administration tolerated these activities until 1864; then the army insisted that they be brought to a halt. In that year and the next, Union Order No. 65 was enforced in St. Louis, Louisville, and other large industrial cities supplying army needs. This order forbade striking and picketing and authorized the protection of strikebreakers.

While skilled trades were successful in organizing during the war, labor as a whole failed to win wage increases at a rate commensurate with the skyrocketing cost of living. Industrial businessmen used the conflict to wrest political leadership from agriculture and commerce, bankers used it to make fortunes speculating in gold and marketing government bonds, manufacturers used it to make extraordinary profits from government contracts, speculators in railroads and western lands used it to prepare a great fortune for themselves; and speculators in contraband used it, in effect, to ruin the morale of the army. But through all the war years industrial workers suffered privations because of rising commodity prices, and white-collar workers and salaried professionals, their incomes less elastic even than those of organized industrial workers, often fell into dire need. Some businessmen made legitimate profits, while others secretly grasped opportunities for fraud. "Bribery and corruption seem to go into every branch of service," complained General Hurlbut. General Butler complained that smugglers of contraband and southern cotton were so successful his soldiers at New Orleans were anxious to go home, "not wishing to risk their lives to make fortunes for others." In or out of the army, the majority of the people found it increasingly difficult to make ends meet while more and more of their liberties were curtailed. Not only were strikes forbidden during the last years of the war but newspapers were gagged, objectors were cast into jail without trial, and martial law was imposed in many areas.

The Civil War began when a northern party captured the federal government. During the war that conquest was made more secure. Men friendly to industrial business were elected to office. Others were absorbed into the civil service; still others consolidated their positions in local government. Founded as a party of protesting western farmers, the Republican party soon became the instrument of Big Business. Those farmers who escaped the call to the colors profited during the war, but agriculture lost its previous political power. Southern planters, their wealth destroyed, and western farmers, their party captured, could do no more than complain about eastern exploitation.

SPECULATION

The wartime economy with its inadequate taxation and massive spending created inflationary pressures both North and South. Inflation was a serious problem in the Union economy, but it never went the ruinous length it did in the South. As can be seen from this article by Jeremiah Best published in Harper's New Monthly Magazine, *April 1865, speculators were one group who throve on inflation and on the erratic fiscal policies of the Federal government.*

JEREMIAH BEST, *Wall Street in War Time*

"The battle of Bull Run," said a late eminent financier, who would have been worth millions and might have ruled the monetary spheres, had he only kept to the straight path, and eschewed Indiana State Bonds—"the battle of Bull Run makes the fortune of every man in Wall Street who is not a natural idiot."

He foresaw a long war, great expenditures, and consequently, taxes being almost unknown, vast issues of paper-money, with their inevitable results, namely, active speculation, an advance in the price of all articles exchangeable for money, and unparalleled vicissitudes of fortune. And he went to work and bought 75,000 shares of stock on the spot. It was moderate, under the circumstances, considering the low prices of stocks, and the improving condition of the railways to look for an average advance of twenty per cent. This would give him a profit of $1,500,000. But the advance would probably be nearer forty than twenty. Forty would give him three millions. With that he would for the present remain satisfied. So he counted his brood in the egg. . . .

Paper-money brought every one into Wall Street, and interested every family in the ups and downs of stocks. It circulated like fertilizing dew throughout the land, generating enterprise, facilitating industry, developing

---

Jeremiah Best, "Wall Street in War Time," *Harper's New Monthly Magazine,* Vol. XXX, No. 179 (April 1865), pp. 615–623.

internal trade; the railways found their business increase beyond their most sanguine expectations; dividend-paying roads had extra profits to divide; embarrassed enterprises cleared off their debts, and became lucrative to their owners; every body wanted to own railway property. Within a few weeks after the first issue of legal tenders, stocks began to rise, and rose steadily, with slight interruptions . . . .

It is keeping within bounds to say that $250,000,000—in paper-money—was realized as profits by the operators in stocks between 1862 and 1864. The difference between the aggregate price of the railroad and miscellaneous shares and bonds dealt in on our Stock Exchange at mid-summer, 1862, and the price of the same securities on 1st August, 1864, is more than that sum. Many popular shares rose 300 per cent.

This profit was divided among many thousands of people. In 1863, and in the first quarter of 1864, every body seemed to be speculating in stocks. Nothing else was talked of at clubs, in the streets, at the theatres, in drawing-rooms. Ladies privately pledged their diamonds as margin with brokers, and astonished their husbands with the display of their gains. Clergymen staked their salary, and some of them realized in a few months more than they could have made by a lifetime of preaching. . . .

The labors and profits of the brokers were enormous. One house checked more than once for $4,000,000 in a day. A day's commissions, in the case of a leading firm, were not unfrequently $5000. Nearly all the leading members of the board lost their voices from constant bawling, and talked in the evening as though they were in the last stage of bronchitis; clerks seldom left their offices before 11 or 12 p.m., a liberal dinner at Delmonico's being allowed by their employers as a stimulus to exertion. The day was not long enough for the gamblers.

At half past 8 a.m. they began to collect in William Street, and by half past 10 the police could hardly keep the thoroughfare open. All day long the crowd ebbed and flowed between the boards and the street, shouting, screaming, swearing, quarreling, tussling, and not a few of them cheating and lying. A man-milliner from up-town, of short stature but prodigious lungs, was always a leading personage in the crowd: his bids rose like muffled thunder from under other men's coat-tails. The little rogue made $100,000, and went off to Europe with it, to study, as he said, "de newe fashions for my emporium." When evening fell the throng adjourned to the Fifth Avenue Hotel, and the rooms adjacent, which were hired for the purpose. There night was made hideous by discordant bids and offers—often till every one in the neighborhood was or wished to be asleep. The Fifth Avenue Board, on an exciting night, was probably the nearest approach to Pandemonium we can hope to witness on this earth.

OF BULLS AND BEARS

Nobody needs to be told that a bull is an operator who buys stocks for the rise, and a bear one who sells them for the fall. The former is said, in Wall Street parlance, to "go long" of a stock when he buys; the other to "sell short." When a man has bought 500 Erie expecting it to rise he is said to be "long of Erie;" if he has sold 500 Hudson for future delivery, expecting it to fall, he is pronounced "short of Hudson." There are many ways of buying and selling stocks. People who have plenty of money buy for cash or "regular"—which means that the stock will be delivered and paid for next day. Others buy on "buyer's option," so many days; in which case the buyer has a right to call for the stock at any time before the maturity of the contract, and does not pay for it till then. Stocks may be sold for cash, or regular; or on seller's option, so many days, in which case the seller may deliver on any day prior to the maturity of the contract and can not be called upon for the stock till then. As a rule, outsiders—by which term is meant all persons who speculate in stocks without being brokers or professional speculators—buy on buyers' options, and sell on sellers' options.

Most Wall Street operators are bull or bear by turns, according to their views of the tendency of the market. These persons very seldom make money. The gift of average foresight is rare, and the variety of circumstance which influence prices in Wall Street so vast, that no mortal can presume to foresee them all. Exceptional periods occur every few years when shrewdness will enable an operator to discern the general drift of the market. But, in ordinary times, chance rules the day. If Smith or Brown makes $100 to-day by bulling Erie, ten to one he loses it to-morrow by bearing Central or bulling Hudson. There are, and always have been, a very large number of persons in Wall Street who have no other means of living than speculations in stocks, and yet who live and live well. But if the private affairs of these gentry were known, it would be found that all or nearly all have been "lame ducks" at some time or other; that is to say, owe money which they can not pay. It was a saying of one of the oldest and boldest operators of the street that he intended some day to paper his study with the promissory notes of his brethren. His own are cheap enough now. . . .

A man who buys Erie because he knows that the earnings of the road are increasing largely, or who sells Hudson because he knows it has a floating debt which will interfere with dividends, has some reason for his act . . . . But the bulk of the Wall Street operators buy and sell with very little more ground for the faith that is in them than the man who bets on the red, or "goes his pile" at poker.

The true bull and the true bear are born so. They do not change. . . .

From *Frank Leslie's Illustrated Newspaper*, Vol. XXIX, No. 732 (October 9, 1869), p. 72.

"The bull and bear fight—two to one on the bear."

Both classes of operators are useful and even essential. But for the bulls no enterprise would ever be carried into effect. And when rogues try to gull the public with fraudulent schemes, and to foist worthless stock on unsuspecting investors, the bear looms up as the protector of his species, and by selling the trash "short" develops its want of value and warns the dupes of their danger. When values are too low, the bull reinstates them. When they rise too high, the bear interposes and checks the enthusiasm of the sanguine.

The bulls had their carnival in 1863 and the beginning of 1864. The bears had theirs in 1857, and again in the later months of 1864, and the commencement, thus far, of 1865. The contest of 1857 was severe, though the result was never doubtful. Our railroads were inefficiently managed. There was not traffic enough for all of them, and a large number were declaring dividends which had not been earned. Most of them were groaning under constantly increasing floating debts. Under these circumstances it was clear that they must decline in public favor as investments, and it was merely a question of time when the fall would come. An organization of about a dozen large operators was formed under the title of "The Observatory," comprising a large proportion of the capital and financial skill of the street. They operated for the fall with vigor and ability. It is not a little curious to note, however, that their ultimate success was due to an event which had by no means entered into their calculations. They had based their sales exclusively on the unsound condition of the railways, whereas the crisis of 1857, which caused the great decline in values, was the result of general overtrading and an excessive drain of specie to Europe. The Observatory made a net profit of $1,500,000 @ $2,000,000 less than some individuals realized on the bull side in 1863. The loss to the public, exclusive of losses in merchandise, was not less than $200,000,000.

The bulls had a carnival, based on the development of gold in California, which lasted from 1852 to 1855, and made many fortunes. But the most brilliant of their campaigns was that of 1863. Paper-money was its base; its success was due to the large earnings of the railroads caused by the development of internal trade.

The crisis of 1857, and the short crops which followed, had impoverished the West, reduced railroad receipts to so low an ebb that they barely paid expenses, and destroyed public confidence in railroad property. Many railroads had passed out of the hands of their owners into those of receivers, and had been reorganized. Others were struggling painfully under an intolerable load of floating debt. The bountiful crops of 1859 and 1860 were beginning to restore them to something like prosperity when the war panic—which followed the election of Mr. Lincoln—again revived distrust, checked trade, and plunged holders of railroad property into despair. It was not till two years afterward that the depression began to be overcome.

In 1862 the bulls showed their heads again—fortified by paper-money and increased railroad earnings. Two brothers, not associated in business, but both clear-headed [and] bold . . . began to attract attention by the boldness of their purchases. Another man, whom few persons knew, but who was said to have been an unlucky curbstone operator for some years, commenced dealing on a capital of two or three thousand dollars, and soon became a prominent figure at the "coal-hole." He enjoyed the acquaintance if not the patronage of a great millionaire; and when he was most audacious in his purchases, it was always suspected that he was acting for his potential friend—which helped his credit and gave him prestige to no small extent. Keen, shrewd, and now at last lucky, his first ventures were successful beyond his hopes; in six months his $3000 had swelled to one hundred times that amount, and he was recognized as a leader. When he rose in the coal-hole to bid, as he generally did, "seller three or thirty," with his eyes flashing, and his slender frame vibrating with excitement—an associate or friend beside him with book and pencil to note down his purchases—by-standers looked on with admiration, bears hastened to cover their shorts, and the large class of speculators, who get their thinking done by other people, lost no time in following in his track. A man with prestige . . . has always following enough to relieve him of his stocks at a profit if he repents his purchases. This was the fortune of this man; for a long time every thing he touched turned to gold, because he could make his operations certain. And his shrewdness did not fail him at the last. For some time before the great crash of April he had foreseen and foretold it. It found him prepared; and of the great fortunes won in 1863, his is one of the very few which has been preserved.

Another leading operator made a display not less brilliant, but more meteoric. He, too, had read the signs of the times, and after feeling his way for some months, at length struck a vein. He achieved fame and fortune in a few days. His personal prestige was at one time greater than was ever enjoyed by any man in Wall Street. People of all kinds thronged his office and begged him to give them just a hint—the least hint, and they would be his friends forever. If he whispered "Rock Island," scores of sensible men rushed to their brokers and ordered Rock Island bought. Not that they knew why they were buying it: they had a hint from the Great Man, and that was sufficient. A Company, respectable enough, and with a fine property which they were desirous of bringing before the public, actually paid him the enormous fee of $165,000 to allow the subscription books to be opened at his office, and his name to appear in the list of directors. Speculators paid him extravagant commissions to buy stocks for them, in the hope that the public might think he was buying them for himself. To his friends he was a generous fellow, and in his wild, extravagant way would tell them:

"Boys, I'll make a million for each of you before I've done."

He was something more than a mere gambler. As an arithmetician he never had his equal in the street, and his grasp of financial questions was so true and comprehensive that at one meeting, he persuaded one of our soundest Boards of railroad managers to depart from the policy they had established, and pursue a new one under his guidance. The misfortune with him was that at last he began to believe in himself. From that moment he was a doomed man. The moment a man in Wall Street begins to think he knows more than other people his ruin is a mere question of time. When this misfortune befell the operator of whom we speak, he determined to make not two or three millions but eight or ten; not to control one stock, but half a dozen. Bankers and banks were ready enough to humor him. Where he had borrowed a million they lent him two; and president and cashier slyly examined his collaterals, and laid in a couple of hundred each of the same sort for their private pocket. If Mr. Chase had not been seized with the fine notion of selling gold for greenbacks, and if nothing else of the like nature had happened, there is no saying how many millions this great operator might not have realized, and what income-tax he would have paid. Unfortunately, the dread day of April came, and found him expanded to the utmost extent. Banks and bankers called for their money, and would hear of no excuse. Private lenders called for more margin. Customers called for their balances. The struggle was brief. One morning the word was passed round:

"M—— has failed!"

It was the culminating point of the crisis of April. The great leader went down, under full sail, with all hands on board, and all the little smacks and other craft which had followed in his wake shared his fate.

It was a bad time for Uncle Sam's income-tax commissioners. The decline was so rapid that not only did speculators lose, but brokers, money-lenders, and others, who had no interest in the operations of the day, were involved in the general catastrophe. Stocks fell 15 per cent on Saturday, and then, though every body said they would naturally react on Monday, they fell 15 per cent more on that day. No such decline had ever been witnessed in Wall Street, and people were new to the alternate inflations and panics which are the characteristics of paper-money eras. Very few had time to save themselves. Several thousands of individuals who had made during the year preceding fortunes varying from $25,000 to $250,000 found themselves stripped in a week. Of those who survived the subsequent decline slaughtered the greater part. Speculation in stocks received a blow from which it has not since recovered.

A few figures will explain the extent of the losses which have fallen upon stock gamblers since last 1st of April. Erie, which sold when the war began at 30, rose to 130, fell in April to 105, and has since sold at 66. Reading, which sold in 1861 at 55, rose to 160, and has since sold at 102. Toledo sold at 28 in 1861, at 160 in 1863, and at 103 since. Michigan Southern sold at 30 in 1862, at 118 in 1863, and at 61 since. Pittsburg rose from 22 to 129, and has since fallen to 80. Rock Island rose from 40 to 150, and has since sold at 88. It will be remembered that the figures at which these properties sold at the beginning of the war were in gold, and that the roads were not then earning money; whereas the subsequent figures are in a currency worth 50 per cent in gold, and the roads are all earning dividends.

OF CORNERS

Every body knows what the corner of a street is, or the corner of a room. A Wall Street "corner" has no affinity with either of these. It is derived from the popular verb to "corner," *i.e.,* to embarrass beyond chance of escape. A stock operator is cornered when he has sold stock short which he can not procure for delivery, and a stock is said to be cornered when a bold operator or a clique buys it all up, and then calls upon the bears who have sold it short to "stand and deliver." Great corners are among the memorable events of the street. . . .

There have been three great corners within the past year or two; one in Hudson River, one in Harlem, one in Rock Island—each of the three organized by a master of the art. Of these the most profitable was the one in Hudson River, the most thorough the one in Harlem.

Hudson came to be cornered accidentally. In a dull, inanimate state of the market the chronic bears were amusing themselves by "hammering," *i.e.,* pressing down the price of Hudson, which did not happen to have any particular friend in the Board. This pastime of theirs was not relished by a large holder of Hudson, then disporting himself during the dog days on board his yacht; and chancing to revolve the matter in his head as he lay with a friend on a pile of deals on a wharf in the North River one morning between four and five, it occurred to him that with proper ingenuity a rod might be set in pickle for these trespassers. Orders went that morning to confidential brokers to take all the sellers' options in Hudson. This was repeated for several days, until the buyers had a pretty large pile of options. Cash stock was then taken as quietly as possible, until the market was bare. A brief calculation showed that the buyers had secured either as cash or contract stock, all the Hudson in existence, with the exception of a very few shares which were not likely to come on the market. A new manœuvre was then developed. Application was made to several leading bear houses to "turn" Hudson; that is to say, to buy it for cash from the cornering party, and to sell it back to them on buyers' option for ten, twenty, or thirty days. This indicated or was regarded as indicating weakness on the part of the cornerers; it looked as though they were short of money; the bears eagerly "turned" several thousand shares for the usual difference, and instantly threw on the market the cash stock, which the cornerers privately bought.

All being now ripe, the trap was sprung. Many of the sellers' options began to mature. There was no Hudson to be had. On that morning when the chief of the party lay on the deals thinking of his margins Hudson was 112; it now rose to 180. On one hundred shares, thoughtlessly sold, the loss was $6800. There could not have been less than 50,000 shares contracted to be delivered to the party which had cornered the stock by members of the Board and others. Bear cries of anguish rose to heaven. In the course of a day or two the clique notified the parties who had turned the stock to deliver. They considered themselves very badly treated. They claimed to have turned the stock merely to oblige the bulls, and now to be asked to lose $5000 or $6000 on every 100 shares! But the bulls were inexorable. They must have their property. On one point they were willing to oblige their foes. They would lend stock at the modest rate of 5 per cent a day. Enormous as this charge was, there were many who, believing that the corner was a mere spasm of a day or two, paid it and borrowed stock. They were the worst punished of all. The corner lasted many days, over two weeks. After paying 5 per cent a day for several days, the victims despaired, and bought the stock. Never in its history had Wall Street been so cruelly scourged.

What distinguished the Hudson River corner from almost all others was the skill with which the clique extricated themselves at last. Every one can see that with plenty of money it is an easy matter to buy up all the shares of a stock which the rank and file of Wall Street are blindly selling short, and to bleed the sellers for their presumption. But the natural end of such an operation is to load the bulls with the entire capital stock of the concern cornered. And no man wants to buy a stock which has just been cornered. Now the clique in Hudson secured the services of a prominent bear broker, and directed him to sell all the stock he could on seller's option during the heat of the contest. While the unfortunate bears were buying stock for delivery at 170 @ 180, this broker was selling at 140, or even lower, on sellers' thirty-day options, which were taken by many in the belief that he was prosecuting the contest and would fail in the end. Whereas, when most of the stock really sold short had been delivered, and the bears squeezed as thoroughly as they could be, the clique quietly delivered the stock apparently sold short by their broker, and found themselves loaded with no exorbitant amount remaining.

The Harlem corner is an instance of the opposite style of management. We have seen lately two corners in Harlem; one in which Commodore Vanderbilt cornered the Common Council and their friends by way of punishment; the other, in which like measure was meted out to the Legislature and their friends for operating on the repeal of the Broadway grant. This was an operation in which feeling seems to have predominated over calculation. The severity of the punishment was unequaled. Many contracts to deliver Harlem at 110 were settled at 280. Probably no less than $3,000,000 in money were taken out of the pockets of the bears in

Harlem. Several houses went down in the struggle, and others which survive still wear its scars. But the end of the campaign saddled the bulls with the entire capital stock of the Harlem, which, as it doesn't pay dividends, and may never do so, is not a cheerful load to carry. A man who bid 60 for Harlem—the last sales being at something like 240—would probably be promptly supplied. People won't buy it at any price.

A fair joke was developed in the course of the Harlem corner. The bulls had purchased from a leading operator certain "calls" on Harlem. A call is a document which states that for value received the bearer may call upon the subscriber for so many shares of such a stock at such a price within a stated time. It need hardly be mentioned that the shrewd old speculator who sold these calls on Harlem did so in perfect ignorance of the fact that the stock was being cornered at the time. When he discovered the trap into which he had fallen his wrath was pungent. The calls were sold at 130 or thereabouts. When the stock rose to 250 or so, the holders "called." The seller refused to deliver. Being asked his reasons, he replied in the language of the Morris Canal victims, that the corner was a conspiracy, and furthermore, said he:

"This paper says you may call on me for Harlem. Well, call. I don't mind it. Call again, as often as you like. I don't see any thing here about my delivering any stock."

The Rock Island corner made a great noise in its time, and some of its features were brilliant. The bulls bought, counting cash and contract stock together, about 20,000 more shares of Rock Island than exist. Of course when the deliveries were called for the bears were at the mercy of their opponents, and the price rose from 110 to 150. In the middle of the contest the bull leader suddenly sold out with such surprising swiftness and dash that none of the bears had an opportunity of disputing the market with him. Fully 40,000 shares were sold in a day, the price falling from 141 to 118. Had he hesitated, or attempted to rally the price, the bears would infallibly have pressed him with their options, and deprived him of a market on which to sell.

Corners, as a rule, are not profitable operations, unless the stock cornered be of such quality that the bulls are satisfied to own the whole of it, and they have the means to do so. The Hudson River corner paid 12 per cent; the Rock Island showed a profit of 4½. In the old days before 1857, the leading operator was once or twice broken by corners, but I doubt whether the cornerers made much, even when he didn't break. In London, they have a horror of corners. One important reason why they objected to putting our railway shares on their exchange list was that their capitals were generally so small that they were liable to be cornered by any one of several great operators.

OF GOLD GAMBLING

The legal tender Acts demonetized specie, and rendered it an article of merchandise, like flour or pork. At first there were many who contended that it should not rise to any premium. It had not done so during the suspension of 1857; and had the war ended as soon as some sanguine patriots expected, legal tender notes might have maintained their value in coin. As the war did not end, but, on the contrary, pursued its weary course with the usual vicissitudes of fortune, it soon became evident to sound thinkers that gold must eventually command a substantial premium. Leading foreign houses put their capital in gold, and converted their profits into gold as fast as they made them. Speculators began to buy gold for the rise.

At that time dealings in gold were confined to the Board of Brokers and the outside Board, popularly known, from the dinginess of its apartments, as the "Coal-hole." There were bear operators enough in the Board to sell on time all the gold wanted to the disbelievers in the currency. Their sales on sellers' options carried interest; and one house believed that it had discovered the royal road to fortune by selling so many millions of gold short that its monthly receipts from interest amounted to $10,000. No better business, as the partners boasted, could possibly be discovered. Unfortunately, one day, the Union arms met with a reverse, and gold jumped up five or six per cent. This gave courage to the buyers for a rise, and they bought with freedom. In three days the profits from interest account were swallowed up, and the confident bears were forced to cover their contracts at a severe loss.

Gold was then about 125. It rose from that point, almost without a check, to 173. This steady advance in a few weeks was mainly due to the large issues of paper-money at Washington, and the poor success of the Union armies. But the rise was considerably aided by the operations of a clique known as the "Washington party."

The Washington party consisted, as its name imported, of men resident at or temporarily placed at Washington. They were members of Congress, Republicans and Democrats; newspaper correspondents; clerks high in office in the Departments; lobby agents; and Washington bankers. They enjoyed remarkable facilities for procuring early intelligence from the armies, and correct information regarding the designs of Government. Commencing with a small capital and a few adherents, they attracted money and associates by the rumor of their large profits, and in January, 1863, they were by far the most powerful body of operators in this market. No one knows precisely the rules which governed their method of operating, but they were bulls in every thing, and their ostensible engineers were Washington bankers, who hailed from some one of our up-town hotels. Not content with buying gold, they bought exchange in enormous amounts, and likewise tobacco, cotton, and other merchandise. It was currently reported in February, 1863, that they had made not less than $6,000,000.

Their operations were so vast that concealment of them was impossible, and they were traced with ease. More than once, at the closing Board of the day in the "coal-hole," the well-known broker of the party would beg the President to "dwell" on gold, as he had "a little order." Members knew what that meant. He wanted a million or so. The report would run through the Board into the street, and through Wall Street to all the brokers' offices, that the Washington party were buying. There must be news. Every body wanted to buy too. Before the close of business a substantial advance in the premium had been established. At that time large dealings in gold were rare. Now a man buys or sells a million, and nobody is surprised or curious.

In February, 1863, a New York banker went to Washington. He had some talk with the Secretary of the Treasury and the members of the Committee of Ways and Means. He was known in this city as a man who had always been a believer in gold, and a holder of at least a million. One morning he telegraphed his partners here:

"Sell my gold!"

It was then 172 @ 173. The order was obeyed, and many were the surmises to which the laconic message gave birth. The market was in that condition that it seemed impossible for gold not to rise. It had risen steadily for several months, and every one who had sold it had lost money. The Washington party was said to hold over $4,000,000 of gold, besides exchange. There was no prospect of a diminution of paper-money, and the military horizon was not brilliant.

A day or two after the New York banker had sold his gold a little bill was rushed through Congress. It was a silly little bill. It forbade loans of over par on gold, and threw some other pottering little difficulties in the way of traffic in coin. But though it was "neither as wide as a church door nor as deep as a well, it was enough" to prick the bubble which had been inflated by the Washington party. A panic in gold ensued.

It fell from 173 to 160, from 160 to 140, from 140 to 130, and at last, at midsummer, sold at 120. The dismay in Wall Street and William Street was appalling. Men with haggard faces and woebegone expression hung listlessly on the corners of the streets. . . . The fall in gold involved a corresponding fall in exchange, and in produce, groceries, and dry-goods. How many millions of apparent wealth were wiped out by this panic imagination only can figure. The Washington party were overwhelmed. They might possibly have stood their losses on gold. But when to these were added their losses on exchange, on tobacco, and other merchandise, even their gains were insufficient to carry them through, and they went down and were heard of no more. Some bankers who sold them options are said to remember them still.

The panic culminated in August, 1863, when Fort Wagner was taken, and our sanguine people pictured General Gillmore razing Charleston to the earth and sowing its site with salt. Gold then sold, for a day at least, at 120. From that point it rose, with many fluctuations, under the influence of natural causes, to 167 @ 175. Merchants were recovering from the losses they had suffered; exports were increasing; trade was improving; farmers were getting better prices for their produce. Every thing seemed quiet and, under the circumstances, as satisfactory as could have been expected.

At this conjuncture, Mr. Chase put his foot in it. Mr. Chase is now Chief Justice of the United States, and will probably make the best Chief Justice we have had for half a century. But it is due to truth to say that he was a most miserable financier at this crisis. In the first place, instead of confining himself to his proper business, which was the providing of ways and means for the war, he persuaded himself that he was called upon to regulate prices. And then, instead of seeking light in history, he must needs repeat all the blunders which were made by France, Austria, and England during their suspensions of specie payments, though every book of history shows plainly how fatal those blunders had been. He first calmly swept aside the law which requires a sinking fund to be set apart for the redemption of the debt, and the other law which requires the customs duties to be paid in coin. He announced that he would receive payment of duties in paper at 165 cents for the gold dollar. Then he took a lesson from the example of the French Directory, and gave out that he would announce the price of gold every morning at the sub-treasury, and that this price should be the price for all day, no matter what news came to hand to vary it.

These absurd measures had their natural effect. The shrewd operators in gold—who by this time had established an exchange of their own—played on Mr. Chase as a man plays with a child. They made him vary his rate for gold to suit their speculations. They could easily foresee how long he could continue to dispense with gold receipts for customs; when the limit was reached, they knew he was at their mercy. Among merchants, the effect was still more grave. The violation of law perpetrated by the Secretary of the Treasury alarmed them, and shook their confidence in Government credit. Enormous quantities of goods were entered at the Custom-house, in the belief that when the time came for the resumption of the payment of duties in gold, the premium would advance. A general distrust in the wisdom of Government began to pervade the mercantile community. When Mr. Chase stopped receiving duties in paper, gold jumped up five to ten per cent.

Still the Secretary was not satisfied. He had borrowed a hint from the French Directory. He now took a lesson from the Committee of Public Safety, and persuaded Congress to pass the most insane measure ever placed on our statute book—the Gold Bill, as it was called. This preposterous enactment, seeking to prevent all dealings whatsoever in gold, pronounced a variety of ordinary and legitimate acts of commerce criminal, and exposed all persons engaged in foreign trade to prosecutions at law. Had this measure retained its place among our laws, the trade of the seaboard cities would have been destroyed, and the currency would long ere this have been worth no more than the rebel shinplasters. The day the gold bill passed gold was quoted 200. It rose next day to 210, next day to 220, next day to 240, and in a week to 280. One reason alone sufficed to account for the advance. There were a large number of persons who believed in the Union, in the success of our armies, and in the ultimate redemption of the currency in coin. These persons had either sold gold short, believing it to be too high, or had postponed their payments of gold for duties and their remittances to Europe. When the gold bill passed, the gold-room was closed, and the trade in gold was at an end. One or two gold brokers still professed to deal in the article, but they were unwilling to make large engagements. A man who had to pay $100,000 duties on a cargo of teas or silks could not tell where to get the coin. The bears in gold—who were generally extra loyal men—were still more embarrassed. One man was short half a million of gold. He was called upon by his buyers to deliver. He went to every broker in the city; no one would sell him so large an amount. Of course he broke—owing to his excessive faith in the currency and in the soundness of Mr. Chase's system. If he had been a Copperhead and a believer in the worthlessness of greenbacks he would have made a fortune. Many contracts were settled during the few days of panic which followed the passage of the gold bill at a loss of 80 per cent, or $80,000 on every $100,000. Mr. Chase had certainly slaughtered his friends most thoroughly.

After a few days' experience of this monstrous bill Congress came to its senses and repealed it. Gold fell 25 per cent on the repeal. The gold-room was re-opened, and merchants and speculators dealt therein as before. It has fluctuated since then with the fluctuations in public confidence, rising as high as 260 on bad news from the war, and falling on peace rumors to 185. But the trade in gold has been free, and hence, in the long-run, the fair trader may rely upon its finding its level.

Large fortunes have been made in gold, but it is very doubtful whether any of them have been kept. The fluctuations have been so severe that the most fortunate operators have been caught sooner or later. At least half a dozen men have been pointed out in Wall Street at different times as having realized their million by gold gambling; but not one of them has taken any of his gains away. There was a clique of rebels at Montreal, and another clique at Louisville, Kentucky, which used to operate largely in gold. So long as the premium advanced they did well enough, and not only made money, but laid the flattering unction to their souls that they were discrediting our currency. But by-and-by some victory of Sherman's or some peace *canard* in the papers caused a stampede *in* the gold-room, and away went profits and margins too. So with the loyal gamblers. So long as all seemed bright they saw money piling up on their side fast enough. But some day a reverse in the field, or a new currency issue—necessitated by the inexorable wants of Government—swept away their gains, and left them poorer than when they began. Whether it be the destiny of gold to advance even after the peace, as many now seem to think will be the case, in consequence of the enormous accumulation of debt which the Government will have to liquidate; or whether it fall to or near par, on the success of our armies and the restoration of the prolific South to the fold of the Union, one thing seems pretty clear: little or no money will be made by gambling in gold. Gentlemen in the country, who aspire to this short and easy road to fortune, try certain well-known "hells" at Newport and Saratoga. If you can make a fortune in the comfortable *salons* of these worthies, you may also make it in gold. But it is as easy to do it in one as in the other.

CONFEDERATE MUNITIONS MAKER

Josiah Gorgas, a northerner and a graduate of West Point, headed the Confederate Ordnance Department during the war. This paper which he prepared for the Southern Historical Society demonstrates that the North had no monopoly on organizational talent. Considering the fact that the Confederacy was predominantly agricultural, Gorgas performed one of the more brilliant achievements of the war. His work behind the lines compares favorably with Lee's in the field. Had he stayed with the North, he might well have rivaled Carnegie and Rockefeller in his ability to coordinate and manage diverse enterprises.

JOSIAH GORGAS,
Notes on the Ordnance Department of the Confederate Government

At the formation of the Government, or at the beginning of the war, the arms at command were distributed as follows:

	Rifles	*Muskets*
At Richmond, Va. (about)	4,000	—
Fayetteville Arsenal, North Carolina (about)	2,000	25,000
Charleston Arsenal, South Carolina (about)	2,000	20,000
Augusta Arsenal, Georgia (about)	3,000	28,000
Mount Vernon Arsenal, Alabama	2,000	20,000
Baton Rouge Arsenal, Louisiana	2,000	27,000
	15,000	120,000

There were at Richmond about 60,000 old, worthless flint muskets, and at Baton Rouge about 10,000 old Hall's rifles and carbines.

Besides the foregoing, there were at Little Rock, Ark., a few thousand stands, and some few at the Texas arsenals, increasing the aggregate of serviceable arms to, say, 143,000. To these must be added the arms owned by the several States and by military organizations throughout the coun-

"Notes on the Ordnance Department of the Confederate Government," *Southern Historical Society Papers*, Vol. XII (Jan.–Dec., 1884), pp. 67–88.

try, giving, say, 150,000 in all for the use of the armies of the Confederacy. The rifles were of the calibre 54, known as Mississippi rifles, except those at Richmond, taken from Harper's Ferry, which were calibre 58; the muskets were the old flint-lock, calibre 69, altered to percussion. Of sabres there were a few boxes at each arsenal, and some short artillery swords. A few hundred holster pistols were scattered here and there. There were no revolvers.

There was little ammunition of any kind, or powder, at the arsenals in the South, and that little relics of the Mexican war, stored principally at Baton Rouge and Mount Vernon arsenals. I doubt whether there were a million rounds of small-arm cartridges in the Confederacy. Lead there was none in store. Of powder the chief supply was that captured at Norfolk, though there was a small quantity at each of the Southern arsenals, say 60,000 pounds in all, chiefly old cannon powder. The stock of percussion caps could not have exceeded one-quarter of a million.

There were no batteries of serviceable field artillery at any of the Southern arsenals. A few old iron guns, mounted on Gribeaural carriages, fabricated about the time of the war of 1812, composed nearly the entire park which the Confederate States fell heir to. There were some serviceable batteries belonging to the States, and some which belonged to volunteer companies. There were neither harness, saddles, bridles, blankets, nor other artillery or calvary equipments.

Thus to furnish 150,000 men on both sides of the Mississippi, on say the 1st of May, 1861, there were on hand no infantry accoutrements, no cavalry arms or equipments—no artillery and, above all, no ammunition; nothing save small arms, and these almost wholly smooth-bore, altered from flint to percussion. Let us see what means we had for producing these supplies.

Within the limits of the Confederate States, there were no arsenals at which any of the material of war was constructed. No arsenal, except that at Fayetteville, N.C., had a single machine above a foot-lathe. Such arsenals as there were, had been used only as depots. All the work of preparation of material had been carried on at the North; not an arm, not a gun, not a gun carriage, and except during the Mexican war—scarcely a round of ammunition had, for fifty years, been prepared in the Confederate States. There were consequently no workmen, or very few of them, skilled in these arts. No powder, save perhaps, for blasting, had been made at the South; and there was no saltpetre in store at any point; it was stored wholly at the North. There was no lead nor any mines of it, except on the Northern limit of the Confederacy, in Virginia, and the situation of that made its product precarious. Only one cannon foundry existed: at Richmond. Copper, so necessary for field artillery and for percussion caps, was just being produced in East Tennessee. There was no rolling mill for bar iron south of Richmond; and but few blast furnaces, and these small, and with trifling exceptions in the border States of Virginia and Tennessee.

Such were the supplies and such the situation when I took charge of the Ordnance Department on the 8th of April, 1861.

The first thing to be attended to was the supply of powder. Large orders had been sent to the North, both by the Confederate Government and some of the States, and these were being rapidly filled at the date of the attack on Fort Sumter. The entire product of one large Northern mill was being received at a Southern port. Of course all the ports were soon sealed to such importations from the North. Attention was at once turned to the production of nitre in North Alabama and in Tennessee—in the latter State under the energetic supervision of its Ordnance Department. An adequate supply of sulphur was found in New Orleans, where large quantities were in store to be used in sugar-refining. The entire stock was secured, amounting to some four or five hundred tons.

The erection of a large powder-mill was early pressed by President Davis, and about the middle of June, 1861, he directed me to detail an officer to select a site and begin the work. The day after this order was given Colonel G. W. Rains, a graduate of West Point, in every way qualified for this service, arrived in Richmond, through the blockade, and at once set out under written instructions from me to carry out the President's wishes. He, however, went first to East Tennessee to supervise and systematize the operations of two small private mills, which were then at work for the State of Tennessee.

Thus, in respect to powder and our means of making it, we had, perhaps, at this time (June 1st, 1861), 250,000 pounds, chiefly cannon, at Norfolk and in Georgia, and as much more nitre (mainly imported by the State of Georgia). We had no powder-mills, except the two rude ones just referred to, and no experience in making powder or in getting nitre. All had to be learned.

As to a further supply of arms, steps had been taken by the President to import these and other ordnance stores from Europe; and Major Caleb Huse, a graduate of West Point, and at that moment professor in the University of Alabama, was selected to go abroad and secure them. He left Montgomery under instructions early in April, with a credit of £10,000 (!) from Mr. Memminger. The appointment proved a happy one; for he succeeded, with a very little money, in buying a good supply, and in running the Ordnance Department into debt for nearly half a million sterling—the very best proof of his fitness for his place, and of a financial ability which supplemented the narrowness of Mr. Memminger's purse.

Before this, and immediately upon the formation of the Confederate Government, Admiral Semmes had been sent to the North by President Davis as purchasing agent of arms and other ordnance stores, and succeeded in making contracts for, and purchases of, powder, percussion caps, cap machinery (never delivered), revolvers &c. He also procured drawings for a bullet-pressing machine, and other valuable information.

The sets of machinery for making the rifle with sword bayonet and the rifle-musket model of 1855, had been seized at Harper's Ferry by the State of Virginia. That for the rifle-musket was being transferred by the State to her ancient armory at Richmond, under the direction of Lieutenant-Colonel Burton, an officer in the service of Virgina, whose experience in the armories of the United States and in the erection of the works at Enfield, near London, qualified him above all for the work. The other set of machines was sent to Fayetteville, N.C., by consent of the State of Virginia, to be there re-erected, as there was at that point an arsenal with steam power, and some good buildings, which had heretofore never been put to any use. These two setts of machinery—capable, if worked with but one set of hands to each, of producing 2,000 to 2,500 stands per month in all—were the only prospective resources at home. With additional workmen, and some extension of the machinery, much larger results could be obtained. But the workmen were not to be had. As it was, it would take many months to put it in working order. Parts were missing, and some injury done in the hasty transfer (partly under fire) from Harper's Ferry. There were no private armories at the South; nor was there any inducement, prior to the war, to turn capital in that direction. Thus, the class of skilled operatives needed were unknown to this region. In New Orleans the Brothers Cook were embarking in the business of making small arms, assisted by the purses and encouraged by the sympathy of patriotic citizens.

In *field artillery* the production was confined almost entirely to the Tredegar Works, in Richmond. Some castings were made in New Orleans, and foundries were rapidly acquiring the necessary experience to produce good bronze castings. The Ordnance Department of Tennessee was also turning its attention to the manufacture of field and seige artillery at Nashville. At Rome, Ga., a foundry—Noble & Son—was induced to undertake the casting of three-inch rifles, after drawings furnished at Montgomery; but the progress made was necessarily slow. The State of Virginia possessed a number of old four-pounder iron guns, which were reamed out to get a good bore, and were rifled with three grooves, after the manner of Parrott. The army in observation at Harper's Ferry, and that at Manassas, were supplied with old batteries of six-pounder guns and twelve-pounder Howitzers. A few Parrott guns purchased by the State of Virginia were with Magruder at Big Bethel.

For the ammunition and equipments required for the infantry and artillery a good laboratory and shops had been established at Richmond by the State, but none of the Southern arsenals were yet in a condition to do much work. The arsenal at Augusta, Ga., was directed to organize for the preparation of ammunition and the making of knapsacks, of which there were none wherewith to equip the troops now daily taking the field. The arsenal at Charleston and the depot at Savannah were occupied chiefly with local work. The arsenal at Baton Rouge was rapidly getting under way; and that at Mt. Vernon, Ala., was also being prepared for work. None of them had had facilities for the work usually done at an arsenal. Fayetteville, N.C. was in the hands of that State, and was occupied chiefly in repairing some arms, and in making up a small amount of small arm ammunition. Little artillery ammunition was being made up, except for local purposes, save at Richmond.

Such was the general condition of supplies when the Government, quitting Montgomery, established itself at Richmond.

PROGRESS OF MANUFACTURE

Colonel Rains, in the course of the Summer of 1861, established a refinery of saltpetre at or near Nashville, and to this point chiefly were sent the nitre, obtained from the State of Georgia, and that derived from caves in East and Middle Tennessee. He supplied the two powder mills in that State with nitre, properly refined, and good powder was thus produced. A small portion of the Georgia nitre was sent to two small mills in South Carolina—at Pendleton and Walhalla—and a powder produced, inferior at first, but afterwards improved. The State of North Carolina established a mill near Raleigh, under contract with certain parties to whom the State was to furnish the nitre, of which a great part was derived from caves in Georgia. A stamping mill was also put up near New Orleans, and powder produced before the fall of the city. Small quantities of powder were also received through the blockade from Wilmington to Galveston, some of it of very inferior quality. The great quantity of artillery placed in position from the Potomac to the Rio Grande, required a vast supply of powder (there was no immediate want of projectiles) to furnish even the scant allowance of fifty rounds to each gun. I think we may safely estimate that on the 1st of January, 1862, there were 1,500 sea coast guns of various calibres in position, from Evansport on the Potomac to Fort Brown on the Rio Grande. If we average their calibre at thirty-two pounders, and the charge at five pounds, it will at forty rounds per gun, give us 600,000 pounds of powder for these. The field-artillery—say 300 guns—with 200 rounds to the piece, would require, say 125,000 pounds, and the small arm cartridges, 10,000,000, would consume 125,000 pounds more—making in all 850,000 pounds. If we deduct 250,000 pounds, supposed to be on hand, in various shapes, at the beginning of the war, we have an increment of 600,000 pounds. Of this, perhaps 200,000 pounds had been made at the Tennessee and other mills, leaving 400,000 to have been supplied through the blockade, and before the commencement of actual hostilities.

The site of the Government Powder-Mills was fixed at Augusta, Georgia, on the report of Colonel Rains, and progress was made on the work in this year. There were two large buildings, in the Norman (castellated) style of architecture; one contained the refinery and store-rooms—the other being the mills, twelve in number. They were arranged in the best way on the canal which supplied water-power to Augusta. This canal served as the means of transport for the material from point to point of its manufacture, though the mills were driven by steam. All the machinery, including the very heavy rollers, was made in the Confederate States. The various qualities of powder purchased, captured and produced were sources of irregularity in the ranges of our artillery and small arms—unavoidably so of course. We were only too glad to take any sort of powder; and we bought some brought into Florida, the best range of which scarcely exceeded one hundred and sixty yards with the *eprouvette.*

Contracts were made abroad for the delivery of *nitre* through the blockade, and for producing it at home from caves. The amount of the latter delivered by contracts was considerable—chiefly in Tennessee.

The consumption of *lead* was in part met by the Virginia lead mines (Wytheville), the yield from which was from 100,000 to 150,000 pounds per month. A laboratory for the smelting of other ores, from the Silver Hill mines, North Carolina, and Jonesboro, East Tennessee, was put up at Petersburg, under the direction of Dr. Piggott, of Baltimore. It was very well constructed; was capable of smelting a good many thousand pounds per day, and was in operation before midsummer of 1862. Mines were opened on account of Government in East Tennessee, near the State line of Virginia. They were never valuable, and were soon abandoned. Lead was collected in considerable quantities throughout the country by the laborious exertions of agents employed for this purpose. The battle-field of Bull Run was fully gleaned, and much lead collected.

By the close of 1861 the following arsenals and depots were at work, having been supplied with some machinery and facilities, and were producing the various munitions and equipments required: Augusta, Ga.; Charleston, S.C.; Fayetteville, N.C.; Richmond, Va.; Savannah, Ga.; Nashville, Tenn.; Memphis, Tenn.; Mount Vernon, Ala.; Baton Rouge, La.; Montgomery, Ala.; Little Rock, Ark.; and San Antonio, Texas—altogether eight arsenals and four depots. It would, of course, have been better, had it been practicable, to have condensed our work and to have had fewer places of manufacture; but the country was deficient in the transportation which would have been required to place the raw material at a few arsenals. In this way only could we avail ourselves of local resources, both of labor and material. Thus by the close of 1861 a good deal had been done in the way of organization to produce the material of war needed by an army, as far as our means permitted. But our troops were still very poorly armed and equipped. The old smooth-bore musket was still the principal weapon of the infantry; the artillery had the six-pounder gun and twelve-pounder howitzer chiefly; and the cavalry were armed with anything they could get—sabres, horse-pistols, revolvers, Sharp's carbines, musketoons, short Enfield rifles, Hale's carbines (a wretched apology), muskets cut off, etc., etc. Equipments were in many cases made of stout domestic, stitched in triple folds and covered with paint or rubber, varnished. ...

About December, 1861, arms began to come in through the purchases of Major Huse, and we had a good many Enfield rifles in the hands of our troops at Shiloh, which were received in time for use there through the blockade. Major Huse had found the market pretty well cleaned of arms by the late war in Europe, but he had succeeded in making contracts with private manufacturers of which these arms were the result. ...

The winter of 1861–62 was the darkest period of my department. Powder was called for on every hand—Bragg, at Pensacola, for his big ten-inch Columbiads: Lovell, at New Orleans, for his extended defences, and especially for his inadequate artillery at Forts Jackson and St. Phillips; Polk, at Columbus, Kentucky; Johnston, for his numerous batteries on the Potomac; Magruder, at Yorktown. All these were deemed most important points. Then came Wilmington, Georgetown, Port Royal, and Fernandina. Not a few of these places sent representatives to press their claims—Mr. Yulee from Fernandina, and Colonel Gonzales from Charleston. Heavy guns, too, were called for in all directions—the largest guns for the smallest places.

The abandonment of the line of the Potomac, and of the upper Mississippi from Columbus to Memphis; the evacuation of the works below Pensacola, and of Yorktown, somewhat relieved us from the pressure for heavy artillery; and after the powder-mills at Augusta went into operation in the fall of 1862, we had little trouble in supplying ammunition.

To obtain the iron needed for cannon and projectiles, it became necessary to stimulate its production in Virginia, North Carolina, Tennessee, Georgia, and Alabama. To this end, contracts were made with iron-masters in these States on liberal terms, and advances of money made to them, to be refunded in products. These contracts were difficult to arrange, as so much had to be done for the contractor. He must have details from the army and the privilege of transport of provisions and other supplies over the railroads. And then the question of the currency was a continually recurring problem. Mr. Benjamin, who succeeded Mr. Walker in the War Department, gave me great assistance in the matter of making contracts, and seemed quite at home in arranging these details. His power of work was amazing to me; and he appeared as fresh at 12 o'clock at night after a hard day's work, as he had been at 9 o'clock in the morning.

About May, 1862, finding that the production of nitre and of iron must be systematically pursued, and to this end thoroughly organized, I sought for the right person to place in charge of this vital duty. My choice fell on Colonel I. M. St. John (afterwards Commissary-General of Subsistence), and was eminently fortunate. He had the gift of organization, and I placed him in charge of the whole subject of producing nitre from caves and from other sources, and of the formation of nitre beds, which had already been begun in Richmond. Under his supervision beds were instituted at Columbia, S.C., Charleston, Savannah, Augusta, Mobile, Selma, and various other points. We never extracted nitre from these beds, except for trial; but they were carefully attended to, enriched and extended, and were becoming quite valuable. At the close of 1864 we had, according to General St. John, 2,800,000 cubic feet of earth collected and in various stages of nitrification, of which a large proportion was prepared to yield one and a half pounds of nitre per foot of earth, including all the nitre-beds from Richmond to Florida.

Through Colonel St. John, the whole nitre-bearing area of country was laid off into districts; each district in charge of an officer, who made his monthly reports to the office at Richmond. These officers procured details of workmen, generally from those subject to military duty in the mountain regions where disaffection existed, and carried on extended works in their several districts. In this way we brought up the nitre production, in the course of a year, to something like half our total consumption of nitre. It was a rude, wild sort of service; and the officers in charge of these districts, especially in East Tennessee, North Carolina, and North Alabama, had to show much firmness in their dealings with the turbulent people among whom, and by whose aid, they worked. It is a curious fact that the district on which we could rely for the most constant yield of nitre, having its headquarters at Greensboro, N.C., had no nitre-caves in it. The nitre was produced by the lixiviation of nitrous earth dug from under old houses, barns, &c.

The nitre production thus organized, there was added to the Nitre Bureau the duty of supervising the production of iron, lead, copper, and, in fine, all the minerals which needed development, including the making of sulphuric and nitric acids; which latter we had to manufacture to insure a supply of fulminate of mercury for our percussion caps. To give an idea of the extent of the duty thus performed: Colonel Morton, Chief of the Nitre and Mining Bureau, after the transfer of General St. John, writes: "We were aiding and managing some twenty to thirty furnaces, with an annual yield of 50,000 tons or more of pig metal. We had erected lead and copper smelting furnaces [at Petersburg, before referred to] with a capacity sufficient for all our wants, and had succeeded in smelting zinc of good quality at the same place." The Chemical Works were placed at Charlotte, N.C., where a pretty large leaden chamber for sulphuric acid was put up. Our chief supply of chemicals continued to come, however, from abroad, through the blockade, and these works, as well as our nitraries, were as much preparation against the day when the blockade might seal all foreign supply, as for present use. These constituted our reserves, for final conflict.

We had not omitted to have a pretty thorough, though general exploration of the mountain regions from Virginia to Alabama, with the hope of finding new deposits of lead. One of the earliest of these searches was made by Dr. Maupin, of the University of Virginia. No favorable results came from it. I remember an anecdote he told touching one of his researches. An old settler showed the Doctor a small lump of lead which he had extracted from ore like some he had in his possession. There was the lead and here was the ore, but it was not an ore of lead. The Doctor cross-examined: "Did he smelt it himself?" "Yes." "What in?" "An iron ladle," such as is used for running lead balls. "Was there nothing in the ladle but this sort of ore?" "No, nothing." "Nothing at all? No addition—no flux?" "No, nothing but a little handful of common shot, thrown in to make it melt more easy!"

Much of the nitre region was close to the lines of the enemy, and here and there along its great extent became debatable ground. Not seldom the whole working force had to be suddenly withdrawn on the approach of the enemy, the "plant" hurried off, to be again returned and work resumed when the enemy had retired. Much of the work, too, lay in "Union" districts, where our cause was unpopular and where obstacles of all kinds had to be encountered and overcome. It was no holiday duty, this nitre digging, although the service was a good deal decried by such as knew nothing of its nature.

MANUFACTURE OF INFANTRY, ARTILLERY, AND CAVALRY EQUIPMENTS

In equipping the armies first sent into the field the supply of these accessories was amazingly scant; and these deficiencies were felt more keenly, perhaps, than the more important want of arms. We had arms such as they were, for over 100,000 men; but we had no accoutrements nor equipments; and these had to be extemporized in a great measure. In time, knapsacks were little thought of by the troops and we at last contented ourselves with supplying haversacks, which the women (Heaven reward their labors) could make, and for which we could get cotton cloth. But cartridge boxes we *must* have: and as leather was also needed for artillery harness and for cavalry saddles, we had to divide the stock of leather the country could produce, among these much needed articles. But soldiers' shoes were even more needed than some of these; so that as all could not be fully provided, a scale of preference was established. Shoes and cartridge boxes were most needed, and then saddles and bridles. The President, whose practical sagacity was rarely at fault, early reduced these interests to logical sequence. He said, "For the infantry, men must first be fed, next armed, and even clothing must follow these; for if they are fed and have arms and ammunition they can fight." Thus the Subsistence Department had in a general way, a preference for its requisitions on the Treasury; my department came next, and the Quartermaster's followed. Of course the Medical Department had in some things the lead of all, for its duties referred to the men themselves, and it was necessary first of all to keep the hospitals empty and the ranks full.

To economize leather, the cartridge-boxes and waist-belts were made of prepared cotton cloth, stitched in three or four thicknesses. Bridle-reins were also so made, and even cartridge-boxes covered with it, except the flap. Saddle skirts, too, were sometimes made in this way, heavily stitched. An ardent admirer of the South came over from Washington to offer his patent for making soldiers' shoes with no leather except the soles. The shoes were approved by all except those who wore them. The soldiers exchanged them with the first prostrate enemy who no longer needed his leathern articles. To get leather, each Department bargained for its own hides—made contracts with the tanner—procured hands for him by exemption from the army—got transportation over the railroads for the hides and for supplies—and finally, assisted the tanner to procure food for his hands, and other supplies for his tannery. One can readily see from this instance how the labors of the heads of the departments became extended. Nothing but thorough organization could accomplish these multiplied and varied duties. We even established a fishery on the Cape Fear river to get oil for mechanical purposes, getting from the sturgeon *beef* at the same time for our workmen.

In cavalry equipments, the main thing was to get a good saddle—one that did not ruin the back of the horse; for that, and not the rider's seat is the point to be achieved. The rider soon accommodates himself to the seat provided for him. Not so the animal's back, which suffers from a bad saddle. We adopted Jenifer's tree, which did very well while the horses were in good condition, and was praised by that prince of cavalrymen, General J. E. B. Stuart; but it came down on the horses backbone and withers as soon as the cushion of fat and muscle dwindled. The McClellan tree did better on the whole, and we finally succeeded in making a pretty good saddle of that kind—comfortable enough, but not as durable as the Federal article. In this branch of the service, one of the most difficult wants to supply was the horseshoe for cavalry and artillery. The want of iron and labor both were felt. Of course such a thing as a horseshoe machine, to turn out thousands an hour, was not to be dreamed of; besides, we would have had little store of iron wherewith to feed it. Nor could we set up such machinery without much prevision; for to concentrate all work on one machine required the transportation of the iron to one point, and the distribution of the shoes from it to all the armies. But the railroads were greatly over-tasked, and we were compelled to consider this point. Thus we were led to employ every wayside blacksmith shop accessible, especially those in and near the theatre of operations. These, again, had to be looked after, supplied with material, and exempted from service.

BUREAU OF FOREIGN SUPPLIES

It soon became obvious that in the Ordnance Department we must rely greatly on the introduction of articles of prime necessity through the blockade ports. As before stated, President Davis early saw this, and had an officer detailed to go abroad as the agent of the department. To systematize the introduction of the purchases, it was soon found advisable to own and run our steamers. Major Huse made the suggestion also from that side of the water. Accordingly, he purchased and sent in the Robert E. Lee at a cost of £30,000, a vessel capable of stowing six hundred and fifty bales of cotton. This vessel was kept running between Bermuda and Wilmington, and made some fifteen to eighteen successive trips before she was finally captured—the first twelve with the regularity of a packet. . . . Other vessels . . . were added, all devoted to carrying ordnance supplies, and finally general supplies.

The arsenal at Richmond soon grew into very large dimensions, and produced all the ordnance stores that an army may require, except cannon and small arms in quantities sufficient to supply the forces in that part of the field. I have by accident preserved a copy of the last number of the Richmond *Enquirer*, published under Confederate rule. It is dated April 1st, 1865, and contains the following "Statement of the principal issues from the Richmond arsenal, from July 1st, 1861, to January 1st, 1865":

341 Columbiads and seige guns (these were made at the Tredegar works, but issued from the arsenal); 1,306 field-pieces, made chiefly at Tredegar works or captured; 1,375 gun carriages; 875 caissons; 152 forges; 6,852 setts of artillery-harness; 921,441 rounds field, seige, and sea-coast ammunition; 1,456,190 friction primer; 1,110,996 fuses; 17,423 port-fires; 3,985 rockets; 323,231 infantry arms (most of these were turned in from the army, from battle-fields and from the Richmond armory); 34,067 cavalry arms (same remark); 44,877 swords and sabres (from army, battle-field and contractors); 375,510 setts of infantry and cavalry accoutrements; 180,181 knapsacks; 328,977 canteens and straps; 72,413,854 small arm cartridges; 115,087 gun and carbine slings; 146,901,250 percussion caps; 69,418 cavalry-saddles; 85,139 cavalry-bridles; 75,611 cavalry-halters; 35,-464 saddle-blankets; 59,624 pairs [of] spurs; 42,285 horse-brushes; 56,903 curry-combs.

This "statement" appears as an editorial, but the items were furnished from the office of the arsenal, and may be relied on. . . . In the items of cavalry-saddles, bridles, harness, infantry accoutrements, canteens and other articles of this character much assistance was received from contractors. A small part of the percussion caps also came from other arsenals. When we reflect that the arsenal grew to these great dimensions in a little over two years, it must be confessed that good use was made of the time. . . .

Besides the cap machinery, which was a very large and improved plant, machinery for pressing balls, for driving time fuses, for drawing friction primers and metallic cartridges, and other labor saving machines were invented, made and used with effect. In all respects the establishment, though extemporized, and lodged in a cluster of tobacco warehouses, was equal to the first-class arsenals of the United States in extent and facilities.

The arsenal of Augusta, Ga., was in great part organized in the city, where suitable buildings were obtained, and did much the same class of work done at Richmond, though on a smaller scale. It was very serviceable to the armies serving in the South and West, and turned out a good deal of field artillery complete, the castings being excellent. Colonel George W. Rains, in charge of arsenal and powder works, found that the fusion of a small per cent of iron with the copper and tin improved the strength of the bronze castings very much.

The powder mills at Augusta, Ga., which I have already mentioned as the direct result of the order of President Davis, were wonderfully successful and never met with serious accident—a safe indication of the goodness of its arrangements. It showed, too, that under able direction the resources of Southern workshops and the skill of its artisans had already become equal to the execution of great enterprises involving high mechanical skill.

The arsenal and workshops at Charleston were also enlarged, steam introduced, and good work done in various departments.

The arsenal at Mount Vernon, now furnished with steam power and having a good deal of machinery, was considered out of position after the fall of New Orleans, and was moved to Selma, Ala., where it grew into a large, well-ordered arsenal of the best class, under the charge of Lieutenant-Colonel White. It was relied on to a great extent for the equipment of the troops and fortifications in the Southern part of the Confederacy. . . .

The foundry and rolling-mills then grew into large proportions, supplied by the iron and coal of that region. Had the Confederacy survived, Selma bid fair to become the Pittsburgh of the South. The iron obtained from the brown haematite at the furnaces in Bibb county (Brierfield), and from the Shelby Works, was admirable, the former being of unusual strength. . . .

Besides the Arsenals, a brief account of which has just been given, we had the armories at Richmond and Fayetteville, N.C.; and arms were also made at other points.

The State of Virginia claimed all the machinery captured at Harper's Ferry, and was bringing it all to Richmond. It was agreed, however, with the State of North Carolina, that that part of the machinery which was specially adapted to make the Mississippi rifle (calibre 54) should go to Fayetteville, where there was an arsenal with good steam-power, the machinery to be returned at the close of the war to the State of Virginia. Colonel Burton, an admirably-educated machinist, superintended the re-erection of the works at Richmond. He was subsequently made Superintendent of Armories, and given full charge of the entire subject of manufacture of arms in the Confederacy. The machinery of the rifle-musket (calibre 58), retained at Richmond, got to work as early as September, 1861. If we had possessed the necessary number of workmen this "plant" could have been so filled in as to have easily produced 5000 stands per month, working night and day. As it was, I don't think it ever turned out more than 1,500 in any one month. Fayetteville did not get to work until the spring of 1862, and did not average 400 per month, for want of hands. . . .

The want of cavalry arms caused me to make a contract with parties in Richmond to make the Sharp's carbine—at that time the best cavalry arm we had. A set of machinery capable of turning out one hundred arms a day was driven to completion in less than a year, nearly all the machinery being built up "from the stumps." The arms were never perfect, chiefly for want of nice workmanship about the "cut-off." It was not gas-tight. We soon bought out the establishment, and converted it into a manufactory of rifle-carbines, calibre 58, as the best arm our skill would enable us to supply to the cavalry. ...

One of the earliest difficulties forced upon us in the manufacture of arms was to find an iron fit for the barrels. The "skelps" found at Harper's Ferry served for awhile, and when these were exhausted Colonel Burton selected an iron produced at a forge in Patrick county, Va., and by placing a skilled workman over the rolling process at the Tredegar Works he soon produced "skelps" with which he was satisfied. We found that almost any of the good brown haematite ores produced an iron of ample strength for the purpose, and the even grain and toughness could be attained by careful re-rolling. ...

A great part of the work of our armories consisted in repairing arms brought in from the battle-field or sent in from the armies in too damaged a condition to be effectually repaired at the arsenals. In this way only could we utilize all the gleanings of the battle-fields. My recollection is that we saved nearly ten thousand stands of arms from the field of Bull Run, and that the battle-fields about Richmond in 1862 gave us about twenty-five thousand excellent arms through the labors of the armory at Richmond.

The original stock of arms, it will be remembered, consisted almost wholly of smooth-bore muskets, altered from flint to percussion, using ounce-balls (cal. 69). ... All this original stock disappeared almost wholly from our armies in the first two years of the war, and were replaced by a better class of arms, rifled and percussioned. It is pretty safe to assume that we had altogether, east and west of the Mississippi, 300,000 infantry, pretty well-armed, by the middle of 1863. We must therefore have procured at least that number for our troops. But we must also have supplied the inevitable waste of two years of active warfare. Placing the good arms thus lost at the moderate estimate of 100,000, we must have received from various sources 400,000 stands of infantry arms in the two years of fighting, ending July 1st, 1863. I can only estimate from memory the several sources from which this supply was derived, as follows:

Good rifled arms on hand at the beginning of the war (this includes the arms in the hands of volunteer companies)	25,000
New arms manufactured in the Confederacy and in private establishments	40,000
Arms received from the battle-fields and put in good order (this includes the great number of arms picked up by the soldiers)	150,000
Imported from January 1st, 1862, to July 1st, 1863	185,000
Total	400,000

This estimate does not include pistols and sabres, of which a small supply was imported.

To account for the very large number obtained from the enemy (rather an under than an over estimate), it must be remembered that in some fights, where our troops were not finally successful, they were so at first; and swept over the camps and positions of the enemy. Whenever a Confederate soldier saw a weapon better than his own, he took it and left his inferior arm; and although he may have been finally driven back, he kept his improved musket. So, too, on every field there were partial successes which in the early part of the war resulted in improved weapons; and although on another part of the field there may have been a reverse; the enemy had not the same advantage; the Confederate arms being generally inferior to those of their adversaries. The difference of arms was not so marked at a later day except in cavalry arms, in which we were always at a disadvantage, the celebrated Spencer carbine being generally in the hands of the enemy cavalry during the last two years of the war.

A CENTRAL LABORATORY

The unavoidable variation in the ammunition made at the different arsenals pointed out, early in the war, that there should be a general superintendent of all the laboratories, invested with authority to inspect and supervise their manipulations and materials. To this end Lieutenant-Colonel Mallet, a chemist and scientist of distinction, who had for some years been professor in the University of Alabama, was selected and placed in charge of this delicate and important duty. . . .

Among the obvious necessities of a well-regulated service, was one large, central laboratory, where all ammunition should be made—thus securing absolute uniformity where uniformity was vital. The policy of dissemination so necessary to husband our transportation, and to utilize the labor of non-combatants, must here yield to the greater necessity of obtaining our ammunition uniform in quality and in dimensions. Authority was, therefore, obtained from the War Department to concentrate this species of work at some central laboratory. Macon, Ga., was selected, and Colonel Mallet placed in charge of the Central Laboratory, as Burton was later placed in charge of a National Armory. Plans of the buildings and of the machinery required were submitted to the Secretary of War, approved, and the work begun with energy. This pile of buildings had a façade of 600 feet, was designed with taste, and comprehended every possible appliance for good and well-organized work. The buildings were nearly ready for occupation at the close of the war, and some of the machinery had arrived at Bermuda. In point of time, this project preceded that of the National Armory, and was much nearer completion. These, with our admirable powder-mills at Augusta, would have completed a set of works for the Ordnance Department; and in them we would have been in condition to supply arms and munitions to 300,000 men. To these would have been added a foundry for heavy guns at Selma or Brierfield, Ala.; at which latter place the strongest cast-iron in the country was produced, and where we had already purchased and were carrying on a furnace for the production of cold blast charcoal pig for this special purpose. All these establishments were in the heart of the country, not readily reached by the enemy; and were, in fact, never reached by them until just at the close of the war. Being in or near an excellent agricultural region, they would have had the advantage of cheap living for operatives; and they had all sufficient facilities for transportation, being situated on main lines of railroad.

SUMMARY

I have thus, from memory, faintly traced the development of the means and resources by which our large armies were supplied with arms and ammunition. This involved manufacturing, mining and importation. The last two were confided in time to sub-bureaus created *ex-necessitate*, which were subsequently detached. The first was carried on by the armories, arsenals, laboratories and depots above mentioned. We began in April, 1861, without an arsenal, laboratory or powder mill of any capacity, and with no foundry or rolling mill, except at Richmond, and before the close of 1863, in little over two years, we had built up, during all the harassments of war, holding our own in the field defiantly and successfully against a powerful and determined enemy. Crippled as we were by a depreciated currency; throttled with a blockade that deprived us of nearly all means of getting material or workmen; obliged to send almost every able-bodied man to the field; unable to use the slave labor with which we were abundantly supplied, except in the most unskilled departments of production; hampered by want of transportation even of the commonest supplies of food; with no stock on hand even of the articles, such as steel, copper, lead, iron, leather, which we must have to build up our establishments; and in spite of these deficiencies we preserved at home as determinedly as did our troops in the field against a more tangible opposition, and in a little over two years created, almost literally out of the ground, foundries and rolling mills (at Selma, Richmond, Atlanta, and Macon), smelting works (at Petersburg), chemical works (at Charlotte, N. C.), a powder mill far superior to any in the United States and unsurpassed by any across the ocean, and a chain of arsenals, armories and laboratories equal in their capacity and their improved appointments to the best of those in the United States, stretching link by link from Virginia to Alabama. Our people are justly proud of the valor and constancy of the troops which bore their banners bravely in the front of the enemy; but they will also reflect that these creations of skill and labor were the monuments which represented the patience, industry and perseverance of the devoted and patriotic citizens; for of the success which attended the operations of any department of the Confederate Government the larger moiety was due to the co-operation of the body of the people—a co-operation founded in their hearty sympathy with and their entire faith in the cause which that government represented.

ORGANIZATION IN IRON AND STEEL

When the war began, Andrew Carnegie, an ambitious Scottish immigrant, 26 years old, was associated with Thomas Scott, President of the Pennsylvania Railroad. Scott, who had early recognized young Carnegie's abilities, brought him to Washington, where for a time he operated all the military railroads and telegraph systems in the Union. After his tour of duty, Carnegie saw the great possibilities in the iron industry, which was then expanding to meet wartime demands. At Pittsburgh, the center of his activities, Carnegie had an ideal location for expansion. Through his intimate connection with the railroads he had a ready market for his products, especially iron bridges, rails, and later steel. As these excerpts from his autobiography show, Carnegie understood the importance of product quality, of technological innovation, and of systematic management.

ANDREW CARNEGIE, *Autobiography*

In 1861 the Civil War broke out and I was at once summoned to Washington by Mr. Scott, who had been appointed Assistant Secretary of War in charge of the Transportation Department. I was to act as his assistant

---

Andrew Carnegie, *Autobiography* (Boston: Houghton Mifflin, 1920), pp. 99–101, 115, 116, 122, 123, 130–132, 134–136, 146, 147. Reprinted by permission of the publisher.

in charge of the military railroads and telegraphs of the Government and to organize a force of railway men. It was one of the most important departments of all at the beginning of the war.

The first regiments of Union troops passing through Baltimore had been attacked, and the railway line cut between Baltimore and Annapolis Junction, destroying communication with Washington. It was therefore necessary for me, with my corps of assistants, to take train at Philadelphia for Annapolis, a point from which a branch line extended to the Junction, joining the main line to Washington. Our first duty was to repair this branch and make it passable for heavy trains, a work of some days. General Butler and several regiments of troops arrived a few days after us, and we were able to transport his whole brigade to Washington.

I took my place upon the first engine which started for the Capital, and proceeded very cautiously. Some distance from Washington I noticed that the telegraph wires had been pinned to the ground by wooden stakes. I stopped the engine and ran forward to release them, but I did not notice that the wires had been pulled to one side before staking. When released, in their spring upwards, they struck me in the face, knocked me over, and cut a gash in my cheek which bled profusely. In this condition I entered the city of Washington with the first troops, so that with the exception of one or two soldiers, wounded a few days previously in passing through the streets of Baltimore, I can justly claim that I "shed my blood for my country" among the first of its defenders. I gloried in being useful to the land that had done so much for me, and worked, I can truly say, night and day, to open communication to the South.

I soon removed my headquarters to Alexandria,* Virginia, and was stationed there when the unfortunate battle of Bull Run was fought. We could not believe the reports that came to us, but it soon became evident that we must rush every engine and car to the front to bring back our defeated forces. The closest point then was Burke Station. I went out there and loaded up train after train of the poor wounded volunteers. The rebels were reported to be close upon us and we were finally compelled to close Burke Station, the operator and myself leaving on the last train for Alexandria where the effect of panic was evident upon every side.

---

* "When Carnegie reached Washington his first task was to establish a ferry to Alexandria and to extend the Baltimore and Ohio Railroad track from the old depot in Washington, along Maryland Avenue to and across the Potomac, so that locomotives and cars might be crossed for use in Virginia. Long Bridge, over the Potomac, had to be rebuilt, and I recall the fact that under the direction of Carnegie and R. F. Morley the railroad between Washington and Alexandria was completed in the remarkably short period of seven days. All hands, from Carnegie down, worked day and night to accomplish the task." (Bates, *Lincoln in the Telegraph Office*, p. 22. New York, 1907.)

Some of our railway men were missing, but the number at the mess on the following morning showed that, compared with other branches of the service, we had cause for congratulation. A few conductors and engineers had obtained boats and crossed the Potomac, but the great body of the men remained, although the roar of the guns of the pursuing enemy was supposed to be heard in every sound during the night. Of our telegraphers not one was missing the next morning.

Soon after this I returned to Washington and made my headquarters in the War Building with Colonel Scott. As I had charge of the telegraph department, as well as the railways, this gave me an opportunity of seeing President Lincoln, Mr. Seward, Secretary Cameron, and others; and I was occasionally brought in personal contact with these men, which was to me a source of great interest. Mr. Lincoln would occasionally come to the office and sit at the desk awaiting replies to telegrams, or perhaps merely anxious for information. . . .

During the Civil War the price of iron went up to something like $130 per ton. Even at that figure it was not so much a question of money as of delivery. The railway lines of America were fast becoming dangerous for want of new rails, and this state of affairs led me to organize in 1864 a rail-making concern at Pittsburgh. There was no difficulty in obtaining partners and capital, and the Superior Rail Mill and Blast Furnaces were built.

In like manner the demand for locomotives was very great, and with Mr. Thomas N. Miller I organized in 1866 the Pittsburgh Locomotive Works, which has been a prosperous and creditable concern—locomotives made there having obtained an enviable reputation throughout the United States. It sounds like a fairy tale to-day to record that in 1906 the one-hundred-dollar shares of this company sold for three thousand dollars—that is, thirty dollars for one. Large annual dividends had been paid regularly and the company had been very successful—sufficient proof of the policy: "Make nothing but the very best." We never did.

When at Altoona I had seen in the Pennsylvania Railroad Company's work the first small bridge built of iron. It proved a success. I saw that it would never do to depend further upon wooden bridges for permanent railway structures. An important bridge on the Pennsylvania Railroad had recently burned and the traffic had been obstructed for eight days. Iron was the thing. I proposed to H. J. Linville, who had designed the iron bridge, and to John L. Piper and his partner, Mr. Schiffler, who had charge of bridges on the Pennsylvania line, that they should come to Pittsburgh and I would organize a company to build iron bridges. It was the first company of its kind. I asked my friend, Mr. Scott, of the Pennsylvania Railroad, to go with us in the venture, which he did. Each of us paid for a one fifth interest, or $1250. My share I borrowed from the bank. Looking back at it now the sum seemed very small, but "tall oaks from little acorns grow."

In this way was organized in 1862 the firm of Piper and Schiffler which was merged into the Keystone Bridge Company in 1863—a name which I remember I was proud of having thought of as being most appropriate for a bridge-building concern in the State of Pennsylvania, the Keystone State. From this beginning iron bridges came generally into use in America, indeed, in the world at large so far as I know. My letters to iron manufacturers in Pittsburgh were sufficient to insure the new company credit. Small wooden shops were erected and several bridge structures were undertaken. Cast-iron was the principal material used, but so well were the bridges built that some made at that day and since strengthened for heavier traffic, still remain in use upon various lines. . . .

The Keystone Bridge Works have always been a source of satisfaction to me. Almost every concern that had undertaken to erect iron bridges in America had failed. Many of the structures themselves had fallen and some of the worst railway disasters in America had been caused in that way. Some of the bridges had given way under wind pressure but nothing has ever happened to a Keystone bridge, and some of them have stood where the wind was not tempered. There has been no luck about it. We used only the best material and enough of it, making our own iron and later our own steel. We were our own severest inspectors, and would build a safe structure or none at all. When asked to build a bridge which we knew to be of insufficient strength or of unscientific design, we resolutely declined. . . .

This policy is the true secret of success. Uphill work it will be for a few years until your work is proven, but after that it is smooth sailing. Instead of objecting to inspectors they should be welcomed by all manufacturing establishments. A high standard of excellence is easily maintained, and men are educated in the effort to reach excellence. I have never known a concern to make a decided success that did not do good, honest work, and even in these days of the fiercest competition, when everything would seem to be matter of price, there lies still at the root of great business success the very much more important factor of quality. . . .

I was very much pleased to hear a remark, made by one of the prominent bankers who visited the Edgar Thomson Works during a Bankers Convention held at Pittsburgh. He was one of a party of some hundreds of delegates, and after they had passed through the works he said to our manager:

"Somebody appears to belong to these works."

He put his finger there upon one of the secrets of success. They did belong to somebody. The president of an important manufacturing work once boasted to me that their men had chased away the first inspector who had ventured to appear among them, and that they had never been troubled with another since. This was said as a matter of sincere congratulation, but I thought to myself: "This concern will never stand the strain of competition; it is bound to fail when hard times come." The result proved the correctness of my belief. The surest foundation of a manufacturing concern is quality. After that, and a long way after, comes cost. . . .

The Keystone Works have always been my pet as being the parent of all the other works. But they had not been long in existence before the advantage of wrought- over cast-iron became manifest. Accordingly, to insure uniform quality, and also to make certain shapes which were not then to be obtained, we determined to embark in the manufacture of iron. My brother and I became interested with Thomas N. Miller, Henry Phipps, and Andrew Kloman in a small iron mill. Miller was the first to embark with Kloman and he brought Phipps in, lending him eight hundred dollars to buy a one-sixth interest, in November, 1861. . . .

Andrew Kloman had a small steel-hammer in Allegheny City. As a superintendent of the Pennsylvania Railroad I had found that he made the best axles. He was a great mechanic—one who had discovered, what was then unknown in Pittsburgh, that whatever was worth doing with machinery was worth doing well. His German mind made him thorough. What he constructed cost enormously, but when once started it did the work it was intended to do from year's end to year's end. In those early days it was a question with axles generally whether they would run any specified time or break. There was no analysis of material, no scientific treatment of it.

How much this German created! He was the first man to introduce the cold saw that cut cold iron the exact lengths. He invented upsetting machines to make bridge links, and also built the first "universal" mill in America. All these were erected at our works. When Captain Eads could not obtain the couplings for the St. Louis Bridge arches (the contractors failing to make them) and matters were at a standstill, Kloman told us that he could make them and why the others had failed. He succeeded in making them. Up to that date they were the largest semicircles that had ever been rolled. Our confidence in Mr. Kloman may be judged from the fact that when he said he could make them we unhesitatingly contracted to furnish them. . . .

Unfortunately Kloman and Phipps soon differed with Miller about the business and forced him out. Being convinced that Miller was unfairly treated, I united with him in building new works. These were the Cyclops

Mills of 1864. After they were set running it become possible, and therefore advisable, to unite the old and the new works, and the Union Iron Mills were formed by their consolidation in 1867. . . .

We were young in manufacturing then and obtained for the Cyclops Mills what was considered at the time an enormous extent of land—seven acres. For some years we offered to lease a portion of the ground to others. It soon became a question whether we could continue the manufacture of iron within so small an area. Mr. Kloman succeeded in making iron beams and for many years our mill was far in advance of any other in that respect. We began at the new mill by making all shapes which were required, and especially such as no other concern would undertake, depending upon an increasing demand in our growing country for things that were only rarely needed at first. What others could not or would not do we would attempt, and this was a rule of our business which was strictly adhered to. Also we would make nothing except of excellent quality. We always accommodated our customers, even although at some expense to ourselves, and in cases of dispute we gave the other party the benefit of the doubt and settled. These were our rules. We had no lawsuits.

As I became acquainted with the manufacture of iron I was greatly surprised to find that the cost of each of the various processes was unknown. Inquiries made of the leading manufacturers of Pittsburgh proved this. It was a lump business, and until stock was taken and the books balanced at the end of the year, the manufacturers were in total ignorance of results. I heard of men who thought their business at the end of the year would show a loss and had found a profit, and *vice-versa.* I felt as if we were moles burrowing in the dark, and this to me was intolerable. I insisted upon such a system of weighing and accounting being introduced throughout our works as would enable us to know what our cost was for each process and especially what each man was doing, who saved material, who wasted it, and who produced the best results.

To arrive at this was a much more difficult task than one would imagine. Every manager in the mills was naturally against the new system. Years were required before an accurate system was obtained, but eventually, by the aid of many clerks and the introduction of weighing scales at various points in the mill, we began to know not only what every department was doing, but what each one of the many men working at the furnaces was doing, and thus to compare one with another. One of the chief sources of success in manufacturing is the introduction and strict maintenance of a perfect system of accounting so that responsibility for money or materials can be brought home to every man. Owners who, in the office, would not trust a clerk with five dollars without having a check upon him, were supplying tons of material daily to men in the mills without exacting an account of their stewardship by weighing what each returned in the finished form.

The Siemens Gas Furnace had been used to some extent in Great Britain for heating steel and iron, but it was supposed to be too expensive. I well remember the criticisms made by older heads among the Pittsburgh manufacturers about the extravagant expenditure we were making upon these new-fangled furnaces. But in the heating of great masses of material, almost half the waste could sometimes be saved by using the new furnaces. The expenditure would have been justified, even if it had been doubled. Yet it was many years before we were followed in this new departure; and in some of those years the margin of profit was so small that the most of it was made up from the savings derived from the adoption of the improved furnaces.

Our strict system of accounting enabled us to detect the great waste possible in heating large masses of iron. This improvement revealed to us a valuable man in a clerk, William Borntraeger, a distant relative of Mr. Kloman, who came from Germany. He surprised us one day by presenting a detailed statement showing results for a period, which seemed incredible. All the needed labor in preparing this statement he had performed at night unasked and unknown to us. The form adapted was uniquely original. Needless to say, William soon became superintendent of the works and later a partner, and the poor German lad died a millionaire. He well deserved his fortune.

I was always advising that our iron works should be extended and new developments made in connection with the manufacture of iron and steel, which I saw was only in its infancy. All apprehension of its future development was dispelled by the action of America with regard to the tariff upon foreign imports. It was clear to my mind that the Civil War had resulted in a fixed determination upon the part of the American people to build a nation within itself, independent of Europe in all things essential to its safety. America had been obliged to import all her steel of every form and most of the iron needed, Britain being the chief seller. The people demanded a home supply and Congress granted the manufacturers a tariff of twenty-eight per cent *ad valorem* on steel rails—the tariff then being equal to about twenty-eight dollars per ton. Rails were selling at about a hundred dollars per ton, and other rates in proportion.

Protection has played a great part in the development of manufacturing in the United States. Previous to the Civil War it was a party question, the South standing for free trade and regarding a tariff as favorable only to the North. The sympathy shown by the British Government for the Confederacy, culminating in the escape of the *Alabama* and other privateers to prey upon American commerce aroused hostility against that Government, notwithstanding the majority of her common people favored the United States. The tariff became no longer a party question, but a national policy, approved by both parties. It had become a patriotic duty to develop vital resources. No less than ninety Northern Democrats in Congress, including the Speaker of the House, agreed upon that point.

Capital no longer hesitated to embark in manufacturing, confident as it was that the nation would protect it as long as necessary. Years after the war, demands for a reduction of the tariff arose and it was my lot to be drawn into the controversy. It was often charged that bribery of Congressmen by manufacturers was common. So far as I know there was no foundation for this. Certainly the manufacturers never raised any sums beyond those needed to maintain the Iron and Steel Association, a matter of a few thousand dollars per year. They did, however, subscribe freely to a campaign when the issue was Protection *versus* Free Trade.

The duties upon steel were successively reduced, with my cordial support, until the twenty-eight dollars duty on rails became only one fourth or seven dollars per ton. [To-day (1911) the duty is only about one half of that, and even that should go in the next revision.] . . .

THE ERIE PRINCE

James Fisk, Jr., was considered a vulgar, unprincipled man who combined the tricks of a Yankee peddler with the taste of a Roman emperor. The war made Fisk as it made Carnegie. But where the wry, little Scotsman was a builder and a manager, the gaudy, brash, Green Mountain boy was a speculator and a promoter. Each in his own way illustrates the turbulent cross currents of the war and its aftermath. Both were supreme individualists, representative men of the Gilded Age.

WILLOUGHBY JONES, *James Fisk, Jr., The Life of a Green Mountain Boy*

Mr. Fisk purchased his goods from the house of Jordan, Marsh & Co., in Boston. This firm was attracted by the frequent large bills of goods which their young customer from Vermont purchased, and was also struck by his

---

Willoughby Jones, *James Fisk, Jr., The Life of a Green Mountain Boy* (Philadelphia: W. Flint, 1872), pp. 21–56.

general bearing and manner of doing business. Detecting in him abilities worthy of a wider sphere of action, and wishing to secure the services of such a stirring man, they proposed to take him into their establishment as a salesman. This proposition was accepted and with that promptitude which was one of his most marked traits, he wound up his business at Brattleboro immediately and entered the house of Jordan, Marsh & Co. on a salary.

The rebellion of the Southern States and the war that followed, brought the opportunity for the exercise of Mr. Fisk's peculiar powers of mind. He instantly grasped the whole situation of the changed status in commercial affairs. The Government will require large quantities of stores, especially of woolen and cotton fabrics. Large and profitable contracts will be awarded to somebody, and the young New England clerk resolved that he would secure a large share of these for the house by whom he was employed. His first efforts proved highly successful, and established him in the confidence of his employers. It is said that a Boston lady, through the influence of one of the Massachusetts Senators, had obtained a large contract for supplying underclothing for the army, and had already disposed of a portion of the contract to a prominent Boston house. Mr. Fisk at once set to work to secure a graceful introduction to this lady of much consequence, succeeded, and ingratiated himself with her so speedily that he induced her to annul the sub-contract she had already given out and award it to his rival firm instead. Other contracts soon followed from the same source, and the profits accruing to Jordan, Marsh & Co. therefrom were immense.

This stroke, though brilliant and successful, was soon quite eclipsed by another. The firm had quite a large quantity of blankets that had been on their hands for a long time and which were now stowed away in one of the lofts and regarded as dead stock. One day he went to the head of the firm and simply said, "Mr. Jordan, I'm going to sell those blankets up in the loft." Nothing more explicit in regard to his design or the idea he had conceived could be got out of him; but it had now begun to be felt that when James said he was going to do anything he would do it, and so, with a smile that was a mixture of hope and incredulity, he was answered, "All right! Go ahead and sell them for anything you can get." The next train for Washington carried James Fisk, Jr., among its passengers. A few days thereafter those old blankets stowed away in Jordan, Marsh & Co.'s loft were not only disposed of, for three times as much as the firm would gladly have taken for them, but they also got a contract for a further supply of a million or more dollars in value, and their house must have realized between two and three hundred thousand dollars. This unprecedented success won for the young man a place in the firm, to which he was promptly admitted as a partner.

The new sense of dignity and power which naturally came with the consciousness of being a partner in one of the largest establishments of New England, in nowise diminished the zeal and boldness of the new member. Large contracts continued to flow into their house as the fruit of his tact and energy, and very soon the business of the firm showed various signs of the infusion of new blood into its veins.

Fisk advised his firm to engage in manufacturing their own goods, instead of buying them from manufacturers and agents, thus they could add the manufacturer's profit to their own, and would also in that way be able to undersell rival houses. At first it was tried in a small way; the experiment was a grand success. The firm bought several cotton and woolen mills, built as many more new ones, operated them at a profit that seemed almost fabulous in some cases, and thus for other hundreds of thousands of dollars were indebted to the originality and quick perception of the junior partner.

Being in New York on one occasion, and discovering indications that there was likely to be a great demand soon for a certain kind of goods, and learning that there was but one mill in the country where such goods were manufactured, he immediately telegraphed his firm to send an agent to Gaysville, Vt., to buy that mill at any price demanded, and at the same time he bought up all the goods of that kind to be had in the market. The firm had now learned to obey the laconic and even mysterious direction of James as unhesitatingly as Napoleon's subordinates obeyed his every word. The agent was sent as the telegram ordered and the coveted mill was purchased at a fair price. In less than an hour after the bargain was closed, the former owner received a telegram from New York offering him $5,000 more than the price at which he had sold it. But it was too late. Fisk had been too quick for them. Jordan, Marsh & Co. had an entire monopoly and controlled the market. James Fisk, Jr., had got up his first "corner" and engineered it through to entire success. After running the mill some two years at an annual profit of upwards of $100,000, the Boston firm resold it to the former owner.

He also led his firm into the purchase of cotton in the Confederacy, to be shipped out, and thus realized large profits. . . .

The house of Jordan, Marsh & Co., already prominent among the Boston firms when Mr. Fisk entered it, had, during the four years of his connection with it, rapidly grown to be one of the very foremost and probably now stood at the head of the list in extent of business done and profits realized. While the era of government contracts and large outside speculative enterprises continued, this was Fisk's special field, and while thus engaged he was necessarily away much of the time, and was not brought into such close personal contact with the other members of the firm daily as to make his peculiar propensities felt unpleasantly; but as this era waned he was brought more constantly in personal contact with his partners. The very qualities which had made him their most valuable man when government contracts were plenty, stocks rising, and a smile of prosperity rested over everything, were precisely the most dangerous ones to be influenced by now, when business had become unsettled and hazardous, making it necessary to take in much of the sail, that had been spread before the favorable and reliable breeze and manage all affairs with the utmost care and caution. His bold, venturesome, impulsive spirit now clashed at once with the cautious counsels of his partners, and the man's individuality and dominant traits were felt in their full force. . . . The question was easily settled, and the man who had entered the house at one end as a salesman four years ago now made his exit at the other end as a partner, retiring with what he would have considered a princely fortune in his peddling days, and also carrying with him the satisfaction of knowing, that he had been the most important element in the unrivaled success of a great firm for four eventful years.

After a short and unsuccessful attempt to establish a dry goods house in Boston, Fisk closed his business in that city, and in the end of the year 1864 went to New York.

Whilst the war lasted, great manufacturing centers were active in filling army contracts, and there was a field for diplomacy and bold adventure, that brought to the successful manipulator often, a fortune in a day. The close of the war put an end to these opportunities, but the high premium on gold and the frequent fluctuations in stocks gave to the operators in Wall Street unbounded opportunities for the construction of "corners" and the organization of "rings." Thither was attracted James Fisk, just as thousands of other restive, active, bold speculative spirits were and are. He went from Boston to New York in quest of adventure and found it there—most varied and overwhelming.

He entered Wall Street a capitalist, for though his efforts to establish a mercantile house in Boston had absorbed a considerable sum of money, he had, nevertheless, a large surplus on which to operate. He took offices on Broad street, and furnished them in the most sumptuous style, having some original features not found elsewhere. He launched out boldly in all the leading stocks, puting up his margins in pretty much the same way that players put up "chips" in roulette or faro. But in his first experience in the new field the proverbially fickle goddess seemed to turn her smile and face from him. He lost heavily and continually in all his investments. . . . It was but a few months before his capital was exhausted, his bank account cancelled, and the remnant of a once comfortable fortune which he had brought from Boston had wholly disappeared—gone the way of so many others before and since. . . .

For a moment this young man of singular and varied experiences knew the keenest pangs of despair, became pensive and retrospective, and indulged a momentary meditation upon the vanity and mutability of human affairs. But it was only for a moment. His was not a spirit to sit down and acknowledge irretrievable failure. "Never say die!" was his motto, and one to which he was eminently entitled.

Rousing himself from the contemplation of the dark future, he muttered in portentous emphasis, *"Wall Street has ruined me, and Wall Street shall pay for it!"* At the moment of uttering these words he, of course, had no idea as to how they were to be made good. He had not the most remote conception of any plan for recuperating his broken fortune; but, conscious of his personal power, he made the resolve intending that it should be kept. The threat had hardly been uttered ere he bade adieu to the doomed street, packed a carpet bag, and started for Boston, aimless, except to get away from the scene of his disaster.

On this journey to New England, the victim of Wall Street did not sit in moody silence, moaning to himself over his bleeding wounds, but presented an unruffled surface, as though everything had been prosperous. Among the passengers on the train was a young man who seemed sorely troubled and dejected. The two spirits naturally waxed communicative, and soon the young stranger told his story. He proved to be one of the quite numerous class of unfortunates, who own patent rights that nobody wants. He had invented something, got it patented, and spent all his own means and as much more as he could borrow, endeavoring to get it before the public. He, too, was going back to his home, dejected and crest-fallen, for his enterprise had been ill-starred . . . . Like all men with patents, he was ready and eager to explain its great merits and value, and talk about it and nothing else as long as any one would listen. . . . Mr. Fisk saw at once that the patent was of value, and that the young man's dreams of the fortune there was in it had been far from baseless. However, he induced the young man to go on to Boston instead of stopping at home, encouraging him to hope that they might possibly pick up some one there who would purchase it, and whatever he could get now would be so much clear gain, of course, as he was going home to throw it up entirely. Arrived at their journey's end, the young man gladly disposed of his patent-right for a comparatively trifle, and went home somewhat less heavy hearted. The patent was a small improvement of great utility and extensive application in machinery used in cotton and woolen mills, proved to be of immense practical and pecuniary value, and brought the new owners, Fisk being one of them, a handsome income. Thus, the downward tide in his fortunes was stemmed. Confidence and courage were restored, and with the possession once more of capital sufficient for extensive operations he determined to return to Wall Street. He accidentally learned that a company in Boston wished to buy the Bristol line of steamers running on Long Island Sound. It occurred to him that he might turn this circumstance to some account for himself, and this was the pretext of his next visit to New York. He secured a letter of introduction to the president of the company owning the line of steamers. The person to whom he was thus introduced was the celebrated Daniel Drew, a man of note and a great power in financial circles. The introduction to Drew constitutes one of the most prominent and important landmarks in Fisk's life, and turned his career into the course that conducted him to position and rank. Drew was now the magnate of Erie—one of its directors, its treasurer, its sole manipulator, the first to use his position to gamble in the stock of his own corporation, already dubbed the "speculative director," and the acknowledged leader of Wall Street's "bear" brigade. The old warrior was much pleased with his new acquaintance; was quite surprised and fascinated with the grand and liberal ideas which the young man very freely ventilated on the question of steamships and affairs generally, and immediately authorized him to act as his agent in negotiating the sale of the Bristol steamers. This trust was executed in a manner that confirmed and heightened Mr. Drew's first impressions, and gave him entire satisfaction, and at the same time it proved a very profitable transaction for the agent.

Mr. Fisk now looked upon Wall Street as his headquarters again; but as he had learned that the game there was played with stacked cards and loaded dice, he sagely concluded it would be much safer to have a finger in the stacking business. . . . He was not to be caught twice in the same trap. He had seen those "twenty-four jacks" fall out of Ah Sin's sleeves in their first hand of euchre, and he was not going to sit down to the game again till he had a pair of sleeves just like Ah Sin's—only a little larger—and they should be well filled with right bowers. Drew, in the first flush of his admiration for the young man's bearing, spoke the necessary words of encouragement, and shortly after the sign of a new firm of brokers appeared, bearing the firm name of Fisk & Belden. They made a specialty of dealing in Erie, and soon became known among the fraternity as Drew's brokers. The head of the firm being a special favorite, confidant and *protégé* of the crafty director and treasurer, it is more than probable that he was privy to sufficient information and "points" not for general use, to enable him to operate on his own account with all desired safety and make much more than a simple commission as broker for others. It was in the spring of 1866 that Drew executed his first great master-stroke in bear operations, inaugurating a system of manipulations wholly original and unparalleled, making the entire bull clique writhe under his goad, and finally strewing the pavement with their skulls and bones, establishing for himself an enduring fame in the history and traditions of Wall Street. Fisk, being fully behind the scenes in this campaign, enjoyed the sport immensely and turned his opportunity to much substantial account. ... When the pupil had once seen how the cards were stacked, he brought to the work such rare manual skill, that he stacked them under his instructor's very eyes, without his seeing it, and played them upon him before he was aware of it. ... With fortune in his favor, Mr. Fisk soon recovered what he had invested in Wall Street, and it was but a few months after he had lost his last dollar that he again had a bank account of over a million dollars.

James Fisk was elected a member of the board of directors of the Erie Railway Company in October, 1867. Three tickets were put forward for election at that time. The officers in control of the company, headed by Drew, sought re-election. With this party Mr. Fisk was identified. Next came Vanderbilt, who having made himself absolute and undisputed master of the Harlem, Hudson River and New York Central roads, now sought to grasp control of Erie in like manner, that he might have despotic sway over all the roads connecting New York with the great lakes and make himself practical dictator of the material interests of the commercial metropolis. The third party was headed by John S. Eldridge and composed of men largely interested in the Boston, Hartford and Erie Road, a line running from Boston through Connecticut and New York to Fishkill, where it meets a branch of Erie. This corporation was in a desperate struggle for existence and was in bad financial odor. The Massachusetts Legislature had voted to assist the company to the sum of $3,000,000 provided it would raise an additional sum of $4,000,000 elsewhere. The laudable purpose of this third party was to gain a controlling voice in the Erie councils in order to get this corporation to assist them to the much-desired $4,000,000. Under the Eldridge banner Jay Gould was training.

At these elections each share of stock entitled the holder to one vote, consequently a party must control a majority of the stock in order to carry the election. With three parties competing for possession, there was a fine prospect for a rapid and extraordinary rise in the stock, promising a lively time and a rich harvest for the brokers, operators, and owners of Erie. The Eldridge party resorted to diplomacy and secured a coalition with Vanderbilt. These two factions agreed to unite their forces in ousting Drew and electing a board of directors that would manage the road so as to secure both their interests.

On Sunday before the election, Drew called on Vanderbilt at his residence for the purpose of proposing a compromise. The great Commodore was entirely disarmed by this unexpected tender of the olive branch. In such matters it is always better to treat than to fight. Drew had been a dangerous enemy, he might now be made a powerful ally. The proposition to combine forces was, therefore, accepted. The monarch of corporations and the master of the bulls and bears of Wall Street, entered into a solemn compact to stand together against all comers. Cornelius Vanderbilt held by a firm and steady grasp, the New York Central, the Hudson River, and the Harlem railroads; Daniel Drew was the master of the Erie company; the union therefore brought together and made of one interest all the railroad outlets westward from New York city. The Eldridge party was taken off and only one ticket was voted for at the annual election for Erie directors.

Among the new directors chosen at this election were Jay Gould and James Fisk, Jr., who met for the first time at the preliminary meeting of the new board. Mr. Fisk says the date of this election is well fixed in his memory, because it constitutes an "episode" in his life. He dates his grey hairs from that day, and he says he saw more robbery during the next year than he had ever seen before in his whole life—a statement that will receive ready credence. He has also said he had not been in office fifteen minutes before he made up his mind that there was going to be trouble.

The first act of the programme had been successfully performed and it was now time for the next. In pursuance of the agreement to run the Erie stock up, a large "pool" was formed the last of November, and Drew was placed in charge of the fund raised, to conduct the operations in the stock board. It was understood by all the members of the pool that Erie stocks were to be sent up to a high figure and held there long enough to complete the speculation. Many of the members, therefore, made large purchases on their own account, in addition to their contributions to the general fund.

The prices did not make rapid leaps upward at once but fluctuated two or three per cent, "forward and back," rather mysteriously for four or five weeks. The members of the pool, who had made outside investments being surprised that the stock fell back heavily after each advance, instead of rising uniformly and rapidly as anticipated, applied to Drew for information and advice; but he, in his childlike innocence and simplicity, seemed more confused and puzzled than any of the rest and utterly at a loss to account for the strange manner in which their stock acted, yet felt sure it would soon move regularly under their purchases. With this assurance from their sagacious chief they made still further private purchases, some of them even borrowing some of the pool money from Drew to put up as a margin and in addition went "long" extensively. They were confident the looked-for bound upward must come soon, began to count the hours ere their fortunes would be reckoned in millions. They continued their purchases while the stock rose four, five or six per cent and then to their utter amazement, it dropped heavily back to the starting point and was plenty to all purchases. They now became alarmed, for their "long" contracts were near maturity and but a few days could elapse before they would be made or ruined by the operation.

Finally the day came and it was a day of disaster. The members of the pool had been betrayed and sold out by their own leader, and their losses were counted by thousands on operations that had promised hundreds of thousands in clear profits. Daniel Drew caparisoned as a bull had played the bear, squeezing the life out of his confiding confederates.

As soon as these facts became known, a meeting of the pool was held at which Drew coolly and soothingly announced that the pool had made a handsome sum and proceeded to divide the spoil. The grim humor of this situation has but few parallels and will be fully appreciated by all the world now, though the humorous side of it was not at the time at all apparent to the members of the pool, except, perhaps, Fisk and Gould, who had a very lively sense of the humorous, and as they were too sharp to be caught, and probably even profited by the proceeding, it is more than likely that they appreciated the position in all its phases.

The wrath of Vanderbilt knew no bounds; it was like the fury of a mighty storm. Drew chuckled, thought it a huge joke, and carefully treasured the moral thereof.

Vanderbilt was now determined that Erie should come under his power —absolutely and beyond the will of any man or body of men to say him nay. He first submitted to the directors certain propositions expressing his desire as to the management of the road, and the rejection of these by the board showing him that he was not supreme ruler, but had been duped all round, he resolved to make Erie his own by main force, as he had done with the others. A new pool was immediately formed to do what the first one had failed to do. Daniel Drew was not a member of this pool. Jay Gould, however, was. Drew was a man of unbounded resources. As soon as he perceived that he was discarded by his associates he buckled on his armor and resolved to confront his old enemy.

The legislature of New York made it unlawful for any railway company to issue new stock without special authority first obtained, but it permitted the conversion of bonds into stock. Mr. Drew held a large number of Erie bonds, these he quietly converted into stock, amounting in all to several millions of dollars, and then complacently awaited the movements of the new pool.

From *Frank Leslie's Illustrated Newspaper*, Vol. XXIX, No. 733 (October 16, 1869), p. 73. From a photograph by Mathew B. Brady.

James Fisk, Jr.

The collapse of the first combination had come in the middle of January, 1868, and, on the 17th of February the arrangements for the second move were complete. On that day Vanderbilt procured from Judge Barnard an injunction restraining Drew from using 58,000 shares of Erie stock, which were in his possession as collateral securities. Two days later came a second order from the same judge suspending Drew from the office of treasurer and director of the Erie company, and ordering him to appear on the 10th of March and show cause why he should not be permanently removed from the direction of the Erie Railway. Drew was the leading spirit and great arch enemy, and it was felt that with him out of the way and his hands effectually tied, all would be well. The 58,000 shares which he held having been tied up by the injunction of the 17th, he induced the board of directors to pass a resolution to issue $10,000,000 of new bonds to supply various needs of the road. These were of course converted into stock at once, and so for the 58,000 shares which Vanderbilt had tied up 100,000 new shares had been manufactured. This brilliant stroke was achieved on the 19th, before Judge Barnard's order of that date, suspending Drew from office, had been served, and was of course kept a dead secret to all, but the directors concerned, no suspicion of it reaching Wall Street or Vanderbilt. Therefore when the second injunction arrived, it was received with a smile more childlike and bland than ever and did not disturb the old gentleman's nerves in the least. He chuckled and said, "Fire away, with your injunctions, Mr. Barnard! Fire away! An innocent man like me has nothing to fear from the law." Fisk and Gould exchanged winks, chuckled and whispered to each other, "What jolly sport to see these old bucks butt heads!"

Of the new shares thus issued, Drew took 50,000 and James Fisk, Jr., 50,000. Drew immediately divided his into small lots, placed them where they could be used at a moment's notice and waited developments. When the two injunctions had been served, Vanderbilt regarded the hands of Drew tied beyond the power of doing further harm and therefore gave orders for the pool and his brokers to move forward in the purchase of Erie. The order was obeyed with alacrity and the great railroad king was fast gaining possession of the coveted power. The stock was very active, the chief feature of the street and the price tended upward. Drew thought it time to pour in his first broadside, to send the price down so that he could bring in what he required to fill his contracts. On the 29th of February Erie was selling in the morning at 68¾ and the demand for it was strong. Drew gave orders to his brokers, who held the 50,000 shares in small lots, to sell, and the whole load was dumped upon the bulls and eagerly swallowed by them before they were aware of its source. Soon the rumor that there had been a large issue of new stock spread like wildfire, striking terror into the bulls, and in a few minutes Erie reeled and tumbled to 65. A howl of delight went up from the bears and nearly every one was expecting to see it fall to 50, when it as suddenly wheeled again and shot back to 73. Like a great general stemming a panic among his men and turning a rout into victory, Vanderbilt commanded his brokers to stand firm and buy every share of Erie stock offered. Something like $5,000,000 worth of it was loaded upon him that day, but he stood up under it all, holding it with ease. The little bears were all scooped up in his net and the nerves of even their great leader himself were somewhat unsettled by this manifestation of tremendous power and determination. Drew had now flung upon the market all the stock he could command, and yet the price had gone up and left him with large short contracts uncovered. On the 3d of March his nerves received a further shock, for on that day, at the instance of Vanderbilt, Judge Barnard fulminated his third injunction, this time not against Drew alone but against the whole body of Erie directors, peremptorily forbidding the issue or use of any stock of the company in addition to the 251,058 shares outstanding at the last annual report. As 50,000 new shares were already on the market and they had got Vanderbilt's money therefor, they could not restrain a slight smile at the Judge and his patron for this injunction. But Drew could not join in this smile. He could think of nothing but "them shorts" and was alarmed lest this last move had placed him in Vanderbilt's power once more. Nor did any of them long indulge in humor over the comical phase of this last move, but they seriously addressed themselves to the problem of breaking the cordon that was gathering around them.

A week wore on. Vanderbilt pushed Erie steadily upward and it now stood at 78. During these days the directors came to the conclusion that "two can play at that game" of injunctions. The 10th was the day on which Drew was commanded to appear before Judge Barnard and show cause why he should not be turned out of Erie. He knew that the crisis of the whole situation must culminate on that day. But on the morning of the 9th the directors quietly went over to Brooklyn, and upon affidavits stating that a conspiracy had been entered into to injure the Erie Railway and speculate in its stocks, and that Judge Barnard himself was interested in it and was using the power of his court to aid the conspirators, an injunction was obtained from Judge Gilbert staying proceedings in all the suits, that had been instituted, Judge Barnard being included in the restraint, and ordering the directors to proceed in the management of the road precisely as if no suit had been instituted. This placed matters in a very interesting position. On one hand Judge Barnard had forbidden certain things to be done and, therefore, if the directors proceeded, that functionary would visit them with his vengeance for contempt of his court; on the other hand was the order of Judge Gilbert, directing them to move forward in those same matters, if they stood still they were equally liable to be punished by him for contempt of his court. Drew, being a devout Methodist, probably never plays cards, and so had most likely never heard of Hoyle's famous maxim, "When you are in doubt, take the trick," but he had seen quite enough of law in his long life to know that a prisoner is always entitled to the benefit of any doubt, and Judge Barnard was the man the terror of whose process for contempt it was decided to brave. In this position the opposing forces rested on their arms facing each other the last night before the great decisive battle, knowing that on the morrow would come the final crisis of the campaign, and that before the sun set again, the laurels would be awarded to bull or bear, Vanderbilt or Drew.

It had been a case of "love at sight" between Fisk and Gould. They recognized at once the elements of strength which their union would have, and had been putting their heads together through all these months to improve any opportunity that might arise. Gould had retained the confidence of Vanderbilt all this time and he now so far presumed upon this confidence as to suggest to Vanderbilt, that as the day was to be one of much excitement in the courts, the bears might take advantage of it to depress Erie, and it would, therefore, be advisable for the Commodore to give his brokers orders to sustain the market. Vanderbilt saw the propriety of the course suggested. Gould then played upon Drew's nerves by ominously hinting that Fisk was acting a little peculiar, might not put his 50,000 shares upon the market after all, and if he did not, Vanderbilt would triumph and Erie might go to 200, or higher, as Harlem did. This greatly increased the old man's alarm and his weak knees began to tremble.

The morning of the 10th dawned. Vanderbilt gave an unlimited order to sustain the market, then standing at 79. Drew scrutinized Fisk's actions and found they did look dubious, as Gould said. He was seized with a fear that he was going to be duped in the house of his friends, as he had duped others, and immediately sent orders for his brokers to buy Erie to cover his shorts. This was the moment Fisk was waiting for. His 50,000 shares were immediately distributed among numerous brokers in small lots, and orders given to sell when the word came. The stock board met at 10 o'clock, and the street was already tremulous with nervous excitement. The presiding officer commenced calling the list of stocks, all were passed quickly till he called "Erie." At that word, before it was off his lips, the thickly packed crowd of brokers bounded as if a mine had been sprung beneath them. Their united yells rent the air of the large room as had not been done for many a long day. . . . Erie changed hands by the five and ten thousand shares per second. The battle raged madly for ten minutes and the stock was going at 80, when the presiding officer announced that dealings in Erie must cease, and called the next stock on the list. Instantly the whole body now bolted from the room and poured down the long, large staircase into the street like a wild sweeping torrent, leaving the vice-president to go through the formality of calling the list to an empty room. On the street the battle was continued and raged in still greater disorder; each of Vanderbilt's brokers forming the centre of an eddying circle in the grand whirlpool, and quickly catching at all offers to sell, while Drew's men were equally busy and eagerly covering his shorts. The struggle was kept up with unabated fury till noon, when Erie, under the combined purchases of Vanderbilt and Drew, touched 83. Fisk's men now received their word and flung his 50,000 shares on the market. They were snatched up as beggar boys snatch at pennies thrown among them and still ask for more. The contest raged with unabated zeal till those who had purchased got a chance to glance at the shares that had been delivered to them. It was then suddenly discovered that large quantities of brand-new stock, clean and unrumpled, *issued to James Fisk, Jr.,* had been put upon the street that day. Instantly and like a rising storm a panic ran through the heart of Wall Street. Here, even more than elsewhere, rumors gather volume as they fly, and rumor now soon had it that new stock had been dumped upon the street in unlimited quantities. The shock was like the work of magic. . . . The panic extended even to Vanderbilt's allies. The men who were concerned with him in the new pool, and who had made large outside investments under their agreement to run Erie up, became utterly demoralized by the rumors flying wildly around them. Sharing the general conviction that the Drew party had triumphed and Vanderbilt been beaten, and knowing that in such an event Erie must tumble to 40 or even lower, they made haste to sell ere the Commodore could countermand the order to sustain the market, and thus saddled all their loads upon their chief before the news of the situation reached him.

Under the panic Erie reeled heavily and made a sudden lunge down to 71—a fall of 12 per cent in two hours. There it halted quite firmly, making the wonder of the day, not that it fell so quickly, but that it did not tumble 50 per cent further. The whole shock of the battle, the whole huge load of the market, was sustained by one man, standing alone in his mighty power, deserted by his allies, who had sold out upon him at the trying moment and skulked away. . . .

When the panic started, news of the crisis was sent to Vanderbilt, and he was asked if his brokers should sell. "Sell!! *you fool!* No!!! *Buy all the shares offered!"* was the response roared by the man who saw with the quick eye of genius. One moment of hesitation, one faltering word of command, one instant of wavering in his position, and his lines would be hopelessly broken; Erie, of which he now held millions, would break and tumble 50 per cent; Central, Hudson River, and Harlem, all of which he carried on his shoulders, would follow in the panic and he would be hopelessly swamped. He took in the whole situation at a glance, and knew that Erie must be sustained at all hazards now, and by the force of his will alone the tide was stemmed, the panic stopped short, and disaster stayed.

The battle was done. Fisk had triumphed over Vanderbilt, defeating his purpose and hopes, while relieving him of some $10,000,000 of his money, and had also bitten Drew quite severely, by way of a side diversion. Fisk's dubious looks ceased the moment they had produced their desired effect in leading Drew to give orders to cover his contracts, and when the old man learned, an hour later, that Fisk was going to sell, he sent a messenger to countermand his order to buy; but it was too late. His brokers had acted promptly, and his shorts, contracted at about 70, had been covered at about 80. Still, the result of the whole battle of three weeks was such that the veteran leader of the bears was eminently satisfied, and he heartily joined in the chuckle that ran round the self-satisfied circle gathered at Erie headquarters, in West street, that evening, around the uncovered chest containing Vanderbilt's millions, in exchange for the small slips of clean paper ground out by their little mill, only a few days before.

When Judge Barnard discovered that his injunctions were disregarded and his writs defied, he resolved upon summary vengeance. On the morning of the 11th of March he issued warrants for the arrest of all of the Erie Directors. . . . During the time that this tempest was brewing in the "halls of justice," the Erie Directors were assembled at their offices in West street, counting and dividing the net profits of the previous day's operations. Suddenly they were interrupted in this agreeable labor by the arrival of a messenger, "breathless with haste," who, having learned of the dire vengeance concocted by the wrathful Judge, and having "seen, with his own eyes," the marshaling of an army of fierce deputies, armed with writs innumerable, ran with all his speed straight to the office of the doomed Directors, warning them of their fate. The whole company, struck dumb in amazement at the audacity of Barnard, were seized with fear, so that their knees smote one against another. Fisk was calm. He had learned in the Sunday school, at Brattleboro, that a wise man foresees evil and hides himself. He had also learned when a boy, that when a man in Brattleboro wished to avoid an unpleasant interview with the Sheriff of the county, he would walk through the covered bridge across the Connecticut and visit his friends in New Hampshire. Fisk smiled, and said, "Gentlemen, let's go to New Jersey," and they went immediately, carrying the treasury, and the books of the Erie Railway Company, with them.

The Legislature of New Jersey was in session at Trenton, and the terminus of the Erie road was at Jersey City. A bill was passed, without notice, to make the Erie Company a New Jersey corporation, with its officers in Jersey City. Thus, again, Fisk triumphed over all opposition. He had now proved himself to be both a bold operator and a skillful manipulator.

A new danger, however, presented itself. Drew was restless; he could not remain in exile and ease. He therefore resolved to resort to strategy; he made secret visits to New York, and held interviews with Vanderbilt, the arch enemy. Of all this Fisk was fully advised. The young man's detectives were ever on the old man's tracks, and when Drew was in the act of surrendering the treasury of Erie to the enemy, Fisk interposed and saved the prize. To cap the climax, Fisk entered into new combinations with the masters of the New York Legislature lobby and procured the passage of a bill at Albany, legalizing all the acts of the Erie Directors. This achievement brought all parties to terms; the contest ended and the victors sat down to a division of the spoils. Cash, bonds and stock were distributed in sums counted by millions, and the Railway, with its officers, rolling stock and fixtures, was turned over into the possession of Fisk and Gould, to have and to hold for their own use.

Vanderbilt took as his share several millions, Eldridge, for the Boston party, about nine millions, Drew retained all he had made during two years of treasureship, half a million was paid to lawyers and court officers, and then all was peace. . . .

LABOR IN WARTIME

In his history of the labor movement, George E. McNeill recorded events in which he was an actual participant. Twenty-five years old in 1861, he already had ten years of trade union experience behind him. Born into a New England abolitionist family, McNeill combined antislavery sentiment with labor reform. This brief excerpt from his voluminous writings is the best concise treatment of organized labor in the North during the Civil War and the immediate postwar period.

GEORGE McNEILL, *The Labor Movement: The Problem Today*

The war of the chattel labor masters upon the Republic concentrated the whole force of the patriotic labor masses of the North, East, and West. They left their tools of industry and took up the implements of war. Never was there such a patriotic uprising of the common people. They proved themselves worthy of their inheritance. Their hearts made the breast-work of defence, not only of the Union, but of the possessors of wealth. At first the industries trembled, but the demand for arms and equipments, and the distribution of money by bounties, soon compelled more rapid production. Strikes occurred in some places to compel the advance of wages, and the demand for less hours of labor was voiced by factory operatives and trades-unions.

It may be said that the eight-hour movement obtained its great impetus during the war. An intelligent agitation was commenced, and demands were made for labor legislation. Many old unions were re-organized, national and international trades-unions created, and local unions and labor associations sprung up everywhere. In 1861 the horse-car drivers of New York formed a benevolent association, John Walker, who has been a driver on the Third-avenue line for twenty years, being the founder. This organization discountenanced strikes, but as reduction after reduction took place they were compelled to unite upon the question of wages. The coal miners organized a National Association in 1861. The Boston United Laborers' Society was organized in 1862, the hack-drivers in 1863, and the locomotive engineers in the latter year. The Garment Cutters' Association, from whose members sprung the Order of the Knights of Labor, was organized at this eventful period. In California the scattered trades-unions of the cities, and especially those of San Francisco, formed an amalgamation.

This nearly completed the circle of organization of the wage-laborers. Secret associations, with signs and passwords, were established, the largest in point of numbers being the Supreme Mechanical Order of the Sun, an organization with an extensive ritual, having numerous degrees. The Grand Eight-hour League, and other associations whose names were never given to the public, were organized. Through the power of these orders workingmen were elected to legislative bodies in several of the States. At the councils, conventions and congresses of the labor organizations during the war resolutions of a patriotic nature were passed. The cost of living had more than kept pace with the wages of the workers, and

---

George E. McNeill, ed., *The Labor Movement: The Problem Today* (Boston: A. M. Bridgman, 1887), pp. 124–128.

discontent was general. The building trades were especially active in the movement.

In the early part of 1863 strikes were prevalent in many of the industries. Ship carpenters demanded three dollars per day, and mechanics and laborers in the Navy Yard were also moving for an increase of wages. It was during this trying time of the Republic that the organized workingmen of England manifested in unmistakable terms their love for our institutions . . . as acknowledged by President Lincoln in the early part of February of that year. The clerks in different departments pressed their claim for the early-closing movement, and mass-meetings of women were held, at which the terrible condition of the working women of the large cities was exposed and a strong public sentiment created in their favor. The shipwrights of New York City formed an association for intellectual and social improvement, established a reading room and library and listened to a course of lectures.

The draft of 1863, which practically exempted the wealthy by the payment of the small sum of three hundred dollars, was felt to be unjust to the laboring men, and advantage was taken of this feeling to create disloyalty to the Union and bitterness against the negro. A meeting of mechanics was held in Tammany Hall, and Horace Greeley was present. Mr. Greeley was called upon and very unwillingly addressed the assembly. After he had retired, he was shamefully abused by some of the speakers. This was followed by monster meetings in which all disloyal sentiments uttered in the name of labor were strongly condemned. Strikes continued to multiply, generally for an advance of wages.

Among the longshoremen and railroad employees assaults were made upon the non-unionists who took the places of the men on strike. In New York negroes were engaged to take the places of longshoremen. The negroes were assaulted, but the police succeeded in restoring order. It was not many years after this that the white and colored men joined in a trades-union procession for eight hours, some of the colored leaders riding in carriages, and the colored organizations being received into the procession with a salute.

In the spring of 1864 efforts were made in some of the State Legislatures for the enactment of laws, termed laws against intimidation, but really so drawn as to practically destroy all trades-union organizations. Section 1 of the bill presented in the New York Assembly read as follows: "Be it enacted, that if any person shall, by violence to the person or property of, or by threats or intimidation, or by molesting, or in any way obstructing another, force or endeavor to force any workman or other person hired in any manufacture, trade or business, to depart from his work before the same shall be finished," etc., giving then the penalty.

Mr. Greeley, in commenting upon this in the *Tribune,* said: "There is force in the objection that the acts it reprobates are already misdemeanors punishable under existing laws. We are inclined to the opinion that Mr. Folger's bill, if enacted, would do more harm than good."

The organizations continued to increase in membership. In 1864 the Cigar-Makers' International Union was formed. The stone-cutters, blacksmiths, carpenters and laborers in the forts in New York struck for twenty-five per cent advance, the longshoremen asked for $2.50 per day of nine hours, the mechanics in the Brooklyn Navy Yard asked for an advance of wages, pianoforte-makers organized to secure higher wages, the sewing women of New York and Philadelphia held mass-meetings, and the mates of merchant ships held a meeting for an increase of pay. The journeymen tailors formed a national trades-union in Philadelphia in September, 1865.

It was not until the breaking up of the rebellion and the return of the Grand Army of the Republic to the grand army of labor, from the processes of destruction to the processes of production, that the full force of this movement was developed. Labor newspapers began to multiply, perhaps the most important move in this direction being the establishment of the *Daily Evening Voice* by the Boston Typographical Union, which had a continued existence of two or three years. Great public meetings were held, strikes occurred, and labor processions marched through the streets. State conventions of workingmen were held in Indiana, Illinois and New York; at those in Indiana and New York nearly all the trades being represented.

In Massachusetts an order was introduced into the Legislature by a Union soldier, instructing the Judiciary Committee to consider the expediency of regulating and limiting the hours of labor to constitute a day's work. As a result an unpaid commission was appointed by Governor Andrew to investigate the subject of the hours of labor. The report of this committee was unsatisfactory to the labor men, and the next year Governor Bullock appointed three commissioners: the Honorable Amasa Walker, William Hyde and Edward H. Rogers.

The workingmen of some of the large cities celebrated the Fourth of July by processions and orations. The position given the returned soldiers by the labor men contrasted with that given them by the city of Boston, where the Aldermen rode in barouches and the veterans in express wagons. The *Daily Evening Voice,* then published in Boston, in a pungent editorial, commented on this, and said: "When labor is paid as it deserves, and not overworked, it will be impossible to keep the honors of the world from the workingmen, and such an exhibition as that of the Boston procession cannot occur."

The year 1866 witnessed a grand revival of the labor movement. Isolated unions and associations came more and more to see the necessity of amalgamation. An active propaganda was aroused, and new organizations were continually multiplying. From thirty to forty national and international trades-unions and amalgamated societies were in existence, some of them numbering tens of thousands of men. The people of to-day have little conception of the extent of the labor movement of twenty years ago. . . .

POSTWAR LABOR MOVEMENT

Where McNeill emphasized the American penchant for utopian reform through political action, Gompers, deeply influenced by European intellectuals, concentrated on practical objectives through organization and discipline of specific craft unions. Better wages, more leisure, and improved working conditions were to be achieved by collective bargaining directly with the employer.

SAMUEL GOMPERS, *Seventy Years of Life and Labour*

In those early years the fraternal or lodge movement absorbed practically all my leisure. It was its human side that drew me. I saw in it a chance for men to develop and to lend a helping hand when most needed. The lodge was to me a form of education extension. In time its limitations became evident, for I had been making ready to reach out for something bigger and more fundamental. I was a member of the union in my trade for practical reasons, while my idealism and sentiment found expression

---

in fraternalism. As yet I did not understand that the philosophy and scope of the trade union movement could be made broad and deep enough to include all the aspirations and needs of the wage-earner.

I attended union meetings rather casually in the 'sixties. Local Cigarmakers' Union No. 15 met in a room over the saloon of Garrett Berlyn, 46 East Broadway. He was the father of Barney Berlyn who was one of our members and was elected corresponding secretary in 1870. Barney afterwards became an ardent Socialist. Our union was not very strong. It was affiliated to the old National Union of Cigarmakers organized in 1864 and later to the Cigarmakers' International Union of America, as the movement was called after the reorganization in 1867. John J. Junio of Syracuse was president. At that time the cigarmakers of this country were as a rule Armenians, Englishmen, and Hollanders. There were a few Germans who had come to the United States from 1855 to 1867. After the Civil War, when cigarmaking began to develop from a house trade into a factory industry, the proportion of German workmen was largely increased.

There was a vast difference between those early unions and the unions of today. Then there was no law or order. A union was a more or less definite group of people employed in the same trade who might help each other out in special difficulties with the employer. There was no sustained effort to secure fair wages through collective bargaining. The employer fixed wages until he shoved them down to a point where human endurance revolted. Often the revolt started by an individual whose personal grievance was sore, who rose and declared: "I am going on strike. All who remain at work are scabs." Usually the workers went out with him.

I remember being busily at work one day when Conrad Kuhn, president of the Cigarmakers' Unions of New York City, entered the shop and announced: "This shop is on strike." Kuhn was a large, fine-looking man, with a stentorian voice that could be heard in every portion of the shop. Without hesitation we all laid down our work and walked out. That was the way it was done in the early days. We had no conception of constructive business tactics beginning with presentation of demands and negotiation to reach an agreement.

Whether we won or lost that strike I don't remember, but the union had no money at the end. Kuhn gave valiant service to us, but his family was actually suffering. It was after the big strike of 1872 that he had to leave the trade. The Turners helped him find a position where he could earn a living, for of course he was black-listed.

The union was generally in a precarious condition financially. Strike funds were never assured, and there were no other benefits. The union represented a feeling of community of burdens of those working in the same industry. It had to acquire a new meaning before it became an industrial agency. It had to strengthen its defensive resources and develop cohesive forces. But that was not only the embryonic stage of unionism; it was the fledgling period of industry. Industrial production was uncouth, unscientific, just about as planless as unionism. Management, accountancy, salesmanship, elimination of waste were in the rule-of-thumb stage. Factory architecture and industrial sanitation were undeveloped sciences.

Any kind of an old loft served as a cigar shop. If there were enough windows, we had sufficient light for our work; if not, it was apparently no concern of the management. There was an entirely different conception of sanitation both in the shop and in the home of those days from now. The toilet facilities were a water-closet and a sink for washing purposes, usually located by the closet. In most cigar shops our towels were the bagging that came around the bales of Havana and other high grades of tobacco. Cigar shops were always dusty from the tobacco stems and powdered leaves. Benches and work tables were not designed to enable the workmen to adjust bodies and arms comfortably to work surface. Each workman supplied his own cutting board of lignum vitae and knife blade.

The tobacco leaf was prepared by strippers who drew the leaves from the heavy stem and put them in pads of about fifty. The leaves had to be handled carefully to prevent tearing. The craftsmanship of the cigarmaker was shown in his ability to utilize wrappers to the best advantage to shave off the unusable to a hairbreadth, to roll so as to cover holes in the leaf and to use both hands so as to make a perfectly shaped and rolled product. These things a good cigarmaker learned to do more or less mechanically, which left us free to think, talk, listen, or sing. I loved the freedom of that work, for I had earned the mind-freedom that accompanied skill as a craftsman. I was eager to learn from discussion and reading or to pour out my feeling in song. Often we chose someone to read to us who was a particularly good reader, and in payment the rest of us gave him sufficiently of our cigars so he was not the loser. The reading was always followed by discussion, so we learned to know each other pretty thoroughly. We learned who could take a joke in good spirit, who could marshal his thoughts in an orderly way, who could distinguish clever sophistry from sound reasoning. The fellowship that grew between congenial shopmates was something that lasted a lifetime.

I remember vividly a curious period of deep depression that possessed me soon after my return to New York from Lambertsville. Coming back to the cosmopolitan center from small-town life, I began to feel very keenly my own limitations and my inability to express in words the deep emotions and aspirations that were crowding my mind, seeking form and outlet. I was so ill at ease with myself that for some time I cultivated the habit of silence. Of course, I had had the experience of the companionship of boys and young men in debating, and judge and jury clubs of which I was a member. But they didn't test my metal and make me see my limitations when measured against them. During those early discussions I easily measured above my companions. When I came in contact with men and saw bigger powers and the greater responsibilities and possibilities in life, I became self-critical and self-accusing. There was something escaping the grasp of my mind and my power of expression.

The other cause of my discontent was that nothing was accomplished—nothing constructive was building. When our clubs were merged into the Ancient Order of Foresters, the mutual benefit society of which I was secretary and later president, and later in the Odd Fellows Order of which I was the presiding officer, I had found the sentimental expression of humanitarianism and brotherhood with mutual care for others. I did not speak of my inner conflict to a soul, but my splendid health and natural activity of mind finally broke the spell and again I was reading, studying, acquiring, and doing. Then I found—I won't say myself—but the fact of my life—I found the meaning of the union.

It was in 1869 that the convention of the cigarmakers which met that year in Chicago issued a general amnesty proclamation to all unfair cigarmakers offering to take them into unions without payment of initiation fees and unpaid obligations. The declaration temporarily made considerable stir in New York. A number of workers drifted in, but they just as easily drifted out—no permanent growth came from offering union membership at a bargain sale. The organization was then making its fight against the introduction of molds and methods that seemed destined to destroy individual skill. In old Turner Hall, Orchard Street, New York City, our members divided into those favoring a strike against the introduction of molds and those opposed. The crowd of boys with whom I was associated voted for a strike and I followed along. The strike came. It was a hard struggle. From that time I began to realize the futility of opposing progress. The organization lost that fight as molds and bunch-breaking machines enabled immigrant workers to become rapidly adept in producing cheaper grades of cigars. Bohemian cigarmakers began to come in appreciable numbers. In Bohemia cigarmaking was a government monopoly and practically all the work was done by women. This class of workers made the elimination or even the control of mold usage impossible. A prolonged strike against molds in Straiton and Storm's shop ended disastrously. Fred Blend, president of the International at the time, tried to help us, but the International had no money. Members left and union disintegration went on.

This condition of depression extended to the whole labor movement in New York. William Jessup, one of the prominent labor men of New York at that time, was making a heroic but discouraging effort to build up the carpenters' organization. Jessup was also president of the Workingmen's Council—then the English-speaking central body of New York City. The *Arbeiter Union,* the central body for the German workers, was the more virile and resourceful organization. Its members were educated and disciplined in European labor movements and were generally associated with the International Workingman's Association. It was an aggressive, rational body.

A very distinct type of American workingman was that to which Alexander Troup, then of New York, A. C. Cameron of Chicago, Martin A. Foran of Cleveland, Thompson Murch of Maine, and William H. Sylvis of Troy belonged. There was an intellectual quality that kept them from feeling the barriers of a wage-earning class. They looked at industrial problems from the point of view of American citizens and turned instinctively to political activity for reform. Troup was a splendid man, a member of Typographical Union No. 6. He later became editor of a New Haven daily paper. A. C. Cameron of Chicago was widely known through his paper, *The Workingman's Advocate.* Martin A. Foran, a cooper and the founder of the Coopers' International Union, began his political service in an Ohio constitutional convention and for many years was a Representative in Congress. I remember that Foran wrote a labor novel—perhaps not his most valuable service to labor for in Congress he was a respected spokesman for the cause. Thompson Murch, at one time secretary of the National Granite Cutters' Union, was also in Congress several terms.

One of the men who made a most vivid impression on me was William H. Sylvis who became president of the National Labor Union after J. C. C. Whaley. Sylvis was an iron molder who gave the best of his life to building up the Iron Molders' Union. He was a trade unionist but he also had a political slant. He came to New York frequently in the course of his work and in many long talks with him that helped me greatly.

John Fortune was the early leader in the tailoring industry and did much to inspire hope in that trade. The customs tailors early developed an effective organization. They were helped by French, German, and Irish tailors who were members of the International. This was in the days before sewing machines were in general use. In this group was Konrad Carl, a special friend of mine, a splendid man, and a genuine trade unionist. In New York circles the leader of the furniture workers, who were chiefly Germans, was Karl Speyer, a member of the International. These men were prominent in the National Labor Union and approved its venture into the political field. Troup directed the New York State movement that was part of the larger plan. Neither survived the political venture into the presidential campaign of 1872. This policy of condemning existing political parties and building up a labor political machine, did not appeal to me, and although I cast my first presidential vote in 1872, it was for General U. S. Grant.

I was a great admirer of Horace Greeley, and just about a year before the nominations of either of the parties Horace Greeley said that General Grant would be better fitted and qualified for the presidency in 1872 than he was in 1868. I could not see the consistency of Mr. Greeley's then accepting the nomination for President on the Democratic ticket. I believed at that time that the Republican Party had not yet fulfilled its mission. It still had the halo of the anti-slavery movement and there were a number of men who were still living and active in furtherance of the reconstruction policy caused by the Civil War.

It was late in the fall of 1870 my attention was called to a Cooper Union meeting at which the two Englishmen, Mr. Mundella and Thomas Hughes, M.P., were to speak on the scope and influence of trade unions. Mundella was a manufacturer of Nottingham who established the first voluntary board of conciliation and arbitration for the hosiery and glove trades of that locality. It was a voluntary effort toward better industrial organization, for which organization of both employers and employes was a prerequisite. As I was interested to know what changes had come among British workers after I left England as a lad of thirteen, I attended the meeting in Cooper Union. Mundella made the mistake of attempting to instruct the American workingmen and advised co-operation and arbitration in the place of strikes. His declarations were founded on impressions gained at a mutual admiration party and not on observation.

The incident started me to pondering the character and the functions of trade unions. In my own trade, the workmen were powerless against substitution of machines for human skill. Regularly we suffered annual reductions in wages. We had no chance to try either co-operation or arbitration, the remedies recommended by the English speakers, yet we needed protection desperately. I was a good workman, so I fared much better than any others, yet I could not be oblivious to their sufferings. My sense of injustice was stirring and I began going to more labor meetings, seeking the way out. In the labor meetings of the early 'seventies I found passionate feeling, idealism, but little practical aid.

In those days New York was the haven for the over-zealous soldiers in the European struggle for freedom. Europe was struggling against the bonds by which the Congress of Vienna and the Holy Alliance had hoped to strangle the spirit of the French Revolution and the democratic practices of the Napoleonic Empire. East Side New York harbored refugee leaders and soldiers from the successive revolutionary movements of practically all European countries. They were men of imagination, courage, ideals. They sought their ends through revolution. The brilliant color of their thoughts came as a hope-filled alluring light on the gray misery of the New York industrial sky. Their talk stirred me deeply. I began to watch their gatherings.

Back of their activity was an organization called the International Workingmen's Association, whose headquarters were established at London in 1864 and whose presiding genius was Karl Marx. The organization was trade union in inception. It had subsidiary organizations in the various European countries and was controlled by a central General Council. It sought to build up trade unions and held that national trade union movements must act collectively for proper regulation of immigration so that the workingmen of one country could not be used against the workingmen of other countries.

Marx was not consistent in all his writings, but his influence contributed to emphasize the necessity for organization of wage-earners in trade unions and the development of economic power prior to efforts to establish labor government through political methods. The International tried either to establish divisions in the various countries or to secure the co-operation of the national labor organization. In the United States a somewhat loose relationship was established with the National Labor Union, but American workingmen did not feel the same identity of international interests that naturally developed between men of smaller, contiguous countries. Although the International was to concern itself wholly with the affairs of wage-earners, it speedily acquired the reputation of being a powerful revolutionary agency. Great upheavals were taking place in practically all the European countries as they groped their way toward constitutional government, and the men who were interested in economic betterment were naturally interested in uprooting arbitrary political power. The impression given was that the I.W.A. was a powerful secret revolutionary body whose agents permeated all Europe. At any rate, there were revolutionary refugees in New York who were members of the International.

I gathered from various sources that the International was feared by all the reactionary elements and governments of Europe who studiously sought to discredit its work as "Communism." Our American press seized upon the custom of addressing its members as "citizen" as proof of their identification with the French Commune. Later, a more real basis for disfavor developed through the domination gained by a group of intellectuals who were more interested in the thrills of propaganda than in achieving practical industrial betterment. I watched the period not fully understanding and certainly not appreciating how the mistakes of those years were to help me in developing effective policies in later years.

The year 1871 was one of protest and propaganda artistically vivid and throbbing with imagination. My whole being surged with response, though I was a listener in the crowd or only a private in the ranks. Early in the year New York labor inaugurated an eight-hour movement for the enforcement of the eight-hour law and the establishment of that standard in all industries. The movement aroused intense enthusiasm. Sections of the International then organized in New York City joined whole-heartedly.

During that summer, we watched a succession of demonstrations in the streets of New York that were entirely dissociated with American affairs, reflexes only of the European political struggle. There was the bloody procession of Orangemen on July 12 and the riot on East Broadway when the Catholic group descended upon the Orangemen. There was the tremendous peace jubilee celebrating the ending of the Franco-Prussian War, the celebration of Italian unity, and the protest against the court-martial of Hungarian revolutionists. These happenings kept us in touch with the world-pulse of freedom, while we were puzzling over local problems.

Early in September came the great eight-hour parade, intended to visualize the purpose and scope of the movement. On the morning of the day set, rain descended in torrents. New York streets were then cobbled and although the sky cleared by noon the mire under foot was a test of purpose. Curran of the Stone-cutters was grand marshal. Hugo Meyer of the cigarmakers was one of his assistants. The cigarmakers' organization was too weak to make a fight for eight hours at that time, but we joined the parade. We marched down Fourteenth Street to Fourth Avenue along the Bowery to Chatham, from there to the City Hall, then up Broadway to Eighth Street and over to Cooper Union. There were about 25,000 men in line. Two sections of the International and a group of Negro workers attracted the most attention. The Internationals carried the red flag and a banner with the French slogan, "Liberty, Equality and Fraternity." Eight-hour banners appeared along the line of march. Some of the legends they bore were:

PEACEABLY IF WE CAN; FORCIBLY IF WE MUST.

EIGHT HOURS FOR LABOR, EIGHT HOURS FOR SLEEP,
AND EIGHT HOURS FOR NATURAL IMPROVEMENT

WE ARE DETERMINED TO HAVE THE EIGHT-HOUR
LAW ENFORCED; NO MORE PAPER LAWS.

OUR STRENGTH LIES IN THE JUSTICE OF OUR
DEMANDS. LET THE WORKING PEOPLE
OF THE WORLD UNITE.

EIGHT HOURS, OR REMEMBER.

THE NEXT GOVERNOR WILL ENFORCE THE EIGHT-HOUR LAW.

WE WILL FIGHT FOR EIGHT HOURS.

NO MORE TALK—WE MEAN BUSINESS.

WORKINGMEN ARE THE BULWARK OF THE NATION.

DOWN WITH THE PRISON CONTRACT SYSTEM. IF PRISONERS MUST LABOR, LET THE PEOPLE REAP THE BENEFIT THEREOF.

One banner bore the inscription:

EIGHT HOURS FOR WORK. EIGHT HOURS FOR REST. EIGHT HOURS FOR WHAT WE WILL.

This inscription was a fling back at those critics who declared that the shorter work-day would lead to greater dissipation.

The parade ended with a monster mass meeting in Cooper Union under the joint auspices of the Workingmen's Unions and the Arbeiter Union. The parade was apparently an unqualified success, but the unfortunate prominence given to force, to red flags, and the revolutionary element was to impede the constructive work of our movement for years to come.

At that meeting it was resolved to continue the agitation until the eight-hour day should generally prevail. It was evident then that the building trades would probably succeed first.

Meanwhile, trouble was brewing in the International. Section 12 of the American group was dominated by a brilliant group of faddists, reformers, and sensation-loving spirits. They were not working people and treated their relationship to the labor movement as a means to a "career." They did not realize that labor issues were tied up with the lives of men, women, and children—issues not to be risked lightly. Those pseudo-Communists played with the labor movement. This experience burned itself into my memory so that I never forgot the principle in after years.

Victoria Woodhull was then dazzling New York by the brilliancy of her oratory. She was a passionate advocate of woman's suffrage and human freedom even to the length of irresponsible action. An unhappy marriage experience in addition to her philosophical anarchy made her an advocate of free-love as a part of her program of human freedom. She was a slight, sparkling little creature, with expressive brown eyes and short brown hair. Her attractive personality helped to build up a movement in New York which included such people as Theodore Tilton, editor of *The Independent,* Colonel Blood, Osborne Ward, Dr. Maddox, P. J. McGuire, Theodore Banks, John T. Elliott, and Hugh McGregor. Elliott was a fine-looking young man, a southern gentleman, and he was strongly attracted by Mrs. Woodhull. Mrs. Woodhull and her sister, Tenny C. Claflin, published the Woodhull and Claflin *Weekly* which with good reason was dreaded by many a person whose private life did not conform to the conventional moral code, and which added no luster to the movement.

In the fall of 1871, No. 12, to which this group belonged, issued a circular in which they made the International responsible for free-love, anarchy, and every extreme doctrine that appealed to their speculative fancy. The labor movement was appalled. Its enemies rejoiced and hastened to profit. The daily papers utilized the opportunity for a campaign of ridicule and calumny. They classified all labor purposes as Communism.

No program of life that threw overboard the family institution ever appealed to me. That institution was firmly interwoven in my fiber. I saw it in my grandparents, my parents, and then in the lives of my uncles and aunts, all of whom married and set up their homes. My moral training was chiefly by example rather than precept. In my boyhood I knew only those who regarded the home as sacred—one of the ultimate ends of life itself. When only a boy in years, I married a girl a bit younger than I. Soon afterward we set up our own nest—only two rooms, but our own. Before I was eighteen, I had a father's responsibility for a son and regularly thereafter a newcomer found its way into that nest every two years. We hadn't much, but we were bound together for a common fate. I could not understand irresponsibility of word or act.

The pure joy of living is good to know—and I knew it to the utmost in those early days. Red blood ran through a strong body that knew no disease nor hereditary weakness. I enjoyed what was at hand and I spent no time in wishing things were different. Simple wholesome food is very sweet to healthy hunger. A friend's heart and mind were wonderful mysteries to me standing on the threshold of manhood. A poem, a paper, a book was a treasure from which to dig wisdom or pleasure. I loved the touch of soft velvety tobacco and gloried in the deft sureness with which I could make cigars grow in my fingers, never wasting a scrap of material. Body, senses, mind, and heart were thrilling with the wonder of life. I felt a prince in my own realm with never a care for the future. I gave all that was in me to that which was at hand, task or pleasure. Always I was so absorbed in the doing that I did not think of self. This saved me from self-consciousness. And I always wanted a friend with whom to share. Never but once in my life did I seek solitude in any experience or suffer from self-consciousness.

The bona-fide trade unionists in the International repudiated the circular and tried to purge the movement of the reformers and "intellectuals." Men like Fred Bolte of the cigarpackers, Konrad Carl the tailor, Edward Grosse the printer, Fred Bloete the cigarmaker, F. A. Sorge the music teacher took the situation before the General Council in London in order that the administrative body should have the necessary information for disciplinary action. The final result was the expulsion of the "radicals" who then set up dual offices in Spring Street and continued to speak in the name of the International. I was coming to an appreciation of the difference between revolutionary ideals and revolutionary tactics for securing them. But the slow, less spectacular methods of constructive progress were more difficult than the dashing, spotlight tactics of the smaller group.

After the execution of some of the Paris Communists, the Woodhull faction staged another sensational endeavor. It was an international parade and mock funeral ceremony for the executed Communists. The painters' society participated as a body as did the Cuban revolutionists attracted by the libertarian sentiment. Six gray horses drew the catafalque. One of the group rode on horseback draped in the red flag, another impersonated Joan of Arc. Theodore Tilton, Colonel Blood, Mrs. Woodhull, and Miss Claflin rode in a carriage. As a sensational space-getter in the press, the parade for the communist martyrs was an unqualified success. As a constructive labor policy it was a criminal blunder from which, together with similar acts, the labor movement was to suffer for years. It was a hard school in which I was learning the labor movement, but an effective one.

George Francis Train was another of the picturesque characters of that period. Train was so insistent upon his individual rights and his freedom from conventions that the authorities took vengeance by detaining him for years among the abnormal. He was arrested for all manner of infringements of ordinary regulations for ordinary people and spent considerable time in the Tombs as a result of the hostility he aroused in the person of Anthony Comstock, the purist. Train had a little paper, pamphlet-size, that especially aroused the ire of this custodian of public morality. This he placidly edited in the Tombs or any other spot where he happened to be. One time he undertook to circumvent Comstock by quoting passages from the Bible to illustrate that literary indecency is a relative term. But Comstock was not to be foiled and arrested him for sending obscene literature through the mail. This stopped Train from quoting the Bible. I knew Train well and enjoyed his idiosyncrasies.

Winter unemployment was a regular recurring evil in those times. In addition to the seasonal slacking of work which was then unmodified by administrative planning, New York was the winter headquarters of many tramp workers. That was before the time of employment agencies and men had to make their own contacts with jobs—near or far. Often the tramp workman was merely a restless spirit swayed by the *Wanderlust;* sometimes a kindred spirit to the pioneers who served as an advance scout of unionism, scattering the seeds of organization in the more remote towns and villages.

Unemployment hardships were unusually pressing in February and March of 1872. The administrative council of the International Workingmen's Association tried to get the city authorities to take action or at least to secure the use of police and court halls for the discussion of questions affecting public welfare. The Board of Aldermen concurred in the request, but were vetoed by the Comptroller. The papers began gravely to record evidences of the existence of a New York Commune. More definite "proof" was found in the grand mass meeting for the unemployed held in Tompkins Square, March 14, 1872. As the Spring Street faction managed the demonstration, the red flag was in evidence everywhere. For days carts and wagons had been driven over town bearing white canvas announcements of the assemblage. If that Spring Street crowd had only had the same keen appreciation of constructive policies that they had of advertising and propaganda they would have done wonders.

Early in 1872 the agitation for eight hours was resumed. The building trades and several of the German organizations were most active. The directing spirits in the Eight-Hour League were George E. McNeill, Ira Stewart, and George Gunter. These men saw the shorter work-day as the first step necessary in industrial betterment. Workingmen must be able to divide their time so as to best conserve their efficiency as men and consequently as workers. The activity of the League paralleled the revival of trade unionism after the Civil War.

Under the urge of the growing enthusiasm, even the cigarmakers called a mass meeting one Sunday afternoon in Turner Hall on Fourth Street. Benedict Dottler presided. We talked over conditions in our trade, for none other was then so backward, and decided we were not sufficiently organized to join the progressive movement. In a few days we held another meeting at which Jessup, Dottler, Bearman, Hanan, Eswald Schwanderle spoke and Conrad Kuhn introduced a resolution outlining a plan of organization for three language sections under a Central Council. This was the plan upon which we ultimately built up our New York organization. It met our practical difficulties and enabled us to develop community of interests among cigarmakers.

As a part of the eight-hour movement, a great workingmen's parade was arranged in the middle of June (June 10, 1872). German and United States flags, the "Marseillaise" and "Die Wacht am Rhein," vive and hurrah demonstrated the international character of the New York labor as well as that particular eight-hour movement.

Despite all our difficulties, several organizations established the eight-hour day in their trades, but only one, the stone-cutters, maintained that gain through the panic and the industrial depression of the following years.

Unquestionably, in these early days of the 'seventies the International dominated the labor movement in New York City. The older type of labor organization in the United States had been transplanted from England and was of the fraternal benevolent character. The American trade union, the militant economic force, was yet to come. New York City was the cradle of the modern American labor movement. The United States was then preponderantly an agricultural nation, and industry was in its infancy. The factory system was so new that in comparatively few places had it produced its necessary reflex—the organization of labor. Through the gates of Castle Garden were sifting industrial workers from Europe, welcomed by employers who exploited their need and ignorance. The situation produced its own antidote—the workers from the old countries had had more or less experience in the labor movement and they began building their defenses. As the early immigration was dominated by English, Irish, and Scotch, so the early labor movement bore the imprint of British organization and methods. The majority of the immigrants who came from the working class or were forced into it by reversals of fortune found homes and work in New York City from whence they filtered to other industrial communities. But New York was the receiving ground. As the tide of reaction swept down over the movement for democracy in Germany, in Hungary, in Italy, in France, New York gave refuge to those whose only safety lay in flight. New York was vividly cosmopolitan with depths in its life that few understood. There were soldiers from the red-shirted army of Garibaldi; German "forty-eighters," English Chartists, men of big souls and high principles; the *carbonari* of Italy; the home-rulers of Ireland; revolutionaries from Denmark, Austria, Russia. In the early 'seventies New York looked like Paris during the Commune. Each ebb in the forward tide of revolution in Europe brought additions to the rebel group in New York. These refugees regarded America as the platform from which they could freely spread their gospels. Revolutionists are not of the type that readily adapt themselves to the customs of a new land. They inject their own spirit.

These were some of the elements that found their way into the industrial life of New York from which an American labor movement was to be developed. Somehow that movement safely combined the fervor of the revolutionists with the systematic orderliness of constructive minds. This was the great contribution of New York. From that industrial center came the first constructive, efficient American trade union organization, that of the cigarmakers, followed by the furniture workers, the printers, the tailors, the plasterers, and others.

III / POLITICS, RACISM, AND RECONSTRUCTION

A / Lincoln and His Critics

B / Congressional Reconstruction: Design by Committee

A/Lincoln and His Critics

INTRODUCTION

Abraham Lincoln was not cast in the popular image of a great war leader. He did not have the restless, colorful energy of a Churchill or a Napoleon—the ability to inspire a people by sheer force of will. Irresolute perhaps when he should have been tough, he deferred to other opinions at times when his instincts told him he was right. Lincoln had little taste for administration, an aversion that shocked such methodical members of his cabinet as Gideon Welles and Salmon P. Chase. He permitted Seward and Stanton too much latitude in sensitive areas like civil rights. He allowed Chase to build up a personal political machine. He apparently condoned the corrupt practices of treasury agents and speculators who were shipping cotton out of captured southern ports. But Lincoln did have charismatic qualities which became more obvious as he settled into the Presidency. Above all he had an intuitive sense of public opinion. Few American statesmen before or since have practiced the art of politics with his consummate skill.

Politics, like the economy, was in a transitional stage. To manage the Republican party, a grab bag of factions, would have required a strong yet subtle hand, even if no war had intervened. The Democratic party, its ranks thinned by defections in the North and the complete loss of its southern wing, had been reduced to a minority status. Oddly enough, these losses had strengthened its political effectiveness. Stripped to a relatively hard core, the party was weaker in numbers but stronger in organization than its rival. The Democrats always posed a threat to the Administration, particularly in the states where "politics as usual" weakened public morale.

From the beginning of his stormy administration, Lincoln had determined upon a threefold political policy: stronger fusion of the Republican party (hence his careful balancing of prior political affiliations in his Cabinet and in lesser appointments); involvement of as many Democrats as possible in the Union cause; and development of the concept that the President spoke and acted for all the people, irrespective of politics or residence.

On the question of slavery, for strategic and political reasons, Lincoln went slowly at first. Privately, he was as much an antislavery man as Horace Greeley, the influential editor of *The New York Tribune,* who had long been a bitter opponent of the "peculiar institution." As President, however, Lincoln could not take the risk. A careful lawyer, he saw clearly the constitutional problems involved. Slavery was legally established in important loyal border regions—Missouri, Maryland, Kentucky, eastern Tennessee, and western Virginia. Emancipation anywhere by Federal action, he felt, would have serious repercussions that would undermine the Union war effort in these areas. Quite probably it would have also enlarged the rift between the Republicans and the Democrats in the North, which Lincoln at the time was trying desperately to close. Had Union arms been more successful during the first year of the war, the President might have moved more rapidly along the road to emancipation. But he would never have forced emancipation upon the loyal border regions. His correspondence with Horace Greeley early in 1862 shows that restoration of the Union was his prime object in the war. He never changed this priority. Peace terms, of course, were a different matter; here his policy would be influenced by events and by public opinion.

When he finally proclaimed that emancipation would take effect on January 1, 1863, Lincoln stated clearly that this proclamation was a war measure—that it applied only to those states then in rebellion. In effect, it applied to precisely that territory the Federal government did not control. "A paper manifesto," snorted many radicals, but Charles Sumner, for one, applauded the proclamation as a step in the right direction. Practical men of all political persuasions conceded that if freedom were established in the deep South after a Union victory, the border slave states would have to go along. Lincoln, however, had his doubts about the ultimate legality of his action and about the position on emancipation in the loyal border slave states. Rebuffed by those states when he proposed Federal compensation for freeing their slaves, he pushed for the 13th Amendment to the Constitution to abolish slavery everywhere in the Union.

Although the President had been subjected to growing criticism from the more radical elements of his party on the slavery question and on the conduct of the war, he managed to control these restive spirits. After the defeats at Fredericksburg and Chancellorsville, he was hard-pressed by both radical and Peace Democrats. Two events—the Vallandigham arrest and his proclamation on reconstruction—brought stinging criticism from the right and the left. Lincoln's limited suspension of the writ of habeas corpus early in the war had led to arbitrary arrests of suspected southern sympathizers, most of whom were Democrats. More sweeping suspensions followed, mainly confined to the border states where military operations were under way, but also in other areas where antiwar men applied for writs to obstruct enlistments. The peace movement, which fed on repeated Union defeats, came to a head in the spring of 1863 when Clement L. Vallandigham, former Ohio congressman and Democratic candidate for governor of the state, was summarily court-martialed and sentenced to close confinement for subversive activities.

Lincoln was much embarrassed by this rash act of the military in a state where the courts were functioning. Yet he felt he could not completely disavow the commanding officer. In setting aside the sentence, he still upheld the conviction by ordering Vallandigham deported to the Confederacy. Outraged by this action, a group of prominent New York Democrats accused the President in a public letter of tyrannical and unconstitutional behavior. His famous reply points up the problem of fighting a civil war, yet still preserving the democratic process. Was Lincoln's compromise solution a wise one? Did it weaken or strengthen loyal opposition? Is loyal opposition possible in wartime, especially civil-war time? Where does the right of dissent end, and subversion begin?

Meanwhile, Lincoln was faced with another serious problem, which involved control of his own party, the power of his office, and indeed, the future of the nation itself. Emancipation had led directly to the complex question of the postwar settlement. Typically, the President moved cautiously. In late 1863, Union arms controlled substantial portions of the Confederacy. More to test public and congressional reaction (and perhaps also to weaken Confederate morale) than to offer any specific blueprint for reconstruction, the President issued a Proclamation of Amnesty and Reconstruction. The document was moderate in tone, setting forth lenient conditions whereby the rebellious states could return to their former allegiance. In line with his concept of the Presidency, Lincoln saw reconstruction as an executive function. The Congress represented only a part of the states and their people, while he, as properly elected President, had a constitutional obligation to act for all.

His assertion of broad executive powers provoked a bitter reaction. Radicals in Congress insisted that the legislative branch, not the executive, should prescribe reconstruction policy. The South was an armed foe. Lincoln's thesis of an indissoluble union of the states might have the Constitution and logic behind it, but the proposition was an abstract one. How could the people of a given state be separate and distinct from it? If the people were rebels, so were the state governments they elected. These exponents of Northern nationalism were not particularly troubled by states' rights, certainly not where the enemy was concerned. The kind of loyalty oath Lincoln proposed would not, they thought, guarantee loyal behavior. Presidential amnesty put too much power in the hands of a single man. In the words of Henry Winter Davis, an outspoken critic, "The President . . . holds the electoral votes of the rebel states at the dictation of his personal ambition." What about emancipation? It had been achieved by executive fiat. Should not Congress legislate on the subject? Who was to protect the ex-slave from the vengeance or the exploitation of his former master? Congress was the supreme lawmaking body, the only branch of the government competent to protect him, and to restore civil government in the South.

Henry Winter Davis of Maryland and Benjamin Wade of Ohio drew up a bill reflecting these sentiments. Lincoln got the bill postponed until near the end of the congressional session before it was finally passed by a close vote. The President then killed it with a pocket veto. On July 8, 1864, in explaining his reasons for doing so, he declared that he was not "inflexibly committed to any single plan of restoration" and that if the loyal people of an ex-Confederate state chose to adopt the Wade-Davis program, they should be encouraged to do so. As for the emancipation section of the bill, he doubted the "constitutional competency of Congress to abolish slavery in states," but at the same time urged a Constitutional amendment to abolish slavery "throughout the nation." It was an adroit document that goaded the radicals into a furious response—the so-called Manifesto of August 5, 1864.

Had Lincoln lived, would he have stood by his moderate plan of reconstruction, counting on his prestige and his political skill to overcome the opposition? At the time of his death, the radicals were but a minority in the party, though unquestionably they were its ablest men. Knowing the views of the radicals and appreciating their qualities, would he have permitted former Confederate states to organize governments with black codes? Would he have looked aside when these same states promptly elected many of their pardoned wartime leaders to Congress? Could malice for none, charity for all, have meant he had forgotten the pledge in his Gettysburg Address: "that these honored dead shall not have died in vain"? Lincoln was an idealist, but he never lost touch with the hard realities of a complex situation. His phrase that he was not "inflexibly committed to any single plan of restoration" seems especially pertinent. In his last public address he made the same point. In his last Cabinet meeting, he suggested the possibility of suffrage for black veterans and the better educated blacks of the South. Whatever policy he would have chosen, it is safe to say that he would have worked with Congress, and maintained his leadership. Whether this would have had any significant bearing on the problem of race relations—the crucial issue of reconstruction—is open to conjecture.

INTERPRETATION

Reviews and particularly review articles should not be neglected by the student of history. Often the concise and critical form of the review presents insights with a forceful clarity lacking in the more formal article. Thomas Pressly of the University of Washington history department, in reviewing Kenneth Stampp's Era of Reconstruction, *ponders the question of the historian and his environment.*

THOMAS J. PRESSLY,
Racial Attitudes, Scholarship, and Reconstruction: A Review Essay

Professor Kenneth M. Stampp's *Era of Reconstruction* * is an impressive synthesis and summary of those newer views concerning Reconstruction which, foreshadowed in a few writings published before the Second World War, have increasingly been expressed in the past twenty years, to the point that now they seem to be dominant among the publishing scholars in the field. Since the ideas dominant among the publishing scholars in a field almost invariably become, in one form or another, the ideas dominant in the college and high school textbooks and lecture notes, and then in the minds of a generation or more of students, we are witnessing what is apparently a major shift in the perception and understanding of a crucial era in the history of the United States. Both the change in substantive views of Reconstruction and also the process of shifting perceptions of the past raise issues of the most fundamental nature concerning the enterprise which forms the vocation and avocation of historians, the attempt to understand the past.

The change in substantive views of Reconstruction can be seen concretely by comparing Professor Stampp's book with the recently reprinted *Essays on the Civil War and Reconstruction* by William A. Dunning. The

---

Thomas J. Pressly, "Racial Attitudes, Scholarship, and Reconstruction: A Review Essay," *The Journal of Southern History*, XXXII (February 1966), pp. 88–93. Copyright, 1966, by the Southern Historical Association. Reprinted without footnotes, and without page references for quotations, by permission of the Managing Editor and the author.

* Kenneth M. Stampp, *Era of Reconstruction* (New York: Alfred A. Knopf, Inc., 1965). Quotes from this book are reprinted with the permission of the publisher.

first of these seven essays was published in 1886 (when Dunning was twenty-nine years of age), and they were collected in volume form in 1897. A revised edition in 1904 substituted a new concluding essay printed in 1901, and it is this edition which is now reprinted. The Dunning *Essays* occupy a historiographical position somewhat different from Stampp's *Era of Reconstruction,* in that Stampp's volume is a summary of a transformation of ideas which has already taken place among the specialists, a summary based primarily on the findings of scholars other than himself. By contrast, Dunning's essays were among the earliest scholarly expressions of ideas which were later to become widely accepted among historians, and were to become widely accepted in considerable measure through the writing and teaching of Dunning himself. But, despite that difference, it seems accurate to consider Dunning's views as broadly characteristic of many historians from the 1890's to the 1930's and to consider the ideas of Stampp as representative of the perspectives which came into their own among historians of Reconstruction in the 1950's and 1960's.

Reconstruction was described by Dunning in the *Essays* as essentially a racial-political revolution which transferred political power from Southern whites to Negroes. He maintained that Negroes during Radical Reconstruction "exercised an influence in political affairs out of all relation to their intelligence or property," and his description of Negroes was not flattering. "... the negroes who rose to prominence and leadership" in Reconstruction, ran one of his summations, "were very frequently of a type which acquired and practiced the tricks and knavery rather than the useful arts of politics, and the vicious courses of these negroes strongly confirmed the prejudices of the whites." In a similarly unflattering vein was Dunning's description of those Southern whites who supported the Radical Reconstruction program, the "scalawags" or "loyalists": "a class which lacked the moral authority to conduct government in the Southern states," individuals who "ran to open disgrace" in "very frequent instances." Any brief and selective summary of an individual's ideas runs the risk of creating an oversimplified and inaccurate impression, and it should be emphasized that Dunning did not express hostility to all aspects of Radical Reconstruction, that he was not an uncritical defender of all Southern "conservative" whites, and that he was not an uncritical defender of the most highly placed opponent of Radical Reconstruction, Andrew Johnson.

Yet, while the qualifications in Dunning's criticism of Radical Reconstruction and its supporters should be noted, his *Essays* make clear his fundamental and pervasive disapproval of what he described as the "seven unwholesome years" of Reconstruction. The disapproval seems to have rested ultimately upon Dunning's conviction that Reconstruction as revolution had produced a racial-political order which was both undesirable and unstable, because it sought "to stand the social pyramid on its apex," to "maintain the freedmen . . . on the necks of their former masters." The racial-political revolution of Reconstruction had been justified by individuals whom Dunning called "the emotionalists" (Garrison, Sumner, Phillips, Chase), whose "abstract theories of equality" and "trite generalities of the Rights of Man" had come to be accepted "in the frenzy of the war time" and "during the prevalence of the abolitionist fever." Fortunately, in Dunning's view, a different group of leaders (Jefferson, Clay, Lincoln) had correctly seen that whites and Negroes were so "distinct in characteristics as to render coalescence impossible . . . ." The ideas of this second group had re-emerged in reaction to Radical Reconstruction, leading to the realization that slavery must be replaced "by some set of conditions which, if more humane and beneficent . . . must in essence express the same fact of racial inequality." The *Essays* close with a striking and altogether remarkable passage, first published in 1901, in which Dunning cites the events associated with the overseas expansion of the United States around the turn of the century as confirmation of the concept of racial inequality and as evidence that there would probably never be further attempts to establish racial equality in this country: "In view of the questions which have been raised by our lately established relations with other races, it seems most improbable that the historian will soon, or ever, have to record a reversal of the conditions [of racial inequality] which . . . [the undoing of Reconstruction] has established."

If Dunning found confirmation for his views of Reconstruction in the events of his own day, so, too, does Professor Stampp, although both the events of Professor Stampp's day and his own views of Reconstruction differ markedly from those of Dunning. The noteworthy passage with which Dunning closed his volume of essays is matched by an equally striking passage with which Professor Stampp concludes his volume: "The Fourteenth and Fifteenth Amendments, which could have been adopted only under the conditions of radical reconstruction, make the blunders of that era, tragic though they were, dwindle into insignificance. For if it was worth four years of civil war to save the Union, it was worth a few years of radical reconstruction to give the American Negro the ultimate promise of equal civil and political rights."

To historians who share the relativistic views expressed in some of Carl Becker's essays, the comparison between Dunning and Stampp could seem a characteristic example, in which the shift in the concerns of Mr. Everyman over a period of sixty or seventy years has now been reflected in the shift in the outlook of historians. The issues of Dunning's day ("questions which have been raised by our lately established relations with other races") provided him with a base perspective, which he accepted as axiomatic and from which he confidently disapproved of Radical Reconstruction, while recognizing some virtues in it. In a similar fashion, the issues of Professor Stampp's day ("the ultimate promise of equal civil and political rights" for the American Negro) provide him a base perspective, which he accepts as axiomatic and from which he confidently praises Radical Reconstruction, while recognizing some tragic blunders in it. The "climate of opinion" of Dunning's day had exalted "stability" and practical recognition of racial inequality as desirable touchstones for evaluating Reconstruction, whereas the climate of opinion of Professor Stampp's day exalts as a desirable touchstone for evaluation the ideal of achieving equality between whites and Negroes—and Professor Stampp portrays sympathetically the "idealism" of the Radical Republicans, which he ascribes to "faith" mostly derived from religion.

But historians who find unconvincing or unappealing "relativism" of the type expressed by Becker can object that the shift in outlook from Dunning to Stampp should be explained, not in terms of changing "climates of opinion," but in terms of the "progress of historical scholarship." The collecting and sifting of evidence by scholars, it can be maintained, has led historians of today to make descriptive statements of fact which differ from those of Dunning and has thus led to evaluations and interpretations different from those of Dunning. Professor Stampp's descriptive statements are, in actuality, based to a considerable extent upon the findings of scholars since Dunning's era, and Stampp's descriptive statements do differ decidedly from those by Dunning. In contrast, for example, to Dunning's description of Negroes in Reconstruction, Stampp states that Negroes did not control any of the Reconstruction governments and that only a handful reached high office. Of the few Negroes who did occupy high offices in the State governments, "Nearly all . . . were men of ability and integrity." While the mass of Southern Negroes, as portrayed in Stampp's pages, were mostly illiterate, yet they "fully appreciated the importance of achieving literacy, and . . . took advantage of the limited educational opportunities offered them with almost pathetic eagerness." With respect to "scalawags," just as with respect to Negroes, Stampp's descriptions differ from Dunning's. The rather unsavory "scalawags" portrayed by Dunning are replaced in Stampp's volume by a complex group of individuals, some of whom were distinguished leaders of the planter class. A brief and selective summary can distort Stampp's views as much as it can Dunning's, and it should be understood that Stampp depicts some

Negroes who were "aggressive," and some Negroes and "scalawags" who were corrupt, although his characterizations as a whole are sympathetic to the two groups.

Whether the changes in outlook from Dunning to Stampp be explained through the "progress of historical scholarship" or through the shifting "climate of opinion" or through some combination of the two factors, it seems likely that Professor Stampp's *Era of Reconstruction* will prove to be an influential statement of the newer views concerning Reconstruction. Its clear, readable, and expert synthesis of the recent scholarship should have appeal for both specialist and nonspecialist readers. Moreover, since the recent scholarship offers intellectual reinforcement and encouragement to opponents of racial discrimination, the volume will speak to the conviction of many individuals in the 1960's.

It is precisely at this point that the example of Dunning raises fundamental and vexing questions. For Dunning also spoke to the convictions of many individuals of his time, and, from the perspective of the newer Reconstruction scholarships, it would seem that he was so wrapped up in the convictions of his time that it affected adversely his scholarship concerning Negroes, "scalawags," and other individuals and topics in Reconstruction. Dunning's presidential address before the American Historical Association in 1913 still stands as a perceptive and understanding discussion of "Truth in History," and, if the Dunning who wrote that address could be misled as scholar by the ideological convictions of his time, warning is served on us all. The warning applies to every one who tries to understand the past, but in this particular case it is specifically relevant to historians who oppose racial discrimination and who are sympathetic to the newer views of Reconstruction—and I include myself in this group. If Dunning would have been a better historian had he cautioned himself that, since he was convinced of racial inequality, he should check with great care those findings about Negroes and "scalawags" which fitted in so neatly with his belief, should not historians today caution themselves that, since they believe in racial equality, they should examine with particular rigor those findings which coincide with their convictions?

My own view is that more systematic and comprehensive research, using quantitative techniques where feasible and relevant to supplement traditional methods, would help historians guard against potential distortions in understanding the past arising from their own ideological convictions. Until such methods are used, those who share Dunning's views can cite Negroes and "scalawags" who were corrupt and incompetent, while those who favor the newer views can cite examples to the contrary—each group using the same technique of "proof by selective quotation," although holding different ideologies. But, whatever the methods used by historians, the example of Dunning stands as reminder that the passage of time and the shifting of beliefs can starkly reveal the extent to which scholarship rests upon durable evidence and the extent to which it rests upon ideological convictions. What will be the verdict of historians fifty years hence concerning the newer views of Reconstruction?

A PRAYER AND AN ANSWER

By mid-1862 Lincoln's apparent unwillingness to make the war for the Union also a war to emancipate the slaves had come under heavy criticism from the more radical elements within the Republican party. While McClellan's army was withdrawing from the Peninsula, Horace Greeley, editor of The New York Daily Tribune *and one of the most influential advocates of emancipation, published an open letter to the President under the arresting caption, "The Prayer of Twenty Millions." Lincoln, who had already determined on an emancipation course, but who was waiting for a military victory to implement it, replied declaring that the Union was the paramount issue, not the freeing of the slaves.*

An Exchange of Letters between Horace Greeley and Abraham Lincoln

August 19, 1862

To Abraham Lincoln,
President of the United States:

Dear Sir: I do not intrude to tell you—for you must know already—that a great proportion of those who triumphed in your election, and of all who desire the unqualified suppression of the rebellion now desolating our country, are sorely disappointed and deeply pained by the policy you seem to be pursuing with regard to the slaves of rebels. I write only to set succinctly and unmistakably before you what we require, what we think we have a right to expect, and of what we complain.

I. We require of you, as the first servant of the Republic, charged especially and preeminently with this duty, that you EXECUTE THE LAWS. . . .

II. We think you are strangely and disastrously remiss in the discharge of your official and imperative duty with regard to the emancipating provisions of the new Confiscation Act. Those provisions were designed to fight Slavery with Liberty. They prescribe that men loyal to the Union, and willing to shed their blood in her behalf, shall no longer be held, with the nation's consent, in bondage to persistent, malignant traitors, who for twenty years have been plotting and for sixteen months have been fighting to divide and destroy our country. Why these traitors should be

The New York Daily Tribune, August 19, 1862.

THE LATEST FROM AMERICA;

Or, the New York "Eye-Duster," to be taken Every Day.

From *Punch*, Vol. XLIII, No. 1098 (July 26, 1862), p. 33.

An English view of Lincoln's press releases.

treated with tenderness by you, to the prejudice of the dearest rights of loyal men, we cannot conceive.

III. We think you are unduly influenced by the councils, the representations, the menaces, of certain fossil politicians hailing from the Border Slave States. Knowing well that the heartily, unconditionally loyal portion of the white citizens of those States do not expect nor desire that Slavery shall be upheld to the prejudice of the Union—(for the truth of which we appeal not only to every Republican residing in those States, but to such eminent loyalists as H. Winter Davis, Parson Brownlow, the Union Central Committee of Baltimore, and to *The Nashville Union*)—we ask you to consider that Slavery is everywhere the inciting cause and sustaining base of treason: the most slaveholding sections of Maryland and Delaware being this day, though under the Union flag, in full sympathy with the rebellion, while the free labor portions of Tennessee and of Texas, though writhing under the bloody heel of treason, are unconquerably loyal to the Union. . . . It seems to us the most obvious truth, that whatever strengthens or fortifies Slavery in the Border States strengthens also treason, and drives home the wedge intended to divide the Union. Had you, from the first, refused to recognize in those States, as here, any other than unconditional loyalty —that which stands for the Union, whatever may become of Slavery— those States would have been, and would be, far more helpful and less troublesome to the defenders of the Union than they have been, or now are.

IV. We think timid counsels in such a crisis calculated to prove perilous, and probably disastrous. It is the duty of a Government so wantonly, wickedly assailed by rebellion as ours has been, to oppose force to force in a definant, dauntless spirit. It cannot afford to temporize with traitors, nor with semi-traitors. It must not bribe them to behave themselves, nor make them fair promises in the hope of disarming their causeless hostility. Representing a brave and high-spirited people, it can afford to forfeit any thing else better than its own self-respect, or their admiring confidence. For our Government even to seek, after war has been made on it, to dispel the affected apprehensions of armed traitors that their cherished privileges may be assailed by it, is to invite insult and encourage hopes of its own downfall. The rush to arms of Ohio, Indiana, Illinois, is the true answer at once to the rebel raids of John Morgan and the traitorous sophistries of Beriah Magoffin.

V. We complain that the Union cause has suffered, and is now suffering immensely, from mistaken deference to rebel Slavery. Had you, sir, in your Inaugural Address, unmistakably given notice that, in case the rebellion already commenced, were persisted in, and your efforts to preserve the Union and enforce the laws should be resisted by armed force, *you would recognize no loyal person as rightfully held in Slavery by a traitor,* we believe the rebellion would therein have received a staggering if not fatal blow. At that moment, according to the returns of the most recent elections, the Unionists were a large majority of the voters of the slave States. But they were composed in good part of the aged, the feeble, the wealthy, the timid—the young, the reckless, the aspiring, the adventurous, had already been largely lured by the gamblers and negro-traders, the politicians by trade and the conspirators by instinct, into the toils of treason. Had you then proclaimed that rebellion would strike the shackles from the slaves of every traitor, the wealthy and the cautious would have been supplied with a powerful inducement to remain loyal. . . .

VI. We complain that the Confiscation Act which you approved is habitually disregarded by your Generals, and that no word of rebuke for them from you has yet reached the public ear. Frémont's Proclamation and Hunter's Order favoring Emancipation were promptly annulled by you; while Halleck's Number Three, forbidding fugitives from slavery to rebels to come within his lines—an order as unmilitary as inhuman, and which received the hearty approbation of every traitor in America—with scores of like tendency, have never provoked even your remonstrance. . . . And finally, we complain that you, Mr. President, elected as a Republican, knowing well what an abomination Slavery is, and how emphatically it is the core and essence of this atrocious rebellion, seem never to interfere with these atrocities, and never give a direction to your military subordinates, which does not appear to have been conceived in the interest of Slavery rather than of Freedom.

VII. On the face of this wide earth, Mr. President, there is not one disinterested, determined, intelligent champion of the Union cause who does not feel that all attempts to put down the rebellion and at the same time uphold its inciting cause are preposterous and futile—that the rebellion, if crushed out to-morrow, would be renewed within a year if Slavery were left in full vigor—that army officers who remain to this day devoted to Slavery can at best be but half-way loyal to the Union—and that every hour of deference to Slavery is an hour of added and deepened peril to the Union. I appeal to the testimony of your ambassadors in Europe. It is freely at your service, not at mine. Ask them to tell you candidly whether the seeming subserviency of your policy to the slaveholding, slavery-upholding interest, is not the perplexity, the despair of statesmen of all parties, and be admonished by the general answer!

VIII. I close as I began with the statement that what an immense majority of the loyal millions of your countrymen require of you is a frank, declared, unqualified, ungrudging execution of the laws of the land, more especially of the Confiscation Act. That act gives freedom to the slaves of rebels coming within our lines, or whom those lines may at any time inclose—we ask you to render it due obedience by publicly requiring all your subordinates to recognize and obey it. The rebels are everywhere using the late anti-negro riots in the North, as they have long used your officer's treatment of negroes in the South, to convince the slaves that they have nothing to hope from a Union success—that we mean in that case to sell them into a bitter bondage to defray the cost of the war. Let them impress this as a truth on the great mass of their ignorant and credulous bondmen, and the Union will never be restored—never. We cannot conquer ten millions of people united in solid phalanx against us, powerfully aided by Northern sympathizers and European allies. We must have scouts, guides, spies, cooks, teamsters, diggers, and choppers from the blacks of the South, whether we allow them to fight for us or not, or we shall be baffled and repelled. As one of the millions who would gladly have avoided this struggle at any sacrifice but that of principle and honor, but who now feel that the triumph of the Union is indispensable not only to the existence of our country but to the well-being of mankind, I entreat you to render a hearty and unequivocal obedience to the law of the land.

Yours,

Horace Greeley

Executive Mansion
Washington, August 22, 1862

To Hon. Horace Greeley:

Dear Sir: I have just read yours of the nineteenth, addressed to myself through the New-York *Tribune*. If there be in it any statements or assumptions of fact which I may know to be erroneous, I do not now and here controvert them. If there be in it any inferences which I may believe to be falsely drawn, I do not now and here argue against them. If there be perceptible in it an impatient and dictatorial tone, I waive it in deference to an old friend, whose heart I have always supposed to be right.

As to the policy I "seem to be pursuing," as you say, I have not meant to leave any one in doubt.

I would save the Union. I would save it the shortest way under the Constitution. The sooner the National authority can be restored, the nearer the Union will be "the Union as it was." If there be those who would not save the Union unless they could at the same time *save* Slavery, I do not agree with them. If there be those who would not save the Union unless they could at the same time *destroy* Slavery, I do not agree with them. My paramount object in this struggle *is* to save the Union, and is *not* either to save or destroy Slavery. If I could save the Union without freeing *any* slave, I would do it; and if I could save it by freeing *all* the slaves, I would do it; and if I could do it by freeing some and leaving others alone, I would also do that. What I do about Slavery and the colored race, I do because I believe it helps to save this Union; and what I forbear, I forbear because I do *not* believe it would help to save the Union. I shall do *less* whenever I shall believe what I am doing hurts the cause, and I shall do *more* whenever I shall believe doing more will help the cause. I shall try to correct errors when shown to be errors; and I shall adopt new views so fast as they shall appear to be true views. I have here stated my purpose according to my view of *official* duty, and I intend no modification of my oft-expressed *personal* wish that all men, everywhere, could be free.

Yours,

A. Lincoln

OURS IS A CASE OF REBELLION

After the bloody Union defeat at Fredericksburg, followed by the Emancipation Proclamation, the Democratic opposition to the war gained in popular support. In May 1863, Clement L. Vallandigham, an Ohio Democratic leader, was arrested for making inflammatory speeches, tried and found guilty by a military court. The Vallandigham arrest aroused Democrats everywhere. In New York state, where they had gained a notable victory at the polls the preceding November, attacks on the Administration were outspoken and bitter. In his reply to Erastus Corning and other leading New York Democrats, Lincoln justifies his position.

ABRAHAM LINCOLN, *Letter to Erastus Corning and Others*

Executive Mansion, June 12, 1863

Gentlemen: Your letter of May 19, inclosing the resolutions of a public meeting held at Albany, New York, on the 16th of the same month, was received several days ago.

The resolutions, as I understand them, are resolvable into two propositions—first, the expression of a purpose to sustain the cause of the Union, to secure peace through victory, and to support the administration in every constitutional and lawful measure to suppress the rebellion; and, secondly,

---

John G. Nicolay and J. Hay, eds., *Complete Works of Abraham Lincoln* (New York: Lamb, 1905), Vol. VIII, p. 298–311, 313–314.

a declaration of censure upon the administration for supposed unconstitutional action, such as the making of military arrests. And from the two propositions a third is deduced, which is that the gentlemen composing the meeting are resolved on doing their part to maintain our common government and country, despite the folly or wickedness, as they may conceive, of any administration. This position is eminently patriotic and as such I thank the meeting and congratulate the nation for it. My own purpose is the same; so that the meeting and myself have a common object, and can have no difference, except in the choice of means or measures for effecting that object.

And here I ought to close this paper, and would close it, if there were no apprehension that more injurious consequences than any merely personal to myself might follow the censures systematically cast upon me for doing what, in my view of duty, I could not forbear. The resolutions promise to support me in every constitutional and lawful measure to suppress the rebellion; and I have not knowingly employed, nor shall knowingly employ, any other. But the meeting, by their resolutions, assert and argue that certain military arrests and proceedings following them, for which I am ultimately responsible are unconstitutional. I think they are not. The resolutions quote from the Constitution the definition of treason, and also the limiting safeguards and guarantees therein provided for the citizen on trials for treason, and on his being held to answer for capital or otherwise infamous crimes, and in criminal prosecutions his right to a speedy and public trial by an impartial jury. They proceed to resolve "that these safeguards of the rights of the citizen against the pretensions of arbitrary power were intended more especially for his protection in times of civil commotion." And, apparently to demonstrate the proposition, the resolutions proceed: "They were secured substantially to the English people after years of protracted civil war, and were adopted into our Constitution at the close of the revolution." Would not the demonstration have been better if it could have been truly said that these safeguards had been adopted and applied during the civil wars and during our revolution, instead of after the one and at the close of the other? I, too, am devotedly for them after civil war and before civil war, and at all times, "except when, in cases of rebellion or invasion, the public safety may require" their suspension. The resolutions proceed to tell us that these safeguards "have stood the test of seventy-six years of trial under our republican system under circumstances which show that while they constitute the foundation of all free government, they are the elements of the enduring stability of the republic." No one denies that they have so stood the test up to the beginning of the present rebellion, if we except a certain occurrence at New Orleans hereafter to be mentioned; nor does any one question that they will stand the same test much longer after the rebellion closes. But these provisions of the Constitution have no application to the case we have in hand, because the arrests complained of were not made for treason—that is, not for the treason defined in the Constitution, and upon the conviction of which the punishment is death—nor yet were they made to hold persons to answer for any capital or otherwise infamous crimes; nor were the proceedings following, in any constitutional or legal sense, "criminal prosecution." The arrests were made on totally different grounds, and the proceedings following accorded with the grounds of the arrests. Let us consider the real case with which we are dealing, and apply to it the parts of the Constitution plainly made for such cases.

Prior to my installation here it had been inculcated that any State had a lawful right to secede from the national Union, and that it would be expedient to exercise the right whenever the devotees of the doctrine should fail to elect a president to their own liking. I was elected contrary to their liking; and accordingly, so far as it was legally possible, they had taken seven States out of the Union, had seized many of the United States forts, and had fired upon the United States flag, all before I was inaugurated, and, of course, before I had done any official act whatever. The rebellion thus begun soon ran into the present civil war; and, in certain respects, it began on very unequal terms between the parties. The insurgents had been preparing for it more than thirty years, while the government had taken no steps to resist them. The former had carefully considered all the means which could be turned to their account. It undoubtedly was a well-pondered reliance with them that in their own unrestricted effort to destroy Union, Constitution and law, all together, the government would, in great degree, be restrained by the same Constitution and law from arresting their progress. Their sympathizers pervaded all departments of the government and nearly all communities of the people. From this material, under cover of "liberty of speech," "liberty of the press," and *"habeas corpus,"* they hoped to keep on foot amongst us a most efficient corps of spies, informers, suppliers and aiders and abettors of their cause in a thousand ways. They knew that in times such as they were inaugurating, by the Constitution itself the *"habeas corpus"* might be suspended; but they also knew they had friends who would make a question as to who was to suspend it; meanwhile their spies and others might remain at large to help on their cause. Or if, as has happened, the Executive should suspend the writ without ruinous waste of time, instances of arresting innocent persons might occur, as are always likely to occur in such cases; and then a clamor could be raised in regard to this, which might be at least of some service to the insurgent cause. It needed no very keen perception to discover this part of the enemy's program, so soon as by open hostilities their machinery was fairly put in motion. Yet thoroughly imbued with a reverence for the guaranteed rights of individuals, I was slow to adopt the strong measures which by degrees I have been forced to regard as being within the exceptions of the Constitution, and as indispensable to the public safety. Nothing is better known to history than that courts of justice are utterly incompetent to such cases. Civil courts are organized chiefly for trials of individuals, or, at most, a few individuals acting in concert—and this in quiet times, and on charges of crimes well defined in the law. Even in times of peace bands of horse-thieves and robbers frequently grow too numerous and powerful for the ordinary courts of justice. But what comparison, in numbers, have such bands ever borne to the insurgent sympathizers even in many of the loyal States? Again, a jury too frequently has at least one member more ready to hang the panel than to hang the traitor. And yet again, he who dissuades one man from volunteering, or induces one soldier to desert, weakens the Union cause as much as he who kills a Union soldier in battle. Yet this dissuasion or inducement may be so conducted as to be no defined crime of which any civil court would take cognizance.

Ours is a case of rebellion—so called by the resolutions before me—in fact, a clear, flagrant, and gigantic case of rebellion; and the provision of the Constitution that "the privilege of the writ of *habeas corpus* shall not be suspended unless when, in cases of rebellion or invasion, the public safety may require it," is the provision which specially applies to our present case. This provision plainly attests the understanding of those who made the Constitution that ordinary courts of justice are inadequate to "cases of rebellion"—attests their purpose that, in such cases, men may be held in custody whom the courts, acting on ordinary rules, would discharge. *Habeas corpus* does not discharge men who are proved to be guilty of defined crime; and its suspension is allowed by the Constitution on purpose that men may be arrested and held who cannot be proved to be guilty of defined crime, "when, in cases of rebellion or invasion, the public safety may require it."

This is precisely our present case—a case of rebellion wherein the public safety does require the suspension. Indeed, arrests by process of courts and arrests in cases of rebellion do not proceed altogether upon the same basis. The former is directed at the small percentage of ordinary and continuous perpetration of crime, while the latter is directed at sudden and extensive uprisings against the government, which, at most, will succeed or fail in no great length of time. In the latter case arrests are made not so much for what has been done, as for what probably would be done. The latter is more for the preventive and less for the vindictive than the former. In such cases the purposes of men are much more easily understood than in cases of ordinary crime. The man who stands by and says nothing when the peril of his government is discussed, cannot be misunderstood. If not hindered, he is sure to help the enemy; much more if he talks ambiguously—talks for his country with "buts," and "ifs" and "ands." Of how little value the constitutional provision I have quoted will be rendered if arrests shall never be made until defined crimes shall have been committed, may be illustrated by a few notable examples: General John C. Breckinridge, General Robert E. Lee, General Joseph E. Johnston, General John B. Magruder, General William B. Preston, General Simon B. Buckner, and Commodore Franklin Buchanan, now occupying the very highest places in the rebel war service, were all within the power of the government since the rebellion began, and were nearly as well known to be traitors then as now. Unquestionably if we had seized and held them, the insurgent cause would be much weaker. But no one of them had then committed any crime defined in the law. Every one of them, if arrested, would have been discharged on *habeas corpus* were the writ allowed to operate. In view of these and similar cases, I think the time not unlikely to come when I shall be blamed for having made too few arrests rather than too many.

By the third resolution the meeting indicate their opinion that military arrests may be constitutional in localities where rebellion actually exists, but that such arrests are unconstitutional in localities where rebellion or insurrection does not actually exist. They insist that such arrests shall not be made "outside of the lines of necessary military occupation and the scenes of insurrection." Inasmuch, however, as the Constitution itself makes no such distinction, I am unable to believe that there is any such constitutional distinction. I concede that the class of arrests complained of can be constitutional only when, in cases of rebellion or invasion, the public safety may require them; and I insist that in such cases they are constitutional wherever the public safety does require them, as well in places to which they may prevent the rebellion extending, as in those where it may be already prevailing; as well where they may restrain mischievous interference with the raising and supplying of armies to suppress the rebellion, as where the rebellion may actually be; as well where they may restrain the enticing men out of the army, as where they would prevent mutiny in the army; equally constitutional at all places where they will conduce to the public safety, as against the dangers of rebellion or invasion. Take the particular case mentioned by the meeting. It is asserted in substance, that Mr. Vallandigham was, by a military commander, seized and tried "for no other reason than words addressed to a public meeting in criticism of the course of the administration, and in condemnation of the military orders of the general." Now, if there be no mistake about this, if this assertion is the truth and the whole truth, if there was no other reason for the arrest, then I concede that the arrest was wrong. But the arrest, as I understand, was made for a very different reason. Mr. Vallandigham avows his hostility to the war on the part of the Union; and his arrest was made because he was laboring, with some effect, to prevent the raising of troops, to encourage desertions from the army, and to leave the rebellion without an adequate military force to suppress it. He was not arrested because he was damaging the political prospects of the administration or the personal interests of the commanding general but because he was damaging the army, upon the existence and vigor of which the life of the nation depends. He was warring upon the military, and this gave the military constitutional jurisdiction to lay hands upon him. If Mr. Vallandigham was not damaging the military power of the country, then his arrest was made on mistake of fact, which I would be glad to correct on reasonably satisfactory evidence.

I understand the meeting whose resolutions I am considering to be in favor of suppressing the rebellion by military force—by armies. Long experience has shown that armies cannot be maintained unless desertion shall be punished by the severe penalty of death. The case requires, and the law and the Constitution sanction, this punishment. Must I shoot a simple-minded soldier boy who deserts, while I must not touch a hair of a wily agitator who induces him to desert? This is none the less injurious when effected by getting a father, or brother, or friend into a public meeting, and there working upon his feelings till he is persuaded to write the soldier boy that he is fighting in a bad cause, for a wicked administration of a contemptible government, too weak to arrest and punish him if he shall desert. I think that, in such a case, to silence the agitator and save the boy is not only constitutional, but withal a great mercy.

If I be wrong on this question of constitutional power, my error lies in believing that certain proceedings are constitutional when, in cases of rebellion or invasion, the public safety requires them, which would not be constitutional when, in absence of rebellion or invasion, the public safety does not require them: in other words, that the Constitution is not in its application in all respects the same in cases of rebellion or invasion involving the public safety, as it is in times of profound peace and public security. The Constitution itself makes the distinction, and I can no more be persuaded that the government can constitutionally take no strong measures in time of rebellion, because it can be shown that the same could not be lawfully taken in time of peace, than I can be persuaded that a particular drug is not good medicine for a sick man because it can be shown to not be good for a well one. Nor am I able to appreciate the danger apprehended by the meeting, that the American people will by means of military arrests during the rebellion lose the right of public discussion, the liberty of speech and the press, the law of evidence, trial by jury, and *habeas corpus* throughout the indefinite peaceful future which I trust lies before them, any more than I am able to believe that a man could contract so strong an appetite for emetics during temporary illness as to persist in feeding upon them during the remainder of his healthful life.

In giving the resolutions that earnest consideration which you request of me, I cannot overlook the fact that the meeting speak as "Democrats." Nor can I, with full respect for their known intelligence, and the fairly presumed deliberation with which they prepared their resolutions, be permitted to suppose that this occurred by accident, or in any way other than that they preferred to designate themselves "Democrats" rather than "American citizens." In this time of national peril I would have preferred to met you upon a level one step higher than any party platform, because I am sure that from such more elevated position we could do better battle for the country we all love than we possibly can from those lower ones where, from the force of habit, the prejudices of the past, and selfish hopes of the future, we are sure to expend much of our ingenuity and strength in finding fault with and aiming blows at each other. But since you have denied me this, I will yet be thankful for the country's sake that not all Democrats have done so. He on whose discretionary judgment Mr. Vallandigham was arrested and tried is a Democrat, having no old party affinity with me, and the judge who rejected the constitutional view expressed in these resolutions, by refusing to discharge Mr. Vallandigham on *habeas corpus*, is a Democrat of better days than these, having received his judicial mantle at the hands of President Jackson. And still more, of all those Democrats who are nobly exposing their lives and shedding their blood on the battle-field, I have learned that many approve the course taken with Mr. Vallandigham, while I have not heard of a single one condemning it. I cannot assert that there are none such. . . .

. . . And yet, let me say that, in my own discretion, I do not know whether I have ordered the arrest of Mr. Vallandigham. While I cannot shift the responsibility from myself, I hold that, as a general rule, the commander in the field is the better judge of the necessity in any particular case. Of course I must practise a general directory and revisory power in the matter.

One of the resolutions expresses the opinion of the meeting that arbitrary arrests will have the effect to divide and distract those who should be untied in suppressing the rebellion and I am specifically called on to discharge Mr. Vallandigham. I regard this as, at least, a fair appeal to me on the expediency of exercising a constitutional power which I think exists. In response to such appeal I have to say, it gave me pain when I learned that Mr. Vallandigham had been arrested (that is, I was pained that there should have seemed to be a necessity for arresting him), and that it will afford me great pleasure to discharge him so soon as I can by any means believe the public safety will not suffer by it.

I further say that, as the war progresses, it appears to me, opinion and action, which were in great confusion at first, take shape and fall into more regular channels, so that the necessity for strong dealing with them gradually decreases. I have every reason to desire that it should cease altogether, and far from the least is my regard for the opinions and wishes of those who, like the meeting at Albany, declare their purpose to sustain the government in every constitutional and lawful measure to suppress the rebellion. Still, I must continue to do so much as may seem to be required by the public safety.

A. Lincoln

A CONGRESSIONAL GAUNTLET

On December 8, 1863, Lincoln announced a tentative plan establishing certain guidelines for the readmission to the Union of the seceded states. Its moderate tone and the fact that it was presented as an executive proclamation alarmed the radicals in Congress. In response, Benjamin Wade, a rough, outspoken senator from Ohio, and Representative Henry Winter Davis, a handsome lawyer from an old Maryland family, drafted and pushed through Congress a bill that imposed more drastic terms for reconstruction. Lincoln employed delaying tactics, so that the bill did not reach his desk until near the end of the session. He then killed it by a pocket veto, but gave his reasons in another Proclamation of July 8, 1864. The document that follows was written by Davis and countersigned by Wade. It threw down the gauntlet—Congress, not the President, had the ultimate authority to decide such a grave political and social question as reconstruction.

The Wade-Davis Manifesto

To the Supporters of the Government:

We have read without surprise, but not without indignation the proclamation of the President of the 8th of July, 1864. The supporters of the administration are responsible to the country for its conduct, and it is their right and duty to check the encroachments of the executive on the authority of Congress, and to require it to confine itself to its proper sphere. . . .

The President did not sign the bill to "guarantee to certain States, whose governments have been usurped, a Republican form of government," passed by the supporters of his Administration in both houses of Congress, after mature deliberation. The bill did not therefore became a law, and it is therefore nothing. The proclamation is neither an approval nor a veto of the bill; it is therefore a document unknown to the laws and Constitution of the United States. So far as it contains an apology for not signing

---

The New York Daily Tribune, August 5, 1864.

the bill, it is a political manifesto against the friends of the government. So far as it proposes to execute the bill, which is not a law, it is a grave executive usurpation. ...

There is ... no reason to suppose the provisions of the bill took the President by surprise. On the contrary, we have reason to believe them to have been so well known that this method of preventing the bill from becoming a law, without the constitutional responsibility of a veto, had been resolved on long before the bill passed the Senate. We are informed by a gentleman entitled to entire confidence, that before the 22nd of June, in New Orleans, it was stated by a member of General Banks's staff, in the presence of other gentlemen in official position, that Senator Doolittle had written a letter to the Department that the House "Reconstruction Bill" would be staved off in the Senate to a period too late in the session to require the President to veto in order to defeat it; and that Mr. Lincoln would retain the bill, if necessary, and thereby defeat it. The experience of Senator Wade in his various efforts to get the bill considered in the Senate was quite in accordance with that plan, and the fate of the bill was accurately predicted by letters received from New Orleans before it had passed the Senate.

Had the proclamation stopped there, it would have been only one other defeat of the will of the people by an executive perversion of the Constitution. But it goes farther. The President says:

> And whereas the said bill contains, among other things, a plan for restoring the States in rebellion to their proper practical relations in the Union, which plan expresses the sense of Congress upon that subject, and which plan it is now thought fit to lay before the people for their consideration—

By what authority of the Constitution? In what forms? The result to be declared by whom? With what effect when ascertained? Is it to be a law by the approval of the people, without the approval of Congress, at the will of the President? Will the President, on his opinion of the popular approval, execute it as law? Or is this merely a device to avoid the serious responsibility of defeating a law on which so many loyal hearts reposed for security? But the reasons now assigned for not approving the bill are full of ominous significance. The President proceeds:

> Now, therefore, I, Abraham Lincoln, President of the United States do proclaim, declare, and make known that, while I am (as I was in December last when by proclamation I propounded a plan for restoration) unprepared, by a formal approval of this bill, to be inflexibly committed to any single plan of restoration—

That is to say, the President is resolved that the people shall not, *by law,* take any securities from the rebel States against a renewal of the rebellion, before restoring their power to govern us. His wisdom and prudence are to be our sufficient guarantees! He farther says:

> And while I am also unprepared to declare that the Free-state constitutions and governments already adopted and installed in Arkansas and Louisiana shall be set aside and held for naught, thereby repelling and discouraging the loyal citizens who have set up the same as to farther effort—

That is to say, the President persists in recognizing those shadows of governments in Arkansas and Louisiana which Congress formally declared should not be recognized; whose representatives and senators were repelled by formal votes of both houses of Congress, and which, it was formally declared, should have no electoral vote for President and Vice-President. They are mere creatures of his will. They can not live a day without his support. They are mere oligarchies imposed on the people by military orders, under the forms of elections, at which generals, provost-marshals, soldiers, and camp followers were the chief actors, assisted by a handful of resident citizens, and urged on to premature action by private letters from the President. In neither Louisiana nor Arkansas, before Banks's defeat, did the United States control half the territory or half the population. In Louisiana, General Banks's proclamation candidly declared, "*The fundamental law of the State is martial law.*" On that foundation of freedom he erected what the President calls "the free Constitution and government of Louisiana . . . ." At the farce called an election, the officers of General Banks returned that 11,346 ballots were cast, but whether any, or by whom, the people of the United States have no legal assurance. But it is probable that 4000 were cast by soldiers, or employees of the United States, military or municipal; but none, according to any law, State or national, and so 7000 ballots represent the State of Louisiana. Such is the free Constitution and government of Louisiana, and like it is that of Arkansas. Nothing but the failure of a military expedition deprived us of a like one in the swamps of Florida; and before the presidential election, like ones may be organized in every rebel State where the United States have a camp.

The President, by preventing this bill from becoming a law, holds the electoral votes of the rebel States at the dictation of his personal ambition. If these votes turn the balance in his favor, is it to be supposed that his competitor, defeated by such means will acquiesce? If the rebel majority assert their supremacy in those States, and send votes which elect an enemy of the government, will we not repel his claims? And is not that civil war for the presidency inaugurated by the voice of rebel States? Seriously impressed with these dangers, Congress, "the proper constitutional authority," formally declared that there are no govenments in the rebel States, and provided for their erection at a proper time. ... The President's proclamation "holds for naught" this judgment, and discards the authority of the Supreme Court, and strides headlong toward the anarchy his proclamation of the 8th of December inaugurated. If electors for President be allowed to be chosen in either of those States, a sinister light will be cast on the motives which induced the President to "hold for naught" the will of Congress rather than his government in Louisiana and Arkansas. . . .

The Supreme Court has formally declared that, under the fourth section of the fourth article of the Constitution requiring the United States to guarantee to every State a republican form of government, "it rests with Congress to decide what government is the established one in a State"; and "when senators and representatives of a State are admitted into the Councils of the Union, the authority of the government under which they are appointed, as well as its republican character, is recognized by the proper constitutional authority, and its decision is binding on every other department of the government, and could not be questioned in a judicial tribunal.". . .

Even the President's proclamation of the 8th of December formally declares that "whether members sent to Congress from any State shall be admitted to seats constitutionally rests exclusively with the respective houses, and not to any extent with the executive." And that is not the less true, because wholly inconsistent with the President's assumption, in that proclamation, of a right to institute and recognize State governments in the rebel States, nor because the President is unable to perceive that his recognition is a nullity if it be not conclusive upon Congress.

Under the Constitution, the right to senators and representatives is inseparable from a State government. If there be a State government, the right is absolute. If there be no State government, there can be no senators or representatives chosen. The two houses of Congress are expressly declared to be the sole judges of their own members. When, therefore, senators and representatives are admitted, the State government under whose authority they were chosen is conclusively established; when they are rejected, its existence is as conclusively rejected and denied. And to this judgment the President is bound to submit.

The President proceeds to express his unwillingness "to declare a constitutional competency in Congress to abolish slavery in States" as another reason for not signing the bill. But the bill nowhere proposes to abolish slavery in States. The bill did provide that all slaves in the rebel States should be manumitted. But as the President had already signed three bills manumitting several classes of slaves in States, it is not conceived possible that he entertained any scruples touching that provision of the bill respecting which he is silent. He has already himself assumed a right, by proclamation, to free much the larger number of slaves in the rebel States, under the authority given him by Congress to use military power to suppress the rebellion; and it is quite inconceivable that the President should think Congress could vest in him a discretion which it could not itself exercise.

It is the more unintelligible from the fact that, except in respect to a small part of Virginia and Louisiana, the bill covered only what the proclamation covered—added a congressional title and judicial remedies by law, to the disputed title under the proclamation and perfected the work the President professed to be so anxious to accomplish. Slavery as an institution can be abolished only by a change of the Constitution of the United States or of the law of the State, and this is the principle of the bill. It required the new Constitution of the State to provide for that prohibition; and the President, in the face of his own proclamation, does not venture to object to insisting on that condition. Nor will the country tolerate its abandonment; yet he defeated the only provision imposing it. But when he describes himself, in spite of this great blow at emancipation, as "sincerely hoping and expecting that a constitutional amendment abolishing slavery throughout the nation may be adopted," we curiously inquire on what his expectation rests, after the vote of the House of Representatives at the recent session, and in the face of the political complexion of more than enough of the States to prevent the possibility of its adoption within any reasonable time, and why he did not indulge his sincere hopes with so large an installment of the blessing as his approval of the bill would have secured?

After this assignment of his reasons for preventing the bill from becoming a law, the President proceeds to declare his purpose to execute it as a law by his plenary dictatorial power. He says:

> Nevertheless, I am fully satisfied with the system for restoration contained in the bill as the very proper plan for the loyal people of any State choosing to adopt it; and that I am, and at all times shall be prepared to give the executive aid and assistance to any such people as soon as the military resistance to the United States shall have been suppressed in any such State, and the people thereof shall have sufficiently returned to their obedience to the Constitution and laws of the United States, in which cases military governors will be appointed, with the directions to proceed according to the bill.

A more studied outrage on the legislative authority of the people has never been perpetrated. Congress passed a bill, the President refused to approve it; and then, by proclamation, puts as much of it in force as he sees fit, and proposes to execute those parts by officers unknown to the laws of the United States and not subject to the confirmation of the Senate. . . . The bill provided for the civil administration of the laws of the State till it should be in a fit temper to govern itself, repealing all laws recognizing slavery, and making all men equal before the law. These beneficent provisions the President has annulled. People will die, and marry, and transfer property, and buy and sell, and to these acts of civil life courts and officers of the law are necessary. Congress legislated for these necessary things, and the President deprives them of the protection of the law. The President's purpose to instruct his military governors to "proceed according to the bill"—a make-shift to calm the disappointment its defeat has occasioned—is not merely a grave usurpation, but a transparent delusion. He can not "proceed according to the bill" after preventing it from becoming a law. Whatever is done will be at his will and pleasure, by persons responsible to no law, and more interested to secure the interests and execute the will of the President than of the people, and the will of Congress is to be "held for naught," unless "the loyal people of the rebel States choose to adopt it . . . ."

But when we come to the guarantees of future peace which Congress meant to exact, the forms as well as the substance of the bill must yield to the President's will that none should be imposed. It was the solemn resolve of Congress to protect the loyal men of the nation against three great dangers: (1) the return to power of the guilty leaders of the rebellion; (2) the continuance of slavery; and (3) the burden of the rebel debt. Congress required assent to those provisions of the Convention of the State and, if refused, it was to be dissolved. The President "holds for naught" that resolve of Congress, because he is unwilling "to be inflexibly committed to any one plan of restoration"; and the people of the United States are not to be allowed to protect themselves unless their enemies agree to it. The order to proceed according to the bill is therefore merely at the will of the rebel States, and they have the option to reject it and accept the proclamation of the 8th of December, and demand the President's recognition. Mark the contrast! The bill requires a majority, the proclamation is satisfied with one tenth; the bill requires one oath, the proclamation another; the bill ascertains votes by registering, the proclamation by guess; the bill extracts adherence to existing territorial limits, the proclamation admits of others; the bill governs the rebel States *by law,* equalizing all before it, the proclamation commits them to the lawless discretion of military governors and provost-marshals; the bill forbids electors for President, the proclamation and defeat of the bill threaten us with civil war for the admission or exclusion of such votes; the bill exacted exclusion of dangerous enemies from power, and the relief of the nation from the rebel debt, and the prohibition of slavery forever, so that the suppression of the rebellion will double our resources to bear or pay the national debt, free the masses from the old domination of the rebel leaders, and eradicate the cause of the war; the proclamation secures neither of these guarantees.

It is silent respecting the rebel debt and the political exclusion of rebel leaders, leaving slavery exactly where it was by law at the outbreak of the rebellion, and adds no guarantees even of the freedom of the slaves the President undertook to manumit. It is summed up in an illegal oath, without a sanction, and therefore void. The oath is to support all proclamations of the President during the rebellion having reference to slaves. Any government is to be accepted at the hands of one tenth of the people not contravening that oath. Now that oath neither secures the abolition of slavery, nor adds any security to the freedom of the slaves whom the President declared free. It does not secure the abolition of slavery, for the proclamation of freedom merely professed to free certain slaves, while it recognized the institution. Every Constitution of the rebel States at the outbreak of the rebellion may be adopted, without the change of a letter, for none of them contravene that proclamation, none of them *establish* slavery.

It adds no security to the freedom of the slaves, for *their* title is the proclamation of freedom. If it be unconstitutional, an oath to support it is void. Whether constitutional or not, the oath is without authority of law, and therefore void. If it be valid, and observed, it exacts no enactment by the State, either in law or Constitution, to add a State guarantee to the proclamation title; and the right of a slave to freedom is an open question before the State courts on the relative authority of the State law and the proclamation. If the oath binds the one tenth who take it, it is not exacted of the other nine tenths who succeed to the control of the State government, so that it is annulled instantly by the act of recognition. . . .

Such are the fruits of this rash and fatal act of the President, a blow at the friends of his administration, at the rights of humanity, and at the principles of republican government.

The President has greatly presumed on the forbearance which the supporters of his administration have so long practiced, in view of the arduous conflict in which we are engaged, and the reckless ferocity of our political opponents.

But he must understand that our support is of a cause, and not of a man; that the authority of Congress is paramount, and must be respected; that the whole body of the Union men of Congress will not submit to be impeached by him of rash and unconstitutional legislation; and if he wishes our support, he must confine himself to his executive duties—to obey and execute—not to make the laws; to suppress by arms armed rebellion, and leave political reorganization to the Congress. . . .

B/Congressional Reconstruction: Design by Committee

INTRODUCTION

Northern political leaders had done little to plan for peace. By common consent, slavery would be ended. Beyond that, the President and Congress had presented tentative programs, both of which emphasized political readjustment. The government did recognize, however vaguely, the need for refugee relief in the South, and did create the Freedman's Bureau to render assistance. But after moving hesitantly ahead, Washington then drew back. The Bureau was given limited functions, limited tenure (one year after the war's end), and meager resources. As the nation had stumbled into civil war, so it was stumbling into peace. No one, it seems, comprehended the magnitude of the task ahead, nor did anyone understand the complexity of the political, social, and economic questions involved. Over four million landless blacks, and perhaps a half million landless whites, were scattered over the South. The economy of that region was in ruins, its social structure wholly disorganized. Here was a situation that demanded bold, new thinking, the close cooperation of the best minds, North and South. Yet within two years of Appomattox, whatever chance there might have been to restore the nation on equitable terms and to construct a new society in the South had disappeared. Responsibility for failure is difficult to assign. Certainly the new President, Andrew Johnson, must bear a part of the blame, and so must Congress, the political parties, and misguided public opinion—both North and South. In short, Reconstruction was a national disaster which merely postponed critical problems until later generations, problems that still remain unsolved after more than a century.

Andrew Johnson had most of the attributes that make for a strong, competent executive. He was a good administrator, far better than Lincoln. No one doubted his loyalty to the Union, his personal integrity, his courage. As military governor of Tennessee, he had been a pillar of strength to the Union. For his uncompromising stand, he had suffered indignities, hardship, loss of property, and risk of bodily harm. Indeed, Johnson was one of the few authentic civilian war heroes, admired not just by the sturdy mountaineers of his own section, but by Union men everywhere. He was also a highly intelligent man—well read, with a clear, logical mind. All of this he had acquired through his own efforts, for he sprang from the humblest beginnings in the backwoods of North Carolina. These sterling qualities, which had served him so well in Congress and as military governor of his state under the most trying conditions, were to prove his undoing as President. So similar in character and background to his predecessor, he lacked Lincoln's tact and vision. While Lincoln could bend if necessary, Johnson was unyielding when it was a matter of principles as he understood them. An old Jacksonian Democrat, he was inflexibly dedicated to strict construction of the Constitution. "States' rights" was no mere shibboleth; it was intrinsic to his political faith. Within the Federal government, Johnson held tenaciously to a strict separation of powers. Once he had made up his mind that reconstruction was an executive function, nothing would move him. There was to be no conciliation, no compromise. The task, as he saw it, was to organize loyal governments in the South, and to secure the abolition of slavery, along with repudiation of Confederate debts and secession ordinances. The pardoning power would be used liberally once loyalty oaths were taken.

Essentially, this was Lincoln's original plan for reconstruction. But while Lincoln had repeatedly indicated he was open to change as circumstances might dictate, Johnson refused to budge, despite the overwhelming defeat of his program in the congressional elections of 1866. Perhaps even then he might have preserved his leadership, had he recognized that reconstruction was not just a political question, that grave economic and social issue were also involved. But the President should not be made to bear sole responsibility for this narrow view. Most politicians and statesmen of the period can be faulted for their inability to look beyond a political settlement. The mounting quarrel between President Johnson and the Congress was a dramatic affair, and not without great historical significance. The fact remains, however, that for two precious years, the best public men in the North spent their energies and their talents in agonizing debate over legalistic issues, when they might have concentrated their attention more profitably on "binding up the nation's wounds."

Were there any alternatives? Possibly. The Constitution as interpreted by President Johnson was a formidable, but not an impregnable barrier. Distribution of powers between the nation and the states, the very essence of federalism, was the root of the problem. It was difficult to circumvent the Lincoln-Johnson argument that the Constitution prescribed an indissoluble union of the states. If anyone believed otherwise, he would be forced logically to accept secession. But how, the President asked, could

Congress pass legislation when eleven states of the Union were not represented? By this test, all of the legislation passed during the war was unconstitutional. Yet Johnson himself had insisted that the ex-Confederate states approve all laws of the United States (including wartime legislation) as a condition for readmission.

It was evident by early 1866 that whatever practical weaknesses there were in the President's position, he could not be moved. Still, the moderate Republicans hesitated to join with their radical brethren. And when the various factions finally did pass the Civil Rights Act over the President's veto and framed the Fourteenth Amendment, time had already run out for a decisive settlement that might have eased racial and political tensions. During the first year of peace, the defeated South would probably have accepted radical conditions for readmission had the Republican majority in Congress presented a united and militant front against the President. But as each month went by with the continuing deadlock in Washington, southern opinion hardened. Democrats and Republican conservatives in the North also stepped up pressure upon wavering congressional moderates. The great constitutional debate, culminating in the impeachment trial of the President, never did come to grips with basic issues, political or otherwise.

Initially, few radical leaders favored universal manhood suffrage. And the Republican blocs that ruled Congress during the period seemed timid on the subject of clear-cut definitions for the civil rights of the blacks. It was not until 1867 that Congress passed over the President's veto the first of a series of Reconstruction Acts, temporarily enfranchising southern blacks under new, radical state governments. If the Johnson state governments in the South had not outraged northern opinion by passing black codes and foolishly electing many ex-Confederate leaders to Congress, they might well have avoided these harsher conditions that were finally meted out.

The Reconstruction Acts were never meant to be more than temporary measures. Under their provisions, Congress divided the old Confederacy into military districts and delegated civil authority to army officers who would be responsible for governing the southern states until they met certain political conditions, including approval of the pending 14th Amendment to the Constitution. This amendment and the 15th Amendment, which attempted to guarantee Negro suffrage, were the cornerstones of the reconstruction program. But analysis of both amendments suggests that they were general in scope, and sufficiently ambiguous in language to permit wide latitude of interpretation.

Some historians have described the period of military and radical Republican rule over the South as an "Age of Hate," an era of corruption, during which northern "carpetbaggers" and their southern collaborators—black and white—sought personal plunder and political gain at the expense of a stricken people. Others have seen in it a partisan plot to use the newly enfranchised Negro voters as pawns for perpetuating the ascendancy of the Republican party. Still others have suggested that the major thrust of reconstruction was a kind of economic imperialism—the South to be kept in a colonial status, while the North completed its industrial revolution.

More recently, some thoughtful historians have attacked all of these notions. They have insisted that military rule was of brief duration—mild, rather than harsh or vindictive. The "carpetbag" governments of the southern states, they have asserted, were no more corrupt than their counterparts in the North, and they accomplished many important reforms, overlooked by earlier scholars. Far from subjecting the South to a colonial dependency, northern businessmen were anxious to cooperate with southern community leaders for mutual benefits. Such new viewpoints are well taken. Buttressed by careful research, they have contributed significantly to a more balanced view of reconstruction history. Yet one may also argue that national policy, the determining factor, was more often vacillating and inept than imaginative and wise. The fate of the 14th and 15th Amendments to the Constitution is a case in point.

After 1876, when southern whites recaptured control over their state governments, they experienced little difficulty in circumventing the suffrage provisions and other key provisions of both amendments. One distinguished historian has suggested in a recent paper that the amendments were purposely left ambiguous due to fears of a massive black migration into the white North. Whatever the merits of his thesis, the political program of radical reconstruction, which consumed so much time and effort and rhetoric, became essentially a dead letter in less than a decade.

Congressional reconstruction failed even more conspicuously in coping with the economic and social problems of the South after the war. Education, of prime importance for harmonious race relations, was never seriously undertaken by the Federal government, though presumably it had the opportunity, and certainly the resources. Of the 20-odd million dollars appropriated over six years for the reconstituted Freedman's Bureau, only five percent was spent for educational purposes. It was assumed that the southern states would shoulder the burden. The radicals, when they dominated the southern state governments, did what they could with slender resources. Understandably, the results were not impressive. For the year 1868 the Bureau reported that about 250,000 black children and adults were receiving instruction—a bare six percent of the 4,000,000 freedmen. Significantly, that arch radical Thaddeus Stevens was

Chairman of the House Appropriations Committee until his death in 1868. He never suggested any major addition to the Bureau's skimpy budget and never took notice of the pitiful sums earmarked for schools and training. No money was set aside for teaching. Only superintendents received salaries, which amounted to a total of about $23,000 annually for the entire South. While the radicals and the President were engaged in debating Constitutional points, the Negroes were being implored by northern men of goodwill to raise themselves up by their own bootstraps—an exercise in futility, however well-meant. A few Republican leaders urged a complete system of public education, to be funded by the Federal government, for both races in the South. When the Senate refused to accept such a policy, the emotional Charles Sumner left the Senate chamber in tears.

Congress also had a chance to inaugurate sweeping land reform in the South without resorting to widespread confiscation of private property. There were sufficient state-owned and abandoned lands in the former Confederacy to provide every landless head of family with not just 40 acres, but with the 160-acre allotment provided for settlers by the Homestead Act of 1862. Only Thaddeus Stevens presented a land-reform plan, which was conservative enough by modern standards. His colleagues gave it short shrift.

What, then, was needed to make radical reconstruction a landmark in social and economic reform? Larger Federal appropriations and more private capital (a kind of Marshall Plan for the devastated region) would have cured many of the ills that plagued the South for generations. Land reform would have given the poor blacks and the poor whites a stake in the southern economy; and if combined with education and training, it would have had at least a fair chance of creating a more stable society. The scalawags and carpetbaggers did a more creditable job than generally supposed; but this point is too much belabored by some modern historians. If anything, there should have been more and better qualified scalawags, more and better qualified carpetbaggers. A vigorous, farsighted program of reconstruction could have provided the leadership and the resources to attract the best talents from North and South. Less reliance on an impoverished and defeated South and more assistance from the rich and victorious North would have been, in the long run, of inestimable benefit to the entire nation.

Was any such program possible in 1868? The answer would have to be "no." Northern capitalists, heavy with war profits, were looking West, not South. The three-billion-dollar war debt was a frightening specter to political leaders and businessmen, who demanded retrenchment, an end to inflation, and a balanced budget. Land reform, initiated and directed by the Federal government, would threaten property rights. Potentially, it might thwart the designs of politically powerful land speculators and railroad developers who were busy seeking loopholes in the homestead legislation. Northerners tended to consider the racial question a southern problem, to be solved by the blacks themselves through the ballot box. Civil rights did not mean social equality in any sense. As that realistic contemporary observer John W. DeForest wrote prophetically in 1868, "not for generations will respectable whites of the South, any more than those of the North, accept Negroes as their social equals."

THE FREEDMEN SPEAK

About one month after the fall of Savannah, Secretary of War Edwin M. Stanton visited the city to confer with General William T. Sherman. In the course of his visit, he interviewed a group of Negro ministers to gather information on the black population. Only five of the 20 were born free; the rest had been slaves, though four had either purchased their freedom or had been willed it by former masters. Their spokesman made two significant points. He expressed the desire of the freedmen to farm their own land. He also stated that they would rather live among themselves and not be scattered among the white population. "For," said he, "there is a prejudice against us in the South that will take years to get over."

A Conversation between Edwin M. Stanton, Lincoln's Secretary of War, and a Group of Negro Ministers

On the evening of Thursday, the 12th day of January, 1865, the following persons of African descent met, by appointment, to hold an interview with Edwin M. Stanton, Secretary of War, and Major-General Sherman, to have a conference upon matters relating to the freedmen of the State of Georgia, to wit:

1. *William J. Campbell,* aged fifty-one years, born in Savannah; slave until 1849, and then liberated by will of his mistress, Mrs. Mary Maxwell; for ten years pastor of the First Baptist Church of Savannah, numbering about eighteen hundred members; average congregation nineteen hundred; the church property belonging to the congregation (trustees white) worth eighteen thousand dollars.

2. *John Cox,* aged fifty-eight years, born in Savannah; slave until 1849, when he bought his freedom for eleven hundred dollars; pastor of the Second African Baptist Church; in the ministry fifteen years; congregation twelve hundred and twenty-two persons; church property worth ten thousand dollars, belonging to the congregation.

The Journal of Negro History, XVI, No. 1 (January 1931), pp. 88–94. Reprinted by permission of the publisher.

3. *Ulysses L. Houston,* aged forty-one years, born in Grahamsville, South Carolina; slave "until the Union army entered Savannah"; owned by Moses Henderson, Savannah; and pastor of Third African Baptist Church, congregation numbering four hundred; church property worth five thousand dollars, belongs to congregation; in the ministry about eight years.

4. *William Bentley,* aged seventy-two years, born in Savannah; slave until twenty-five years of age, when his master, John Waters, emancipated him by will; pastor of Andrew's Chapel, Methodist Episcopal Church (only one of that denomination in Savannah), congregation numbering three hundred and sixty members; church property worth about twenty thousand dollars, and is owned by the congregation; been in the ministry about twenty years; a member of Georgia Conference.

5. *Charles Bradwell,* aged forty years, born in Liberty County, Georgia; slave until 1851; emancipated by will of his master, J. L. Bradwell; local preacher, in charge of the Methodist Episcopal congregation (Andrew's Chapel) in the absence of the minister; in the ministry ten years.

6. *William Gaines,* aged forty-one years, born in Wills County, Georgia; slave "until the Union forces freed me"; owned by Robert Toombs, formerly United States Senator, and his brother, Gabriel Toombs; local preacher of the Methodist Episcopal Church (Andrew's Chapel); in the ministry sixteen years.

7. *James Hill,* aged fifty-two years, born in Bryan County, Georgia; slave "up to the time the Union army come in"; owned by H. F. Willings, of Savannah; in the ministry sixteen years.

8. *Glasgow Taylor,* aged seventy-two years, born in Wilkes County, Georgia; slave "until the Union army come"; owned by A. P. Wetter; is a local preacher of the Methodist Episcopal Church (Andrew's Chapel); in the ministry thirty-five years.

9. *Garrison Frazier,* aged sixty-seven years, born in Granville County, North Carolina; slave until eight years ago, when he bought himself and wife, paying one thousand dollars in gold and silver; is an ordained minister in the Baptist Church, but, his health failing, has now charge of no congregation; has been in the ministry thirty-five years.

10. *James Mills,* aged fifty-six years, born in Savannah; free-born, and is a licensed preacher of the First Baptist Church; has been eight years in the ministry.

11. *Abraham Burke,* aged forty-eight years, born in Bryan County, Georgia; slave until twenty years ago, when he bought himself for eight hundred dollars; has been in the ministry about ten years.

12. *Arthur Wardell,* aged forty-four years, born in Liberty County, Georgia; slave until "freed by the Union army"; owned by A. A. Solomons,

Savannah, and is a licensed minister in the Baptist Church; has been in the ministry six years.

13. *Alexander Harris,* aged forty-seven years, born in Savannah; free-born; licensed minister of Third African Baptist Church; licensed about one month ago.

14. *Andrew Neal,* aged sixty-one years, born in Savannah; slave "until the Union army liberated me"; owned by Mr. William Gibbons; and has been deacon in the Third Baptist Church for ten years.

15. *James Porter,* aged thirty-nine years, born in Charleston, South Carolina; free-born, his mother having purchased her freedom; is lay-reader and president of the board of wardens and vestry of St. Stephen's Protestant Episcopal Colored Church in Savannah; has been in communion nine years; the congregation numbers about two hundred persons; the church property is worth about ten thousand dollars, and is owned by the congregation.

16. *Adolphus Delmotte,* aged twenty-eight years, born in Savannah; free-born; is a licensed minister of the Missionary Baptist Church of Milledgeville, congregation numbering about three or four hundred persons; has been in the ministry about two years.

17. *Jacob Godfrey,* aged fifty-seven years, born in Marion, South Carolina; slave "until the Union army freed me"; owned by James E. Godfrey, Methodist preacher, now in the rebel army; is a class-leader, and steward of Andrew's Chapel since 1836.

18. *John Johnson,* aged fifty-one years, born in Bryan County, Georgia; slave "up to the time the Union army came here"; owned by W. W. Lincoln, of Savannah; a class-leader, and treasurer of Andrew's Chapel for sixteen years.

19. *Robert N. Taylor,* aged fifty-one years, born in Wilkes County, Georgia; slave "to the time the Union army come"; was owned by Augustus P. Wetter, Savannah, and is class-leader in Andrew's Chapel—for nine years.

20. *James Lynch,* aged twenty-six years, born in Baltimore, Maryland; free-born; is presiding elder of the Methodist Episcopal Church, and missionary to the Department of the South; has been seven years in the ministry, and two years in the South.

Garrison Frazier being chosen by the persons present to express their common sentiments upon the matters of inquiry, makes answers to inquiries as follows:

1. State what your understanding is in regard to the acts of Congress, and President Lincoln's proclamation, touching the condition of the colored people in the rebel States.

Answer. So far as I understand President Lincoln's proclamation to the rebellious States, it is, that if they would lay down their arms and submit to the laws of the United States before the 1st of January, 1863, all should be well; but if they did not, then all the slaves in the rebel States should be free, henceforth and forever: that is what I understood.

2. State what you understand by slavery, and the freedom that was to be given by the President's Proclamation.

Answer. Slavery is receiving by irresistible power the work of another man, and not by his consent. The freedom, as I understand it, promised by the proclamation, is taking us from under the yoke of bondage and placing us where we could reap the fruit of our own labor, and take care of ourselves, and assist the Government in maintaining our freedom.

3. State in what manner you think you can take care of yourselves, and how can you best assist the Government in maintaining your freedom.

Answer. The way we can best take care of ourselves is to have land, and turn in and till it by our labor—that is, by the labor of the women, and children, and old men—and we can soon maintain ourselves and have something to spare; and to assist the Government, the young men should enlist in the service of the Government, and serve in such manner as they may be wanted (the rebels told us that they piled them up and made batteries of them, and sold them to Cuba, but we don't believe that). We want to be placed on land until we are able to buy it and make it our own.

4. State in what manner you would rather live, whether scattered among the whites, or in colonies by yourselves.

Answer. I would prefer to live by ourselves, for there is a prejudice against us in the South that will take years to get over; but I do not know that I can answer for my brethren.

[*Mr. Lynch* says he thinks they should not be separated, but live together. All the other persons present being questioned, one by one, answer that they agree with "brother *Frazier*."]

5. Do you think that there is intelligence enough among the slaves of the South to maintain themselves under the Government of the United States, and the equal protection of its laws, and maintain good and peaceable relations among yourselves and with your neighbors?

Answer. I think there is sufficient intelligence among us to do so.

6. State what is the feeling of the black population of the South toward the Government of the United States; what is the understanding in respect to the present war, its causes and object, and their disposition to aid either side; state fully your views.

Answer. I think you will find there is thousands that are willing to make any sacrifice to assist the Government of the United States, while there is also many that are not willing to take up arms. I do not suppose there is a dozen men that is opposed to the Government. I understand as to the war that the South is the aggressor. President Lincoln was elected President by a majority of the United States, which guaranteed him the right of holding the office and exercising that right over the whole United States. The South, without knowing what he would do, rebelled. The war was commenced by the rebels before he came into the office. The object of the war was not, at first, to give the slaves their freedom, but the sole object of the war was, at first to bring the rebellious States back into the Union, and their loyalty to the laws of the United States. Afterwards, knowing the value that was set on the slaves by the rebels, the President thought that his proclamation would stimulate them to lay down their arms, reduce them to obedience, and help to bring back the rebel States; and their not doing so has now made the freedom of the slaves a part of the war. It is my opinion that there is not a man in this city that could be started to help the rebels one inch, for that would be suicide. There was two black men left with the rebels, because they had taken an active part for the rebels, and thought something might befall them if they staid behind, but there is not another man. If the prayers that have gone up for the Union army could be read out, you would not get through them these two weeks.

7. State whether the sentiments you now express are those only of the colored people in the city, or do they extend to the colored population through the country, and what are your means of knowing the sentiments of those living in the country?

Answer. I think the sentiments are the same among the colored people of the State. My opinion is formed by personal communication in the course of my ministry, and also from the thousands that followed the Union army, leaving their homes and undergoing suffering. I did not think there would be so many; the number surpassed my expectation.

8. If the rebel leaders were to arm the slaves, what would be its effect?

Answer. I think they would fight as long as they were before the bayonet, and just as soon as they could get away they would desert . . . .

9. What, in your opinion, is the feeling of the colored people about enlisting and serving as soldiers of the United States, and what kind of military service do they prefer?

Answer. A large number have gone as soldiers to Port Royal to be drilled and put in the service, and I think there is thousands of the young men that will enlist; there is something about them that, perhaps, is wrong; they have suffered so long from the rebels, that they want to meet and have a chance with them in the field. Some of them want to shoulder the musket, others want to go into the quartermaster or the commissary's service.

10. Do you understand the mode of enlistment of colored persons in the rebel States, by State agents, under the act of Congress; if yea, state what your understanding is?

Answer. My understanding is that colored persons enlisted by State agents are enlisted as substitutes, and give credit to the States, and do not swell the army, because every black man enlisted by a State agent leaves a white man at home; and, also, that larger bounties are given or promised by the State agents than are given by the States. The great object should be to push through this rebellion the shortest way, and there seems to be something wanting in the enlistment by State agents, for it don't strengthen the army, but takes one away for every colored man enlisted.

11. State what in your opinion is the best way to enlist colored men for soldiers.

Answer. I think, sir, that all compulsory operations should be put a stop to. The ministers would talk to them, and the young men would enlist. It is my opinion that it would be far better for the State agents to stay at home, and the enlistments to be made for the United States under the direction of General Sherman.

In the absence of General Sherman, the following question was asked:

12. State what is the feeling of the colored people in regard to General Sherman, and how far do they regard his sentiments and actions as friendly to their rights and interests, or otherwise?

Answer. We looked upon General Sherman, prior to his arrival, as a man, in the providence of God, specially set apart to accomplish this work, and we unanimously felt inexpressible gratitude to him, looking upon him as a man that should be honored for the faithful performance of his duty. Some of us called upon him immediately upon his arrival, and it is probable he did not meet the Secretary with more courtesy than he met us. His conduct and deportment towards us characterized him as a friend and a gentleman. We have confidence in General Sherman, and think that what concerns us could not be under better hands. This is our opinion now from the short acquaintance and intercourse we have had.

[Mr. *Lynch* states that, with his limited acquaintance with General Sherman, he is unwilling to express an opinion. All others present declare their agreement with Mr. *Frazier* about General Sherman.]

Some conversation upon general subjects relating to General Sherman's march then ensued, of which no note was taken.

THE PRESIDENT A NULLITY

John Bigelow, former coeditor with William Cullen Bryant of The New York Evening Post, *had gained a nationwide reputation as a vigorous opponent of slavery and an advocate of free trade. In 1861 he was appointed Consul-General at Paris; then he became Minister to France (1865–1866). Bigelow returned to the United States in early 1867. Absent from the country during the heated partisanship of the wartime period, he was able to view events in Washington during the Johnson administration with considerable objectivity. But it must be remembered that Seward was his close friend and that Bigelow tended to be influenced by the Secretary's moderate position. In his journal and in his illuminating letters to friends, Bigelow describes a situation that resembles in many ways the red scare after World War I and the Joseph McCarthy frenzy after World War II.*

JOHN BIGELOW, *Retrospections of an Active Life*

EXCERPT FROM BIGELOW'S JOURNAL

In the evening I dined again with Seward; Barthelmy, the most recent ambassador from France, his only other guest. ... Mr. Seward uttered an opinion than which nothing could better illustrate the temperamental difference which distinguished Seward from Lincoln. To my remark that Johnson did not know how to be a President, he said Johnson knew a great deal better than Lincoln; that Lincoln succumbed under disaster, but at other times was too indifferent; that he let things go so long as they did not trouble him. Johnson on the other hand let nothing escape. "He reads and examines everything, is a prodigious worker, has the constitution of an ox, and is generally very cheerful, though to-day very much oppressed with the weight of important measures before him involving the future of the country." Seward thought he was not sick and that there was no danger of his health giving way.

These remarks justify a suspicion that Lincoln had more faith in the wisdom and fatherly love of his Creator than Seward; while Seward,

---

John Bigelow, *Retrospections of an Active Life* (New York: Doubleday, Page, 1913), Vol. IV, pp. 43–45, 48, 49, 156–158.

though not altogether lacking faith in either, not infrequently at a pinch was wont to have a little more faith in himself.

He also told me that after I had left the President in the morning, Chase came in. Johnson's patience at his interruptions was exhausted. As he passed Seward to receive Chase, he said in the way of exclamation, but so that Seward only should hear him, "Christ!" Chase, bland as a summer's morning with his little day's work finished, said that he had called to ask a personal favor. He wanted the appointment of a couple of paymasters. After he had gone out Seward said to Stanton, "Sir, you cannot accuse me of ever passing by you and asking the President for an appointment of any kind."...

On the 2d of March the President sent to the Senate two vetoes, perhaps the most important that any President of the United States has up to the present day ever signed. One was the Reconstruction Act, which divided the ten Southern States into five military districts under military governors. The seceded states were to be restored to their places in the Union whenever a convention of delegates elected by the male citizens of whatever race or color, except those disfranchised for participation in the rebellion, should frame a constitution; provided that this constitution, being ratified by the people and approved by Congress, should be put into operation, and the legislature thereby elected should adopt the Fourteenth Amendment of the Constitution of the United States.

The other was the Tenure-of-Office act, designed to frustrate President Johnson in any attempt to carry out the policies of his administration, providing that the consent of the Senate should be necessary to the dismissal of any officer who had been appointed by and with the consent of that body.

Seward and Stanton drafted the President's Veto Message for the Tenure-of-Office act, and Jeremiah Black of Pennsylvania was presumed to have assisted in preparing the other veto.

On the day those vetoes were received I visited the Senate again while the Tenure-of-Office bill was being read. No one but Ira Harris of Albany pretended to listen. Senator Nye of Nevada called my attention to the utter contempt with which anything coming from the White House was treated there. "He is of no account," he said, "we pay no attention any more to what he says." No more they did. I asked Sumner if they were not going to confirm Dix as minister to France. "Perhaps with the Democrats he will get a majority," was the reply, "but I am opposed to it. Congress should require friends in foreign as well as in domestic places; the same loyalty to it that was due to the President, *when we had one. The present incumbent is a nullity and will be treated as such.*" I was so shocked by this kind of talk that I began to doubt whether the Constitution was in safer hands now than it had been when the South was in the saddle. ...

LETTER TO W. H. HUNTINGTON *

New York, March 6, 1867

. . . I returned from Washington on the 2d instant. The President was raining vetoes, which rolled off of Congress like water off a duck's back. There was but one senator who listened to a word of his veto of the Tenure of Office bill, and that was Harris of New York, who wishes a mission or a judgeship or an old pair of pantaloons or something. I never saw Seward looking better nor heard him talk better. His wound has left a great scar upon his face without having seriously deformed its expression. His mind is clear, and he is the only man in Washington who appeared cool and deliberate. Any word of moderation there is a ground of suspicion. To require proof of the most malignant and improbable rumor is attributed to political unsoundness. Seward says it is as much as he can do to escape being tried with Surratt for conniving at the attempt upon his own life. They don't cut throats any longer here, but the work they make of characters is something only paralleled in the declining days of the Girondists. The opposition take the ground that we have no President properly speaking, that the incumbent must be considered & treated as a nullity, and that Congress, therefore, is bound to engross all the executive functions it can lay its hands on. It is acting accordingly. The President has no longer power to remove one of his cabinet. Sumner gave me as a reason for voting against the confirmation of Dix, the necessity of requiring abroad the same loyalty to Congress now that was "due to the President when we had one." In other words, he would unite the legislative & executive power in the same hands.

. . . Oh what a way we have of doing things and of being done! As for my own part, I scarcely know how to behave here. I am not excited enough to share the passions of either side, and yet I find it very difficult to follow the quiet course which my taste & judgment dictate . . . . I have been tempted with offers to return to journalism by people who try to persuade me that I may do so much good by talking a few sober words to the drunken crowd. But I do not flatter myself, nor do I mean to be flattered, out of my independence. This political fermentation is natural, inevitable, & purifying, and useful. It will work out its office without me & I mean that it shall have all the credit of it.

No President was ever so powerless as Johnson is. Even the *Moderados* are afraid to be seen with him.

LETTER TO WILLIAM HARGREAVES †

Washington, Feb. 26, 1868

My dear Friend: I presume you and your friends feel some solicitude about our affairs, and that a letter from our seat of government, where

* A Connecticut-born philanthropist, then residing in France.

† Hargreaves was an English liberal and writer on political affairs.

I have been spending a couple of weeks, will be more than usually welcome. The first question you would ask if I were by your side would be—will the President be convicted and deposed. My impression is that if he exhibits ordinary tact and discretion for the future, which is a great deal more, I am sorry to say, than he has done in the past, he will not be convicted. I base this opinion upon reasons quite independent of his guilt or innocence. He would be convicted to-morrow by the Senate & the country would sustain them probably for the present at least, if that were the end of it. But the moment it is proposed to remove him, the question of the succession looms into view; and many who would be glad to have Johnson put out of the way shrink from the consequences of giving the control of the Executive department of the Government to Benj. Wade, the President of the Senate & ex-officio successor to the vacancy. He is a man of an intemperate character; he says our greenbacks are the best currency in the world, and advocates the addition of 100,000,000 to the present stock at once; and last year made a speech in the west in which he was understood to recommend a redistribution of property occasionally by law. These matters will soon be brought to public attention and their effect will not be favorable to him. Besides which, his elevation would interfere with the aspirations of other Presidential candidates or with the influence of such candidates upon the succeeding administration. Already these jealousies begin to develop. Then again the success of the prosecution will depend to some extent upon the promptitude with which it is accomplished; and that will depend in a great degree upon Chief Justice Chase, who you know is the candidate for the Presidency, of the same wing of the Republican party as Senator Wade. Mr. Chase, like Wade, comes from Ohio, the same State that has just voted to replace Wade in the Senate with a Democrat, but who does not take his seat until next March a year. Chase will feel no particular interest in helping to give the control of the Republican party to another man from his own State who also aspires to the Presidency. Neither will he feel a particular pleasure in assisting to bring the impeachment to a successful issue, which would result in making Wade President and Grant his successor, when, by letting it fail, both those gentlemen would be in great danger of having their respective noses put sadly out of joint. The part which both Wade and Grant have taken, and more especially the part which they will have to take in the contest now pending between Congress and the President, renders the success of the impeachment of vital importance to them politically.

And then again Chase will be placed in an awkward position if he accepts the responsibility of trying the President. He could never be brought to try Jefferson Davis, who was indicted for inciting a rebellion, but he makes no opposition to presiding at the trial of a man who helped to put that rebellion down. If the crisis should terminate in striking all three from the list of possible candidates for the Presidency, I should not be much surprised.

The trial cannot be a very short one, however desirable promptitude may be to the partisans of impeachment; for the President will be interested in prolonging it to the utmost, and of course legal questions will bristle at every stage of the proceedings, which cannot be disposed of without discussion. It will be protracted until the Presidential election advances into the foreground and renders the public indifferent about the result, and then, of course, nothing is to be gained by conviction.

You will observe by the steadiness of our markets that the country takes these things coolly. It is not unwilling to have impeachment held *in terrorem* over the President to make sure that he undoes nothing that the war was intended to accomplish and make permanent; beyond that, the people are indifferent.

The President lacks all requisite qualities for a *coup d'état,* and in this respect has disappointed the Democrats. He consulted no one about the recent appointment of Thomas as acting Secretary of War, not even his Cabinet nor any member of it. Consequently no one was prepared in the Senate or House to say a word for him when the announcement was made. And yet all this secrecy went for nothing, because he sent a man to replace Stanton who has neither the sense nor pluck necessary to do it. . . .

LAND REFORM IN THE SOUTH?

Thaddeus Stevens was the only member of Congress who proposed a land reform bill for the benefit of the black population. His speech on the subject shows that at least one radical was willing to come to grips with basic social and economic problems in the South. Stevens' bill was defeated.

THADDEUS STEVENS, *Speech of March 19, 1867*

This bill is important to several classes of people.

It is important to our wounded and maimed soldiers, who are unable to work for their living, and whose present pensions are wholly inadequate to their support. It is important to those bereaved wives and parents

---

Congressional Globe, 40th Congress, 1st Session (Washington: Government Printing Office, 1867), pp. 204–207.

whose habiliments of woe are to be seen in every house, and proclaim the cruel losses which have been inflicted on them by the murderous hands of traitors.

It is important to the loyal men, North and South, who have been plundered and impoverished by rebel raiders and rebel Legislatures.

It is important to four millions of injured, oppressed, and helpless men, whose ancestors for two centuries have been held in bondage and compelled to earn the very property a small portion of which we propose to restore to them, and who are now destitute, helpless, and exposed to want and starvation under the deliberate cruelty of their former masters.

It is also important to the delinquents whose property it takes as a fine —a punishment for the great crime of making war to destroy the Republic, and for prosecuting the war in violation of all the rules of civilized warfare. It is certainly too small a punishment for so deep a crime, and too slight a warning to future ages. ...

... The cause of the war was slavery. We have liberated the slaves. It is our duty to protect them, and provide for them while they are unable to provide for themselves. Have we not a right, in the language of Vattel, "to do ourselves justice respecting the object which has caused the war," by taking lands for homesteads for these "objects" of the war?

Have we not a right, if we chose to go to that extent, to indemnify ourselves for the expenses and damages caused by the war? We might make the property of the enemy pay the $4,000,000,000 which we have expended, as well as the damages inflicted on loyal men by confiscation and invasion, which might reach $1,000,000,000 more. This bill is merciful, asking less than one tenth of our just claims.

We could be further justified in inflicting severe penalties upon this whole hostile people as "a fierce and savage people," as an "obstinate enemy," whom it is a duty to tame and punish. Our future safety requires stern justice. ...

The first section orders the confiscation of all the property belonging to the State governments, and the national government which made war upon us, and which we have conquered. I presume no one is prepared to object to this unless it be those who condemned the conquest. To them I have nothing to say, except to hope that they will continue consistent in their love of the rebels; to show an exuberant humanity into which is merged and submerged all the exalted feelings of patriotism.

The second section requires the President to execute an existing law which he is sworn to execute, but the performance of which oath is in abeyance. Certainly such law should be enforced or repealed; it is a mockery to allow it to stand on your statute-books and be not only not enforced, but violated every day by the executive government.

Courtesy of Prints and Photographs Division, Library of Congress. Photographed by Mathew B. Brady.

Thaddeus Stevens.

The third section furnishes a more convenient and speedy mode of adjudicating such forfeitures, and more consistent with the military conditions of the conquered States.

The fourth section provides first that out of the lands thus confiscated each liberated slave who is a male adult, or the head of a family, shall have assigned to him a homestead of forty acres of land (with $100 to build a dwelling), which shall be held for them by trustees during their pupilage. Let us consider whether this is a just and politic provision.

Whatever may be the fate of the rest of the bill I must earnestly pray that this may not be defeated. On its success, in my judgment, depends not only the happiness and respectability of the colored race, but their very existence. Homesteads to them are far more valuable than the immediate right of suffrage, though both are their due.

Four million persons have just been freed from a condition of dependence, wholly unacquainted with business transactions, kept systematically in ignorance of all their rights and of the common elements of education, without which none of any race are competent to earn an honest living, to guard against the frauds which will always be practiced on the ignorant, or to judge of the most judicious manner of applying their labor. But few of them are mechanics, and none of them skilled manufacturers. They must necessarily, therefore, be the servants and the victims of others unless they are made in some measure independent of their wiser neighbors. The guardianship of the Freedmen's Bureau, that benevolent institution, cannot be expected long to protect them. It encounters the hostility of the old slaveholders, whether in official or private station, because it deprives these dethroned tyrants of the luxury of despotism. In its nature it is not calculated for a permanent institution. Withdraw that protection and leave them a prey to the legislation and treatment of their former masters, and the evidence already furnished shows that they will soon become extinct, or be driven to defend themselves by civil war. Withhold from them all their rights, and leave them destitute of the means of earning a livelihood, the victims of the hatred or cupidity of the rebels whom they helped to conquer, and it seems probable that the war of races might ensue which the President feared would arise from kind treatment and the restoration of their rights. . . .

Make them independent of the old masters so that they may not be compelled to work for them upon unfair terms, which can only be done by giving them a small tract of land to cultivate for themselves, and you remove all this danger. You also elevate the character of the freedman. Nothing is so likely to make a man a good citizen as to make him a freeholder. Nothing will so multiply the productions of the South as to divide it into small farms. Nothing will make men so industrious and moral as to let them feel that they are above want and are the owners of the soil which they till. It will also be of service to the white inhabitants. They will have constantly among them industrious laborers, anxious to work for fair wages. How is it possible for them to cultivate their lands if these people were expelled? If Moses should lead or drive them into exile, or carry out the absurd idea of colonizing them, the South would become a barren waste. . . .

. . . I do not speak of their fidelity and services in this bloody war. I put it on the mere score of lawful earnings. They and their ancestors have toiled, not for years, but for ages, without one farthing of recompense. They have earned for their masters this very land and much more. Will not he who denies them compensation now be accursed, for he is an unjust man? Have we not upon this subject the recorded decision of a Judge who never erred? Four million Jews were held in bondage in Egypt. Their slavery was mild compared with the slavery inflicted by Christians. For of all recorded slavery—Pagan, heathen, or Mohammedan—Christian slavery has been the most cruel and heartless; and of all Christian slavery American slavery has been the worst. . . .

If the war had been between two regular Governments, both of which survived the war, the victor in the treaty of peace would require the vanquished to pay all such damages as well as all the expenses of the war. If neither had conquered the other they would probably be silent, and each bear his own loss. Congress is dictating the terms of peace. If she does not provide for these meritorious claimants she will be bound in honor to pay them out of the national Treasury. If she does not, individuals will be wronged and the nation dishonored. This bill is very merciful toward a cruel, outlawed belligerent, who, when their armies were dispersed, would gladly have compromised if their lives were saved. Those who will be affected by this bill will not exceed seventy thousand out of a population of six million whites, for this is a people of aristocrats and subjects; of a proud nobility and a cringing, poor peasantry. Those seventy thousand persons own about three hundred and ninety million acres of land out of the five hundred millions in the confederate States. This, together with the town property, cannot be worth less than $10,000,000,000. This estimate includes no man's property who was worth less than $10,000; nor does it include any personal property, which may perhaps swell it to $12,000,000,000. The fine proposed would be but one twentieth of their estates. Were ever such great malefactors so gently dealt with? It were well if all their large estates could be subdivided and sold in small tracts. No people will ever be republican in spirit and practice where a few own immense manors and the masses are landless. Small independent landholders are the support and guardians of republican liberty.

FREEDOM AND CIVIL RIGHTS

The 13th, 14th, and 15th Amendments to the Constitution dealt with civil rights and the abolition of slavery. Well before the 14th Amendment had been ratified (it was imposed as a condition for the readmission of former Confederate states), radicals like Thaddeus Stevens and Charles Sumner felt it did not provide adequate safeguards for the civil rights of freedmen. The 15th Amendment was specifically designed to ensure Negro suffrage. Careful examination of both amendments raises at least two questions. Did the framers adopt general language so that the courts would have wide latitude for interpretation? Were the framers delegating to the states responsibility for specific legislation on the subject—property or literacy qualifications, for example?

The 13th, 14th, and 15th Amendments

ARTICLE XIII

Section 1. Neither slavery nor involuntary servitude, except as a punishment for crime whereof the party shall have been duly convicted, shall exist within the United States, or any place subject to their jurisdiction.

Section 2. Congress shall have power to enforce this article by appropriate legislation. [December 18, 1865]

ARTICLE XIV

Section 1. All persons born or naturalized in the United States, and subject to the jurisdiction thereof, are citizens of the United States and of the State wherein they reside. No State shall make or enforce any law which shall abridge the privileges or immunities of citizens of the United States; nor shall any State deprive any person of life, liberty, or property, without due process of law; nor deny to any person within its jurisdiction the equal protection of the laws.

Section 2. Representatives shall be apportioned among the several States according to their respective numbers, counting the whole number of persons in each State, excluding Indians not taxed. But when the right to vote at any election for the choice of electors for President and Vice President of the United States, Representatives in Congress, the Executive Judicial officers of a State, or the members of the Legislature thereof, is denied to any of the male inhabitants of such State, being twenty-one years of age, and citizens of the United States, or in any way abridged, except for participation in rebellion, or other crime, the basis of representation therein shall be reduced in the proportion which the number of such male citizens shall bear to the whole number of male citizens twenty-one years of age in such State.

Section 3. No person shall be a Senator or Representative in Congress, or elector of President and Vice President, or hold any office, civil or military, under the United States, or under any State, who, having previously taken an oath, as a member of Congress, or as an officer of the United States, or as a member of any State legislature, or as an executive or judicial officer of any State, to support the Constitution of the United States, shall have engaged in insurrection or rebellion against the same, or given aid or comfort to the enemies thereof. But Congress may by a vote of two-thirds of each House, remove such disability.

Section 4. The validity of the public debt of the United States, authorized by law, including debts incurred for payment of pensions and bounties for services in suppressing insurrection or rebellion, shall not be questioned. But neither the United States nor any State shall assume or pay any debt or obligation incurred in aid of insurrection or rebellion against the United States, or any claim for the loss or emancipation of any slave; but all such debts, obligations and claims shall be held illegal and void.

Section 5. The Congress shall have power to enforce, by appropriate legislation, the provisions of this article. [July 28, 1868]

ARTICLE XV

Section 1. The right of citizens of the United States to vote shall not be denied or abridged by the United States or by any State on account of race, color, or previous condition of servitude.

Section 2. The Congress shall have power to enforce this article by appropriate legislation. [March 30, 1870]

IMPEACHMENT

The long editorial that John Bigelow composed for The New York Evening Post *is a reasoned argument for the separation of powers, and, in addition, exposes the absurdity of impeaching a President with but ten months left to serve.*

JOHN BIGELOW, *Retrospections of an Active Life*

May 4, 1868

To the Editors of *The New York Evening Post:*

Gentlemen: The whole difficulty with the case for the conviction of the President is the want of proof of that intent which should distinguish a "high crime and misdemeanor" under our constitution from an ordinary statute or common law crime. Such intent has not been established to the satisfaction of the nation. Till it is established, conviction tends rather to convert Johnson into a great martyr than into a great criminal.

If to be an incompetent or perverse or wicked President were sufficient ground for impeachment, it would undoubtedly be the judgment of the country that Johnson should be impeached; but these words would but mildly express the sentiments entertained of some half dozen of our late Presidents by about half the people of the United States. But impeachment is not designed as a remedy for incompetence or perversity in the executive. The ballot box is the constitutional remedy [for that] and there is no other. Short Presidential terms were provided in contemplation of just such blunders as we made in choosing Johnson for Vice-President. If we are to resort to impeachment whenever a majority turns up in Congress opposed to the policy of the executive, why not elect our Presidents like responsible ministers in England, to hold office so long as they enjoy the confidence of the country, or for life?

If our institutions are as wise as we pretend they are, and if the principle of popular government is as sound as I think it is, it is our duty to stand to our bargain, and worry along through the few remaining months of Johnson's term as well as we can. We committed a great mistake and it was not the first of its kind, in choosing a Vice-President who every one

---

John Bigelow, *Retrospections of an Active Life* (New York: Doubleday, Page, 1913), Vol. IV, pp. 170–175.

knew was not fit for the Presidency. There is only one way in which that mistake can be turned to account. The nation must become thoroughly aroused to the inconveniences of such blunders, that it may not repeat them. It has already manifested more solicitude than usual in reference to the choice of its candidates for the Vice-Presidency next fall; but are we sure that we would not be all the wiser for wandering a few months longer in the wilderness? Do the candidates who have been most prominently brought forward for that office indicate that we have learned all that Johnson is capable of teaching us in regard to the proper mode of discharging our electoral duties? We took Johnson as Christians take their wives for better or for worse. He has disappointed us; but shall we better the matter by familiarizing the country with the degradation of its chief magistrate or by replacing him for the few unexpired months of the current Presidential term with a man who has been chosen by no State and is rejected by his own.

Impeachment, like divorce, is not the proper remedy for mere incompatibility of temper. Wherever they shall be tried, the demoralization and corruption of society will inevitably follow. Nor is that all the evil that would follow. . . . Remove Johnson for no better reason than has yet been proved, and the independence of the executive is gone forever. He is no longer what the Constitution designed him to be, a co-ordinate branch of the government. He becomes the mere sheriff or distaff of Congress, which, like the old Continental Congress, will gradually absorb the executive power, without any ability to exercise it to the advantage of the country. The President will become a mere instrument without power for anything but mischief. His study will be to see that he always has a majority of Congress with him, and that, if he is indifferent about the means—as Presidents elected under such a *régime* would be sure to be—he can always have.

The fear of what Johnson may do between this and the 4th of March next is absurd. With the army, with Congress, and with the people almost unanimously, Democrats as well as Republicans indisposed to link their fortunes in any way with his, it seems like pusillanimity to fear anything he can do to the detriment of the Republic. He can make us more ashamed perhaps of what we did five years ago, when we nominated him, but that is no sufficient reason for disturbing him now.

It is reported that many who feel that there is no sufficient case for the deposition of Johnson, insist upon convicting him on the ground that a verdict of "not guilty" would prejudice the Republican party and probably defeat its candidate at the next election. I am free to say that, if I thought the conviction of Johnson necessary to the success of the Republican candidate at the next Presidential election, it would make me seriously distrust my own judgment in the matter; for it would indicate that the mass of the people who voted for Mr. Lincoln desire Mr. Johnson's conviction. Such, however, I do not believe to be the case. There are many, very many Republicans who have heard charges made against Mr. Johnson, for which, if true, they would wish to see him removed, though they would be better pleased—and this I am persuaded is the feeling of the great body of the people—if proofs should not show a case that would demand a resort to the extreme remedy of deposition.

I know something of the sentiment of the country, and I think there would be a general feeling of relief, if the Court of Impeachment should find that the testimony did not warrant them in degrading the executive just as we are entering upon the canvass for his regular successor. I regard the Republican party at the present time as the bulwark of our liberties and as the legitimate repository of the national power. No proper means should be neglected to secure its ascendency for at least another term, but that result is not to be attained by a judgment upon Mr. Johnson that shall not command the approval of the civilized world. Any verdict wanting such approval will be open to suspicions which the Republican party, strong as it is, cannot afford to incur. The judges who are to pronounce President Johnson guilty of high crimes and misdemeanors are to set to work the day after his deposition to distribute the enormous patronage which that proceeding will let loose. They will require a case which has but one side to it, if they wish to come from their task with unspotted hands. Mr. Wade, too, must be many times more or less Mr. Wade than he is, if he can administer the patronage that will then fall into his hands, without rending this party from end to end. The day he takes the oath of office will there not inevitably be two Republican parties?

Again, looking at the approaching election, it is apparent that a change of administration would be fatal to anything like a free and deliberate choice of candidates. No disposition of patronage could be made that would not be assailed with apparent justice, as an illegitimate interference with the freedom of electors. The Republicans would be accused and in great danger of being found guilty, of having deposed the President that they might use the patronage of his office to prolong their power for another term. This would be one of the inevitable issues of the canvass. In due time the Republicans in Congress will experience the fate to which all parties are exposed and go into a minority. Then come reprisals. The Democrats, if they cannot bully the President into their service, which by that time they will probably be able to do, will take a lesson out of the Republican primer and impeach him. Public sentiment will be too much demoralized to rally against such a mode of warfare, and instead of offering resistance, the politicians will be studying the chances of bettering their condition by new combinations.

But why should a failure to remove Johnson enure to the prejudice of the Republican party? My conviction is that it would strengthen it. The country is satisfied that there was enough presumptive evidence floating about to justify its representatives in putting him on trial. It will be relieved to find that the Court on which the duty of trying him is conferred by the Constitution, with all the temptations to find him guilty which beset them as political partisans, had the firmness and uprightness to find

Courtesy of Prints and Photographs Division, Library of Congress. Photographed by Mathew B. Brady.

John Bigelow.

the proofs insufficient—if they are insufficient—to convict him. This would inspire the country with respect for the Court, and for the party to which a majority of its members belong. Can a contrary verdict on the proofs now before the public inspire a corresponding respect? There can be no doubt that it would not.

I have heard it suggested, and as I think, with great force and propriety, that the senators have the power, and will possibly avail themselves of it, to so render their verdict, as to obviate all the partisan objections that have been made to a discharge of Mr. Johnson. Republicans feel that they cannot afford to give the President and the Democrats a triumph, just at this moment especially. Nor are they entitled to any. But what is to prevent the senators, individually or collectively, when he or they rise to give their verdict, reading an opinion in which they shall briefly recite that they find the President has violated the Civil Tenure Act and any other laws, in such and such particulars, specifying them; that he has used his patronage in ways which have tended to delay reconstruction and to encourage disaffection; that he has been wanting in decorum in his intercourse with his cabinet, with Congress, and with the public; that he has presumed to have a policy which he has sought to force upon the acceptance of the country without a proper deference for the opinions of any of the co-ordinate branches of the government specially delegated to represent the wishes of the people; and that he has in other respects acted in an unbecoming and unpresident-like manner, but that they do not find sufficient proof of criminal intent to sustain the charges, etc., and therefore they vote "Not Guilty."

A verdict conceived upon that basis would be sustained by the nation. It would be as great a humiliation as this country can afford at present to inflict upon its chief magistrate. It would leave no leverage for the opposition to operate upon. It would prevent our party from being distracted during the coming canvass by the ten thousand issues that a change of administration would introduce, and by the jealousies and rivalries that would inevitably ensue, whatever disposition should be made of them. It would show that we are not Mexicans, and that we are not degenerating into that fatal undervaluation of authority and law which has kept Spanish America for half a century the prey of revolution. It would show that we had the courage to abide by the consequences of an occasional unwise exercise of the elective franchise, and that we were prepared to profit like wise men, and not like *sans-culottes,* by our mistake. . . .

POOR WHITES, POOR BLACKS

John W. DeForest, of an old New Haven, Connecticut family, a veteran of the war and an officer for the Freedman's Bureau in South Carolina during 1868, was a distinguished writer who excelled in realistic description. Articles like these, which appeared in Harper's *and in* The Atlantic Monthly, *depict the war-torn South as a degraded society.*

JOHN W. DeFOREST, *Drawing Bureau Rations*

Although October, it was beautiful summer-like weather when I commenced my duties in Greenville.

My office, a vaulted room on the ground floor of the old courthouse, was so warm that I had opened both door and window and was sitting in the draught, when my first visitors of the impoverished classes entered.

They were two tall, lank, ungainly women, one twenty-three, the other twenty-seven, dressed in dirty, grayish homespun, with tallow complexions, straight, light, dead hair, broad cheekbones, and singularly narrow foreheads. One of them was made a little more repulsive than the other by a deformed hand.

"Mornin'," they said, sat down, stared at me a while, and then asked, "Anythin' for the lone wimmen?"

" 'Pears like I oughter git, if any one does," added the elder. "My husband was shot by the Rebs because he wouldn' jine their army."

Supposing that they might object to the smell of tobacco, I had laid down my pipe on their entrance. Presently the eldest one inquired,

"Stranger, is your pipe a-smokin'?"

"It is," I replied, wondering at such extreme sensitiveness. "But I can put it out."

"Ef it's a-smokin', I should like a smoke," was her only comment.

I may have cringed at the idea of putting my pipe between those broken teeth, but I of course made haste to do what was hospitable, and I went into the entry before I allowed myself to smile. She smoked tranquilly

---

John W. DeForest, "Drawing Bureau Rations," *Harper's New Monthly Magazine,* XXXVI (April–May, 1868), pp. 791–799.

and passed the luxury to her sister; then they thanked me, "Much obleeged, stranger"—and departed.

Next came a mother and daughter. The mother was forty-three, looking sixty, short and broadly built, haggard, wrinkled, filthy, with desperate gray eyes and unkempt gray hair. The daughter, fifteen years old, with a white, freckled face and yellow hair, had but one garment, a ragged frock of cotton homespun, unbleached, uncolored, and foul with long wearing. Not large enough to meet in front, it was tied with twine in a loose fashion, exposing entirely one of her breasts. This child had in her arms another child, a wretched-looking baby of six weeks old, tied up in an old rag of carpet, her own illegitimate offspring. Her first words were, "How you git'n 'long?" Her next, "Got anythin' for the lone wimmen?"

A few days later, while on my afternoon constitutional in the neighborhood of the village, I was overtaken by another couple, likewise mother and daughter. The former, dresed in coarse white cotton, ghastly, wrinkled, and eager in face, stooping and clumsy in build, slouching forward as she walked, might have been forty-five, but seemed sixty. The daughter, nineteen years old, as I afterward learned, but looking twenty-seven in the precocity of squalor, had a form so tall and straight and shapely that it could not be otherwise than superb in bearing, despite her miserable poverty of life and raiment. Her face too was almost handsome, notwithstanding its broad cheek bones, narrow forehead, and mustang-like wildness of expression. The first words which I heard from this Juno were, "Mam! don't go so fast. Thar's my shoe ontied."

The mother slackened her speed and opened conversation with me.

"Good evenin'. Git'n cold for the season. Goin' to be a mighty hard winter for poor folks."

After some further complaint they pointed out their cabin to me, and I promised to inquire into their circumstances. A little sleet had fallen, the ground had been more than once stiffened by frost, and the long blue ranges visible from Greenville were white with winter before I chanced to fulfill my promise. The cabin consisted of one large room, with a fireplace, two doorways, and two windows. As in all dwellings of the people of this class, the windows were merely square openings, without glass or sashes, and closed by board shutters. The logs of the walls were unhewn, and on two sides the chinking of mud had entirely fallen out, leaving some fifty long slits, averaging two inches in width, through which the wind drove the inclemencies of winter. The moisture which came through these hen-coop sides and through the porous roof drained off through the rotten and shattered floor. No furniture was visible beyond two broken chairs, two or three cooking utensils, and a pile of filthy rags which seemed to be bedding.

The family consisted of the mother, two daughters named Susie and Rachel, a son of about five, and a grandson of two, named Johnnie. No man; the father had died years ago; the husband of Susie had fallen "in one of the first battles." Johnnie, flaxen-headed, smiling with health and content, as dirty as a boy could desire to be, squatted most of the time in the ashes, warming himself by a miserable fire of green sticks. His mother, Susie, sat in a broken chair in one corner of the chimney, her eyes bloodshot and cheeks flushed with fever. When I uttered a word or two of pity—it seemed such a horrible place to be sick in!—a few tears started down her cheeks.

"What makes me sick," she said, "is going bar'foot in the winter. I an't used to't. I had a husband once, and no call to go bar'foot."

"Oh, mam!" she presently groaned, addressing her mother, "this is an awful house!"

When I asked her how old she was she confessed ignorance. To the same question the other girl answered with a sheepish smile, "You are too hard for me."

The mother, after some reflection, gave their ages as nineteen and thirteen; but, looking in their worn faces, it seemed impossible that they could be so young. There was an elder sister "who had married and gone way off"; and she had carried away the family Bible with all their names and ages. Their father "used to think a heap of the family Bible."

The remembrance of departed days—not very fine, it may be, but still better than these—revived the sick girl's sentiment of self-pity. "Oh!" she groaned, "I've been through a power in the last two years."

"He's a powerful bad boy," she said, twisting Johnnie's flaxen curls with a smile and looking kindly into his sunny face. "I don't know how I can keep him. I've been all over the village and can't git no work. I can put him in the poorhouse," she added, after a brief silence of desperation.

As she talked with me she turned her head from time to time to spit out her tobacco juice.

Such is the destitute class of the South, familiar to us by name as the "poor-white trash," but better known in Greenville District as the "low-down people." It is the dull, unlettered, hopeless English farm laborer grown wild, indolent, and nomadic on new land and under the discouraging competition of slavery. The breed, however, is not all Anglo-Saxon. Among the low-down people you will find names of Irish, Scotch, French, and German origin. Whatsoever stock of feeble or untamed moral nature settles in the South descends rapidly into this deposit of idleness and savagery. The Celtic race seems to possess a special alacrity at sinking; and Irish families left on the track of Southern railroads become vagrant poor-whites in a single generation. The class, in short, is composed of that tenth of humanity which the severe law of natural selection is perpetually punishing for the sin of shiftlessness.

It seems probable that once the poor-whites were small farmers. The great planter bought them out and turned them into "trash," just as the Roman patrician turned the plebeians into a populace. When Colonel Gresham sold 27,000 acres to a German colony at Walhalla, South Carolina, he delivered one hundred and fifty titles as proofs of ownership, showing the extraordinary fact that something like one hundred and fifty families, or a population of from six to nine hundred souls, had given place to one large landholder. Thus it seems to have been everywhere throughout the domain of slavery. The men who had few Negroes or none parted with their lots and cabins to those who had many; and, once cut loose, they went altogether adrift. They might have bought other lands in their old neighborhoods, but they did not. In the vigorous language of Sut Lovengood, "they sot in to rovin' round."

Before emancipation the Negro supported nearly all Southerners. His daily labor produced the great staples which seemed to enrich the planter, and mainly enriched the factor, merchant, hotel keeper, lawyer, and doctor. After nightfall he stole the chickens, pigs, and corn which he sold to Bill Simmins and his tribe for whisky, or for some trivial product of a gipsy-like industry. The planter, aware of this contraband traffic, sometimes quarreled with Bill and drove him out of the neighborhood, but more frequently tried to bribe him into honesty by gifts and favors. Moreover, Bill had a vote and must be endured and even coaxed for that reason. On the whole, the Simminses were treated by the land holders much as the old Roman populace were treated by the patricians. They got no gladiatorial shows, but in one way or other they got hog and hominy. It was a life of rare day's works, some begging, some stealing, much small, illicit bargaining, and frequent migrations.

When the "black 'uns went up," or, in more universal English, when the Negroes were transfigured into freedmen, the "low-downers" were about as thoroughly bankrupted as the planters. No more trading with slaves, and no more begging from masters. Not only was there far less than formerly for the Negroes to steal, but they were far less addicted to stealing, having acquired some self-respect with their freedom and finding the jail more disagreeable than the whip. The planter, being reduced to his last crust, had, of course, nothing to spare for the Simminses; and, furthermore, the male low-downer has roved away to a land whence he will never return, not even with his faculty for migration. Conscripted, much against his will, he was sent to the front, did a respectable amount of fighting, deserted, or died. If a morsel of him survives, it will be pretty sure to tell a Yankee what a Union man it was and how opposed it was to the war before it was "fo'ced in."

His death, although no great loss to him nor to his country, was a more serious matter to his family than one would naturally suppose. "Triflin' creetur" as Bill Simmins was, he was better to his wife than no husband, and better to his children than no father. It is a beggarly fate to be a poor widow or orphan, under any circumstances, but to be one of six hundred soldiers' widows or one of eighteen hundred soldiers' orphans, in a region so lean and so sparsely settled as Pickens District, was a cruel excess of poverty which even a pauper in New England might shrink from.

How to deal with this mass of destitution? Even before hostilities closed it had so far exacted public attention that the Confederacy had been forced to feed the families of its dead or unpaid soldiers. The first Monday of the month, generally known in the South as "sale day" on account of its customary public auction, acquired the additional title of "draw day," because it was used for the issue of rations. Thus, when the Union resumed dominion over the revolted states, it found a population already habituated to corn distributions. "Draw day" disappeared under the first shock of conquest; but it revived as soon as our troops went into garrison; in fact, there came a saturnalia of "draw days." To some extent these monstrous public charities were necessary. There were not only the Simminses to be fed, but many families, once wealthy, who had been stripped by the war or the emancipation, and multitudes of old or infirm or juvenile Negroes who had been set adrift from their homes by the same causes. . . .

JOHN W. DeFOREST, *The Man and Brother*

Dialogues similar in nature to the following were quite frequent in the office of the Bureau Major and will give a fair idea of the Negro's domestic affections.

"I wants to know ef I can't hev my little gal," explains a ragged freedwoman of an uncertain age.

"I suppose you can, if you can prove that she is yours and if you have not bound her out as an apprentice."

"I ha'n't bound her out. I let Mr. Jack Bascom, up to Walhalla, have her to stay with him awhile, an' now I wants her back, an' I sont to Mr. Bascom more'n a month ago to fotch her back, an' 'pears like he ain't gwine to fotch her."

John W. DeForest, "The Man and Brother," *The Atlantic Monthly*, XXII (October 1868), pp. 414–425.

"Perhaps she is very well off with Mr. Bascom; I understand that he is a man of property. What do you want her back for?"

"I wants to see her. She's my little gal, an' I has a right to hev her, an' I wants her."

Here a citizen lounging in the office took part in the conversation:

"Look here, aunty, you had better leave your girl with Mr. Bascom; he is a very kind, honorable man. Besides, he made twenty-five hundred bushels of corn this last season, and it stands to reason that she won't suffer there, while you, probably, don't know whether you'll have enough to go upon through the winter. It's going to be a hard winter for poor folks, aunty, and you'd better take as light a load into it as you can."

"I don't keer for all that," persists the short-sighted, affectionate creature. "Yes, I does keer. But I can't go without seein' my little gal any longer. I ha'n't sot eyes on her for nigh four months, an' I can't stan' it no longer. 'Pears like I don't know how she's gettin' on."

"But you must have faith," I said, attacking her on the religious side, always an open one with the Negroes. However sinful their lives may chance to be in practice, they feel bound to admit the authority of certain doctrines. "It's your duty to have faith," I repeat. "If you have put your child into the hands of a decent man, well off in this world's goods, if you have done by her to the best of your intelligence, you must trust that God will do the rest. You are bound to believe that He will take just as good care of her as if you were there and saw it all."

"Yes, that's so; that's true preachin'," responded the woman, nonplussed at dicovering that preaching could be made so practical as to apply to Bureau business. "But I don't keer for all that. Yes, I does keer, but I wants to see my little gal."

"Suppose you should move up to Walhalla yourself? Then your child could keep her good place, and still you could see her."

"No, no, I can't do that," she affirmed, shaking her head with energy.

"Ah, aunty! I see through you now," said I. "You have a lot of old cronies here; you love to gossip and smoke pipes with them; you care more for them than for your girl. All you want of her is to wait on you while you sit and tattle. You just want her to go for water and to put a chunk of fire on your pipe."

"No, no, no!" denied the aunty, but she looked dreadfully guilty, as though my charge were at least half true. The result was that, by dint of ridicule, coaxing, and arguing, I prevailed upon her to leave her child with Mr. Jack Bascom, in whose care the pickaninny was of course far better off than she could have been with her poverty-stricken parent.

Other women wanted their children, male and female, big and little, brought back from Florida, Louisiana, Tennessee, and Arkansas. It was useless to say, "They have but just gone; they have not fulfilled a quarter of their year's contract; besides, they are earning far more than they can here."

A combination of affection, stupidity, and selfishness easily responded, "I don't keer for all that, an' I wants to see 'em."

The only effective opposition which the Bureau Major could raise consisted in declaring with official firmness and coldness, "I have no transportation for such purposes."

A middle-aged freedwoman came to me with a complaint that her son-in-law would do nothing for the support of his wife and children.

"He's down on the railroad twenty-five miles below yere, an' he's git'n good wages, an' I can't keep 'em no longer."

"Won't he have them with him?" I inquired.

"Yes, he's sont for 'em once or twice; but I ain't gwine to let 'em go so fur off. Ef he wants my da'ter, he's got to live with her, and she's got to live with me."

"Very well; then you may continue to support her," was of course my decision.

Another granny pestered me by the hour for a week together to induce me to save her youngest son, Andy, from being deported. Andy had stolen a pig, and as a result he was in jail, awaiting trial; but the sheriff was willing to release him on condition that he would take a contract out of the state; and consequently a planter who was going to Florida had hired him, paid his jail fees, and secured his liberation.

"He must go," said I. "If he breaks his bargain, I'll have him shut up again."

"Oh, I wouldn't keer for that," whimpered the old creature. " 'Pears like I'd rather hev him in jail all his life than go away from me."

Andy did break his bargain, lurked in the neighborhood a few days, and then, being pursued by the sheriff, absconded to parts unknown.

These aged freedwomen, and many also of the aged freedmen, had the bump of locality like old cats. No place in the world would answer for them except the very place where they had been brought up and had formed their little circle of now venerable gossips. If all their sons and grandsons went to Florida or Louisiana, they would stay with the ancients with whom they were accustomed to smoke and tattle.

And yet the Negroes have a great love for children; it is one of the most marked characteristics of the race. Allowing for their desire to have somebody to wait on them and somebody at hand over whom they can exercise authority; allowing also for their prejudice against everything which in any manner recalls their ancient burden of slavery—they must still be credited with a large amount of natural affection.

One of the strongest objections to the apprenticing of colored children lay in the fact that the relatives soon sickened of their bargain and wanted to regain possession of the youngsters. If the father and mother were not alive to worry in the matter, it would be taken up by grandparents, aunts, and cousins. They coaxed the pickaninny to run away, and they brought horrible stories of cruel treatment to the Bureau officer. Finding, in every case which I investigated, that these tales were falsifications, I invariably refused to break the bond of apprenticeship and instructed the applicants that their only resource was a trial for the possession of the orphan before the judge of the district court. I did this partly from a sense of justice to the master, partly because he was always better able to care for the apprentice than the relatives, and partly because I considered it my duty to aid in setting the civil law on its legs and preparing the community to dispense with military government. As an application for a writ of *habeas corpus* costs money, I never knew mother, grandmother, aunt, or cousin to make it.

One might think that apprentices thus furiously sought for would be gladly let go by their masters; but the Southern whites are themselves noticeably fond of children, and even of Negro children. I have known two small farmers to carry on a long war, involving fights, drawing of knives, suits for assault and battery, and writs of *habeas corpus,* for the possession of a jet black girl only seven years of age and almost valueless except as a plaything. I have known a worthy old gentleman of the higher class to worry away time and money in endeavoring to recover a pet little octoroon from her relatives. . . .

The most hopeful sign in the Negro was his anxiety to have his children educated. The two or three hundred boys and girls whom I used to see around the Bureau schoolhouse—attired with a decency which had strained to the utmost the slender parental purse, ill spared from the hard labor necessary to support their families, gleeful and noisy over their luncheons of cold roasted sweet potato—were proofs that the race has a chance in the future. Many a sorely pinched woman, a widow or deserted by her husband, would not let her boy go out to service, "bekase I wants him to have some schoolin'."

One of the elder girls, a remarkably handsome octoroon with Grecian features and chestnut hair, attended recitations in the morning and worked at her trade of dressmaking in the afternoon. There were some grown men who came in the evening to wrestle, rather hopelessly than otherwise, with the depravities of our English spelling. One of them, a gray-headed person in circular spectacles, bent on qualifying himself for the ministry, was very amusing with his stereotyped remark, when corrected of a mistake, "I specs likely you may be right, mum."

It is a mooted point whether colored children are as quick at learning as white children. I should say not; certainly those whom I saw could not compare with the Caucasian youngster of ten or twelve, who is "tackling" French, German, and Latin; they were inferior to him, not only in knowledge, but in the facility of acquisition. In their favor it must be remembered that they lacked the forcing elements of highly educated competition and of a refined home influence. A white lad gets much bookishness and many advanced ideas from the daily converse of his family. Moreover, ancestral intelligence, trained through generations of study, must tell, even though the rival thinking machines may be naturally of the same calibre. I am convinced that the Negro as he is, no matter how educated, is not the mental equal of the European. . . . There he is in our midst, millions strong; and if he is not educated mentally and morally, he will make us trouble. . . .

I took much pride in the Greenville colored school, for I had aided to establish it. Its real founder, the person who can boast that without him it would not have existed, was Charles Hopkins, a full-blooded black from the low country, for many years a voluntary exhorter among his people and eventually an ordained preacher of the Methodist Church. His education, gathered in the chance opportunities of a bondage of fifty years, was sufficient to enable him to instruct in the lower English branches. He was a meek, amiable, judicious, virtuous, godly man, zealous for the good of the freedmen, yet so thoroughly trusted by the whites that he was able to raise a subscription of two hundred and sixty dollars among the impoverished citizens of Greenville.

During the summer of 1866 Hopkins obtained a room in a deserted hotel which had been seized by the government and, aided by two others of his race, gave spelling and reading lessons to sixty or seventy scholars. For this labor he eventually received a modest remuneration from the New York Freedmen's Union Association. When I assumed command of the sub-district the school had closed for the autumn, the hotel had been restored to its owners, and a schoolroom was needed. The officer whom I relieved had much to say concerning the plans of rent or purchase and earnestly recommended Hopkins to my consideration. It was at this time that the enthusiastic old man raised his subscription. Meanwhile I wrote to the Bureau Superintendent of Education and received assurances of help in case a school was established.

His private purse reduced to a few dollars, his remaining means pledged for the support of his assistants, Hopkins purchased a storehouse belonging to the defunct state arsenal works and took a three years' lease of a lot of ground in the outskirts of the village. A mass meeting of freedmen tore the building to pieces, moved it nearly two miles, and set it up on the new site. Then came much labor of carpenters, masons, and plasterers, and much expense for new materials. By the time the schoolhouse was completed it had cost, together with the rent of the land, five hundred and sixty dollars, or more than twice the amount of the subscription. Hopkins was substantially bankrupt, and, moreover, he was drawing no salary.

It must be understood that the Bureau had no funds for the payment of teachers; by the act of Congress it was limited in the matter of education to the renting and repairing of schoolhouses. Teachers were supported by generous individuals or by benevolent societies at the North, which converged into various larger organizations, and these into the Bureau. For instance, a sewing circle in Lockport might raise five hundred dollars for the blacks, or a wealthy gentleman in Albany might give the same sum from his private purse, and both forward their contributions to the Freedmen's Union Association in New York City. But each of these subscribers naturally desired to know by whom the money would be used, or had in view a worthy person who deserved a mission of some small profit and much usefulness. The consequence was that the Freedmen's Union and the Bureau received few unappropriated contributions and were not able to do much toward the payment of Negro teachers.

Application on application was forwarded, but Hopkins was grievously bullied by his creditors before he received a penny of salary. For his two colored assistants I could obtain nothing, and they left, after two months of unrequited labor, indebted to Hopkins and others for their support. The spirit of the Freedmen's Union was willing, but its purse was weak. The Bureau supplies, on the other hand, were easily obtained, the cost of land and building slipping nicely into the appropriation for "rent and repairs," and the money arriving promptly enough to save Hopkins from falling into the hands of the sheriff. Eventually, too, he secured payment for all his services at the rate of twenty-five dollars a month; and when I last saw him he was as nearly square with the world as the majority of his white fellow citizens.

Meantime he had received ordination from the Charleston missionary branch of the Methodist Church North. With a commission as "Professor" from the Freedmen's Union Association, with the title of clergyman from one of the great branches of the Christian Church, with the consciousness of having founded the Greenville Elementary Freedmen's School, he was a gratified man and worthy of his happiness.

It must not be supposed that he was rolling in pelf. As the school kept open only eight months in the year, as the Methodist missionary society was short of funds and had never paid him the promised annual salary of one hundred dollars, and as the voluntary contributions of his congregation amounted to perhaps seven dollars a quarter, his income was less than he could get by superintending a plantation.

Two white teachers joined the school toward the close of 1866; and the force before I left had been gradually increased to five; Hopkins remaining in charge of the lower classes. The number of scholars on the rolls was something like three hundred. The higher classes were in geography, arithmetic, English grammar and written exercises, and declamation. Class books of the latest issue were gratuitously supplied by a leading New York publishing house. The discipline was admirable; the monotony of study was relieved by gleesome singing; there was a cheerful zeal, near akin to hilarity; it was a charming spectacle. Most of the leading scholars were from one family, a dozen or so of brothers, sisters, and cousins—all of mixed blood and mostly handsome. When I first saw those hazel or blue eyes, chestnut or flaxen heads, and clear complexions, I took it for granted that some of the white children of the village had seized this chance for a gratuitous education. I had met the same persons before in the streets, without suspecting that they were of other than pure Anglo-Saxon race.

The superior scholarship of these octoroons, by the way, is not entirely owing to their greater natural quickness of intellect, but also to the fact that before the emancipation they were petted and encouraged by the family to which they belonged. A man's chances go very far toward making up the actual man.

What is the Negro's social status, and what is it to be? I was amused one Sunday morning by a little tableau which presented itself at the front door of my hotel. The Bureau Superintendent of Education having arrived on an inspecting tour, my venerable friend Hopkins had called to take him to church and was waiting in his meek fashion under the portico, not choosing to intrude upon the august interior of the establishment. Having lately been ordained and conceiving himself entitled to the insignia of his profession, he had put on a white neckcloth, which of course contrasted brilliantly with his black face and clothing. In the doorway stood a citizen, a respectable and kindly man, excellently well reconstructed too, and with as few of the Southern prejudices as one could have in Greenville. But he was lost in wonder at this novel spectacle; he had a smile of mingled curiosity and amusement on his face to which I can not do justice; he seemed to be admitting that here was indeed a new and most comical era in human history. A "nigger" in regular clerical raiment was evidently a phenomenon which his imagination never could have depicted and which, fact alone—so much stranger than fiction—could have brought home to him as a possibility. Whether he believes to this day that he actually did see Hopkins in a black coat and white cravat is more than doubtful.

Not for generations will the respectable whites of the South, any more than those of the North, accept the Negroes as their social equals. That pride of race which has marked all distinguished peoples, which caused the Greeks to style even the wealthy Persians and Egyptians barbarians, which made the Romans refuse for ages the boon of citizenship to other Italians, which led the Semitic Jew to scorn the Hamitic Canaanite, and leads the Aryan to scorn the Jew—that sentiment which more than anything else has created nationality and patriotism, has among us retreated to the family, but it guards this last stronghold with jealous care. Whether the applicant for admission be the Chinaman of California or the African of Carolina, he will for long be repulsed. The acceptance of the Negro as the social equal of the white in our country dates so far into the future that, practically speaking, we may consider it as never to be, and so cease concerning ourselves about it. Barring the dregs of our population, as, for instance, the poor-white trash of the South, the question interests no one now alive. . . .

JUSTICE RECOGNIZES NO COLOR

Under the Reconstruction Acts, the Johnson state governments in the South were declared illegal. Delegates were elected to constitutional conventions throughout the defunct Confederacy on the basis of universal manhood suffrage. During the debate over a new constitution for Arkansas, a Negro delegate, William H. Gray, gave a good account of himself when a white delegate spoke against Negro suffrage. Later, he made some telling remarks on intermarriage. "White men," he said, "have created the difficulty and it will now be impossible to draw the line."

Speeches of William H. Gray at the Arkansas Constitutional Convention, January–February, 1868

. . . It seems not out of place to notice here the sentiments entertained by the negroes of Arkansas (and the same apparently prevail among those of the other Southern States) concerning the Government of the United States, their own right to vote as citizens, their ability to use such right properly, their native intelligence and capacity, as well as that of the white men in general, and other things regarding the relations between the two races under one common government. Mr. Cypert, a delegate from White County, styled in the reports as Conservative, and of note in the convention, having offered, in its fifth sitting, an ordinance "to adopt and submit to the people for their ratification, as the constitution of the State of Arkansas, the same as now in force, being that adopted on the 18th day of March, 1864," and having, in the course of debate thereupon, said that "he was a friend to the negroes, had served in the Freedmen's Bureau, was glad they were free, would have them protected in their just rights, as they were by law, but would never consent to see them enfranchised and made the rulers of white men"—not without referring also to the negroes' natural want of intelligence, their incapability of culture and development, and the consequent impossibility of their properly using the right of suffrage, on which points he and others had frequently spoken at length—William H. Gray, a negro, and delegate to the convention from Phillips County, rose and spoke as follows:

"It appears to me, the gentleman has read the history of his country to little purpose. When the Constitution was framed, in every State but South Carolina free negroes were allowed to vote. Under British rule this class was free, and he interpreted that 'we the people' in the preamble of the Constitution, meant all the people of every color. The mistake of that period was that these free negroes were not represented *in propria persona* in that constitutional convention, but by the Anglo-Saxon. Congress is now correcting that mistake. The right of franchise is due the negroes bought by the blood of forty thousand of their race shed in three wars. The troubles now on the country are the result of the bad exercise of the elective franchise by unintelligent whites, the 'poor whites' of the South. I could duplicate every negro who cannot read and write, whose name is on the list of registered voters, with a white man equally ignorant. The gentleman can claim to be a friend of the negro, but I do not desire to be looked upon in the light of a client. The Government has made a solemn

---

The American Annual Cyclopaedia (New York: Appleton, 1869), Vol. VIII, pp. 33–35.

covenant with the negro to vest him with the right of franchise if he would throw his weight in the balance in favor of the Union and bare his breast to the storm of bullets; and I am convinced that it would not go back on itself. There are thirty-two million whites to four million blacks in the country, and there need be no fear of negro domination. The State laws do not protect the negro in his rights, as they forbade their entrance into the State. [Action of loyal convention of '64.] I am not willing to trust the rights of my people with the white men, as they have not preserved those of their own race, in neglecting to provide them with the means of education. The Declaration of Independence declared all men born free and equal, and I demand the enforcement of that guarantee made to my forefathers, to every one of each race, who had fought for it. The constitution which this ordinance would reënact is not satisfactory, as it is blurred all over with the word 'white.' Under it one hundred and eleven thousand beings who live in the State have no rights which white men are bound to respect. My people might be ignorant, but I believe, with Jefferson, that ignorance is no measure of a man's rights. Slavery has been abolished, but it left my people in a condition of peonage or caste worse than slavery, which had its humane masters. White people should look to their own ancestry; they should recollect that women were disposed of on James River, in the early settlement of the country, as wives, at the price of two hundred pounds of tobacco. When we have had eight hundred years as the whites to enlighten ourselves, it will be time enough to pronounce them incapable of civilization and enlightenment. The last election showed that they were intelligent enough to vote in a solid mass with the party that would give them their rights, and that too in face of the influence of the intelligence and wealth of the State, and in face of threats to take the bread from their very mouths. I have no antipathy toward the whites; I would drop the curtain of oblivion on the sod which contains the bones of my oppressed and wronged ancestors for two hundred and fifty years. Give us the franchise, and if we do not exercise it properly you have the numbers to take it away from us. It would be impossible for the negro to get justice in a State whereof he was not a full citizen. The prejudices of the entire court would be against him. I do not expect the negro to take possession of the government; I want the franchise given him as an incentive to work to educate his children. I do not desire to discuss the question of inferiority of races. Unpleasant truths must then be told; history tells us of your white ancestors who lived on the acorns which dropped from the oaks of Didona, and then worshipped the tree as a God. I call upon all men who would see justice done, to meet this question fairly, and fear not to record their votes."

In the session of January 29th, he said: "Negroes vote in Ohio and Massachusetts, and in the latter State are elected to high office by rich white men. He had found more prejudice against his race among the Yankees; and if they did him a kind act, they did not seem to do it with the generous spirit of Southern men. He could get nearer the latter: he had been raised with them. He was the sorrier on this account that they had refused him the rights which would make him a man, as the former were willing to do. He wanted this a white man's government, and wanted them to do the legislating as they had the intelligence and wealth; but he wanted the power to protect himself against unfriendly legislation. Justice should be like the Egyptian statue, blind and recognizing no color."

Concerning intermarriage between whites and negroes, Mr. Bradley, a delegate to the convention, having offered to insert in the constitution a clause "forbidding matrimony between a white person and a person of African descent," on which point nearly all of the members spoke *pro* and *con* in that and the following days, Mr. Gray said: "It was seldom such outrages were committed at the North, where there are no constitutional provisions of the kind proposed. He saw no necessity of inserting any in the present constitution. As for his people, their condition now would not permit any such marriages. If it was proposed to insert a provision of the kind, he would move to amend by making it an offence punishable with death for a white man to cohabit with a negro woman." At another time he observed on the same subject, that "there was no danger of intermarriage, as the greatest minds had pronounced it abhorrent to nature. The provision would not cover the case, as the laws must subsequently define who is a negro; and he referred to the law of North Carolina, declaring persons negroes who have only one-sixteenth of negro blood. White men had created the difficulty, and it would now be impossible to draw the line which the gentleman desired established."...

SOME ACCOMPLISHMENTS, SOME FAILURES

Looking back almost 40 years to the turbulent times from 1869 to 1877, George Frisbie Hoar of Massachusetts, a member of Congress during those years, concluded that radical reconstruction had failed in some important respects. While underscoring its positive accomplishments, he notes the uncertainties and ambiguities of influential Republican party leaders concerning such key problems as the education of the Negro and the protection of his civil rights.

GEORGE F. HOAR, *Autobiography of Seventy Years*

The reconstruction policy of the Republican Party has been bitterly denounced. Some men who supported it are in the habit now of calling it a failure. It never commanded in its fullest extent the cordial support of the whole party. But it was very simple. So far as it applied to the Southern whites who had been in rebellion it consisted only of complete amnesty and full restoration to political rights. No man was ever punished for taking part in the rebellion after he laid down his arms. There is no other instance of such magnanimity in history. The War left behind it little bitterness in the hearts of the conquerors. All they demanded of the conquered was submission in good faith to the law of the land and the will of the people as it might be constitutionally declared.

Their policy toward the colored people was simply the application to them of the principles applied to the whites, as set forth in the Declaration of Independence and in the Constitution of nearly every State in the Union. There was to be no distinction in political rights by reason of color or race. The States were left to regulate such qualifications as residence, character, intelligence, education and property as they saw fit, only subject to the condition that they were to apply to all alike.

It was the purpose of the dominant party to leave the control of the election of national officers, as it had been left from the beginning, in the hands of the local or State authorities. The power was claimed, indeed it is clearly given by the Constitution, as was asserted in the debates in the Convention that framed it, to conduct those elections under National

---

George Frisbie Hoar, *Autobiography of Seventy Years* (New York: Charles Scribner's Sons, 1903), Vol. I, pp. 254–259.

authority, if it should be found by experience to be necessary. But in fact there was at no time any attempt to go further with National election laws than to provide for punishment of fraudulent or violent interference with elections or for a sufficient provision to ascertain that they were properly conducted, or to protect them against violence or fraud.

Beside this it was the desire of many Republican leaders, especially of Mr. Sumner and General Grant, that there should be a provision at the National charge for the education of all the citizens in the Southern States, black and white, so far as the States were unable or unwilling to afford it, such as had been provided for in the States of the North for all their citizens. It was never contemplated by them to give the right to vote to a large number of illiterate citizens, without ample provision for their education at the public charge. General Grant accompanied his official announcement to Congress of the adoption of the Fifteenth Amendment with an earnest recommendation of such a provision. Earnest efforts were made to accomplish this result by liberal grants from the National treasury. Many liberal and patriotic Southern Democrats supported it. But it was defeated by the timidity, or mistaken notions of economy, of Northern statesmen. In my opinion this defeat accounts for the failure of the policy of reconstruction so far as it has failed. I do not believe that self-government with universal suffrage could be maintained long in any Northern State, or in any country in the world, without ample provision for public education.

It has been claimed with great sincerity and not without plausible reason that a great hardship and wrong was inflicted by the victorious North on their fellow citizens when the political power in their States was given over to their former slaves. This consideration had great force in the minds of many influential Republicans in the North. Governor Andrew of Massachusetts, Governor Morton of Indiana, afterward Senator, men whose influence was probably unsurpassed by any other two men in the country, save Grant and Sumner alone, were of that way of thinking. They thought that our true policy was to let the men who had led their States into the Rebellion take the responsibility of restoring them to their old relations.

It is not unlikely that the strength of the Republican Party would have been seriously impaired, perhaps overthrown, by the division of sentiment on this subject. But the white Democrats in the South were blind to their own interest. President Johnson permitted them in several States to take into their hands again the power of government. They proceeded to pass laws which if carried out would have had the effect of reducing the negro once more to a condition of practical slavery. Men were to be sold for the crime of being out of work. Their old masters were to have the preference in the purchase. So the whole Republican Party of the North came to be united in the belief that there could be no security for the liberty of the freedman without the ballot.

It is said that this reconstruction policy has been a failure. Undoubtedly it has not gained all that was hoped for it by its advocates. But looking back now I do not believe that any other policy would have done as well as that has done, although a large part of what was designed by the Republican leaders of the period of reconstruction never was accomplished.

A complete system of education at the National charge was an essential element of the reconstruction policy. It was earnestly advocated by Sumner and by Grant and by Edmunds and by Evarts. But there were other Republicans of great influence who resisted it from the beginning. Among these was Senator Eugene Hale of Maine, a very accomplished Senator, an able debater and a man of large influence with his colleagues. His public life has been one of great distinction and usefulness. While an earnest partisan he has given an example of independence of action on several notable occasions. But he always seemed to be possessed by what seems to prevail among the Republicans of Maine to a great extent, dislike for what is called sentimental politics. Mr. Hale always seemed to think that the chief function of Congress was to provide for an honest, economical, wise and at the same time liberal public expenditure, to keep in the old paths and leave other matters alone. He dislikes new doctrines and new policies. He is specially adverse to anything like legal restraint. He once in my hearing used a very felicitous phrase, full of wisdom, "Government by good nature." John Sherman, who had originally been an earnest advocate of a liberal National expenditure for education, joined the ranks of its opponents, putting his opposition largely on the ground that he was unwilling to trust the Southern States with the expenditure of large sums of money. He feared that the money would not be fairly expended as between the two races, and that it would be made a large corruption fund for political purposes.

So this most essential part of the reconstruction policy of Sumner and Grant never took effect. Mr. Sumner deemed this matter vital to success. He told me about a week before his death that when the resolution declaring the provision for public education at the National charge an essential part of the reconstruction policy, was defeated in the Senate by a tie vote, he was so overcome by his feelings that he burst into tears and left the Senate Chamber.

Another part of the Republican plan for reconstruction was never accomplished. That was the securing of a fair vote and a fair ascertainment of the result in National elections by National power. Some partial and imperfect attempts were made to put in force laws intended to accomplish this result. They never went farther than enactments designed to maintain order at the polls, to secure the voter from actual violence, and to provide for such scrutiny as to make it clear that the vote was duly counted and properly returned, with a right to appeal to the Courts of the United States in case of a contest, the decision of the Court to be subject to the final authority of the House of Representatives. These laws, although they had the support of eminent and zealous Democrats and although they were as much needed and had as much application to the Northern cities as to the Southern States, were the object of bitter denunciation from the beginning. Good men in the North listened with incredulity to the narrative of well established facts of cruelty and murder and fraud. These stories were indignantly denied at the time, although they are not only confessed, but vauntingly and triumphantly affirmed now. The whole country seems to be made uneasy when the old practice to which it had been accustomed everywhere of having offences tried by a jury taken by lot from the people of the neighborhood, and the result of election ascertained by officers selected from the bystanders at the polls, is departed from. Besides, no strictness of laws which provide only for the proceedings at the elections will secure their freedom if it be possible to intimidate the voters, especially men like the colored voters at the South, from attending the elections, by threats, outrages and actual violence at their homes. Against these the election laws could not guard. Congress attempted some laws to secure the Southern Republicans against such crimes under the authority conferred by the Fourteenth Amendment to the Constitution. But the Supreme Court held that these laws were unconstitutional, it not appearing that the States had by any affirmative action denied protection against such offences to any class of their citizens by reason of race, color, or previous condition. It was idle to expect Southern jurors, or State officers to enforce the law against such crimes in the condition of sentiment existing there.

Further, the people of the North would not maintain the Republican Party in power forever on this one issue alone. They were interested in other things. They could not be expected, year after year, election after election, and perhaps generation after generation, to hold together by reason of this one question, differing on other things. So whenever the Democratic Party should come into power it was apparent that all the vigor would be taken out of the election laws. If there be not power to repeal them the House of Representatives can always refuse to make the appropriation for enforcing them. So it became clear to my mind, and to the minds of many other Republicans, that it was better to leave this matter to the returning and growing sense of justice of the people of the South than to have laws on this subject passed in one Administration, only to be repealed in another. A policy to be effective must be permanent. . . .

ABCDE69

[illegible] of the [illegible] secure [illegible] from [illegible] [illegible] possible for each [illegible] that the [illegible] and properly [illegible] with the right of appeal to the Courts of the United States in case of a [illegible] to be subject to the final [illegible] of the [illegible] of Representatives. [illegible] although [illegible] to confirm the [illegible] Democrats [illegible] they were [illegible] [illegible] [illegible] [illegible] the South [illegible] [illegible] [illegible] [illegible] [illegible] [illegible] [illegible] [illegible] [illegible] [illegible] [illegible] [illegible] [illegible] [illegible]

[illegible]